D0329186

THE HISTORY OF PHILOSOPHY

CONTEMPORARY PHILOSOPHY
—SINCE 1850

THE HISTORY OF PHILOSOPHY
VOLUME VII

CONTEMPORARY PHILOSOPHY —SINCE 1850

BY ÉMILE BRÉHIER

TRANSLATED BY WADE BASKIN

THE UNIVERSITY OF CHICAGO PRESS
CHICAGO AND LONDON

Originally published in 1932 as Histoire de la philosophie:
La Philosophie moderne. IV: Le XIX⁰ siècle après 1850. Le XX⁰ siècle.
© *1932, Presses Universitaires de France*

*The present bibliography has been revised and enlarged to
include recent publications. These have been supplied by
Wesley Piersol.*

*Library of Congress Catalog Card Number: 63–20912
The University of Chicago Press, Chicago 60637
The University of Chicago Press, Ltd., London W.C.1
Translation © 1969 by The University of Chicago
All rights reserved. Published 1969
Printed in the United States of America*

TRANSLATOR'S FOREWORD

Publication of *Contemporary Philosophy* brings to an end a project initiated five years ago—completion of the translation of Émile Bréhier's comprehensive study of the evolution of philosophical thought from its pre-Socratic origins through the first third of the twentieth century. The first volume of Bréhier's monumental *History of Philosophy* had been ably translated by Joseph Thomas and published by the University of Chicago Press early in 1963, under the title *The Hellenic Age*. Mr. Kenneth Douglas, who knew me only as the translator of Ferdinand de Saussure's *Course in General Linguistics,* invited me to translate the second volume of the series. As a student at the Sorbonne a generation earlier, I had been exposed to philosophy and had become aware of the importance of Bréhier's interpretative work, which had already become the standard French work in its field. Somewhat awed but unable to resist the challenge, I set to work immediately. *The Hellenistic and Roman Age* was published early in 1965. The third volume is the series, *The Middle Ages and the Renaissance,* appeared later the same year. *The Seventeenth Century* was completed in 1966, *The Eighteenth Century* in 1967, and *The Nineteenth Century: Period of Systems* in 1968.

If *Contemporary Philosophy* marks the end of a long philosophical journey, it also gives me an opportunity to offer a word of appreciation to my *compagnons de voyage*. Their encouragement, toil, and sacrifices have, I hope, meant the difference between compe-

v

tence and excellence in the finished product. For the shortcomings that persist despite their efforts, I alone must bear full responsibility.

Preeminent among my mentors are Dr. Erwin Bohm of The College of the Ozarks, Dr. Elizabeth McDavid of Cumberland College of Tennessee, Dr. Eva Burkett of the State College of Arkansas, Dr. Dwight Bolinger of Harvard University, Professor André Martinet of the Sorbonne and the École Pratique des Hautes Études, and Dr. Mario Pei of Columbia University. The two scholars on whom I have relied most for help in making Bréhier's authoritative work accessible in English to the inquiring reader as well as the student of philosophy are Mme Nicole Hatfield of Arkansas State College and Dr. Gene Franks of North Texas State University. Mme Hatfield has provided me with clear explanations of recalcitrant passages in Bréhier's text; Dr. Franks has located, verified, and interpreted much pertinent information. On particular problems I have tapped the wisdom of Dr. Howard McCarley of Austin College, Dr. Ernest Trumble of the University of Oklahoma, and many of my colleagues. For the performance of many routine chores, I would also like to acknowledge my indebtedness to a pleiad of students: Miss Judy Bauer, Miss Gayle Brown, Miss Kathryn Kovaciny, Mr. William McCrary, Mrs. Judy Peña, and Mrs. Diane Weger.

Without minimizing the contributions of other members of the faculty and administration of Southeastern State College, I would like to express my appreciation to the following: Dr. Lee Ball, Mr. John Branson, Dr. Donald Brown, Mrs. Mary Frye, Mr. Billy Ray Grimes, Dr. Margaret O'Riley, Miss Mildred Riling, Dr. Eugene Slaughter, and Mr. Lewis Warren; Mr. Raymon Piller, Miss Judith Chandler, Mrs. Mamie Harris, and Mrs. Mildred Williams, who joined me in the search for elusive facts stored on the shelves of our library; and three exemplary men who have helped to create and maintain on our campus conditions favorable to the pursuit of wisdom—Dr. James Morrison, Dean of Instruction, President Leon Hibbs, and his predecessor, Dr. Allen Shearer.

Since reviewers of earlier volumes in the series have praised the

University of Chicago Press for making Bréhier's text available in English translation and preserving its "extraordinary readability and unpretentious scholarship," I would like to acknowledge my debt to those who initiated and worked toward completion of the project as well as the specialists who checked my translation and updated the bibliographies—William Bondeson, Vere C. Chappell, Joseph Betz, and Miss Wesley Piersol.

Finally, for acquiescing to the curtailment of many diversions— and for providing many pleasant interruptions during more than three thousand hours devoted to the task of making Professor Bréhier's continental view of Western philosophy available in English—I owe a debt of gratitude and an apology to Pat, Wade, Danny, and Michael.

W. B.

CONTENTS

FIRST PERIOD
1850-1890

GENERAL CHARACTERISTICS OF THE PERIOD

THE FOND hopes that had been set on the great philosophical and social systems constructed during the first part of the century ceased to exist around 1850. Then began a new period, lasting until around 1890.

The general theme of philosophical speculation during the preceding period had centered on attempts to justify nature and history as conditions determining the advent of a higher reality variously called Spirit, *Geist,* Liberty, Humanity, Harmony, or by many other names. The ultimate goal of liberty counterbalanced rigorous determinism—the law of inexorable development which Comte, Hegel, and even Schopenhauer attributed to things. This liberty was indissolubly linked with necessity, either through consciousness of this necessity, as with Hegel and to a certain degree Comte, or through negation of it and deliverance, as with Schopenhauer. The Romantic hero was a passionate lover who discovered heaven and hell, damnation and redemption in his fatal passion. Philosophical thought was suffused with the same fervor that found its ultimate expression in a flowery letter written by Richard Wagner to Mathilde Wesendonck: "When I lose myself in your holy, bewitching eyes, there is

Since it is impossible to write a complete history of contemporary philosophy, for this and the following period I am restricting myself to brief sketches which are admittedly incomplete; the result is a classification rather than a history.

3

for me no longer subject or object; from this moment everything fuses into one vast, continuous harmony." Then this harmony was broken. It was as if intuitive awareness of the fundamental unity of all things had been lost. Philosophical thought, more sober than before, posited alternatives involving terms the mind was forced to choose between, rather than terms which were to be united. For example, the active wing of the Hegelian party—left-wing Hegelianism or the Hegelianism of Feuerbach and Karl Marx—gave first place to their mentor's idea of the necessity of the social process, leading to materialism. Furthermore, it was not through a misinterpretation of Hegel's works that Taine acquired the idea of a determinism in which all phenomena of mind were related to a *Volksgeist*, which in turn was related to the influence of the physical environment; his interpretation of Hegel was shared by his contemporaries. In contrast, along with the end of the desire for conciliation at any price, this period witnessed the birth of the philosophy of liberty, which was given distinct forms by Renouvier and Secrétan. Particularly in the case of Renouvier, liberty in the form of free will, far from consummating necessity or being a self-imposed necessity, was a break with determinism, defined by pure negation. The historical achievement of mankind was assumed to rest on all the unforeseeable initiative acts of individuals ruled by no law other than that which reason gives to their free wills.

Generally speaking, if we remove from the earlier doctrines everything that confers on them their apocalyptic and visionary character, we obtain new doctrines which have a skeptical, forbidding aspect or which, conversely, place much stress on human effort and little stress on natural necessity. The materialism of Marx is the Hegelian doctrine of the state shorn of its religious overtones, and the positivism of Littré is Comte's doctrine stripped of its whimsical notions concerning the church of the future and the organization of definitive relations between the temporal world and the spiritual world. Forcibly, almost violently, Hegel had separated history and philology—history, which describes the advent of mind, in contrast to philology, which restricts itself to the critical study of documents and divests history of the epic aspect conferred on it by an immediate reading of texts.[1] This distinction vanishes completely in the period under consideration: Renan, Max Müller, Éduard Zeller, Burckhardt, and many others who called themselves philologists were at the same time historians. The general result of this criticism was to transform the appearance of the past, making it much less mysterious and much more similar to the present. History in the strict sense in which the word was used by Bossuet or St. Augustine—to designate a period distinguished specifically by its spiritual structure as a whole—tended to disappear in Renan. Like Rohde, Renan saw in the distant past the operation of faculties identical in every way with our own, with the result that from his perspective each period becomes contemporaneous with our own. As Hegel had feared, criticism robs us not only of the sense of a clear distinction between the present and the past but also of the presentiment of an ultimate future to which history is leading us. Everything is brought into harmony, and Lucretius' *Semper eadem omnia* often reappears—for example in linguistic investigations— as an indispensable methodical principle, though the tone is more ironical and reserved than pessimistic. Cournot, with his views on chance and accidents, formulated the theory of historical knowledge which eliminated the possibility of finding a meaning in history by revealing the convergence of a vast number of unrelated causes in the production of any event. Of course there is a contrast between Marxist determinism and Cournot's indeterminism, but both agree on one point: the absence of any esoteric doctrine concerning the final stage of history.

A strange situation resulted. Affecting ignorance or skepticism with respect to the determination of ends, philosophers shifted their attention to the realm of cognitive thought or active will and the formal conditions governing this thought or will. The period abounds in general theories of knowledge and studies of logic as

[1] He takes issue time after time, for example, with Niebuhr's attempt to show that the beginnings of Roman history are all mere legends.

well as in speculations concerning the foundation of moral philosophy. Tired of pursuing an imaginary object, the human mind became introspective and studied the laws of its functioning, in stark contrast to the attitude of Comte and Hegel, who spent their whole lives combating just such formalism. Attention was directed toward Kantian criticism, especially the *Critique of Pure Reason,* marking the beginning of German and French neocriticism. The same spirit also accounted for Taine's Condillacian analysis and for the popularity of J. S. Mill's *Logic,* which goes beyond the study of logic to provide an empirical theory of knowledge. Finally, the new spirit manifested during the period under consideration culminated in the birth of criticism of the sciences, which developed mainly during the following period.

The same period also witnessed the production of many cold, harsh, ironical works, all characterized by one essential trait—indifference to objects. This indifference, which vividly impressed Nietzsche and caused him to heap criticism upon historians, was characteristic of the whole period. Formalism in philosophy corresponded to Parnassianism in French poetry; moreover, Mallarmé carried his art to the extreme in his search for the purely formal conditions of a poem. "An admirable undertaking," wrote Paul Valéry. "Where Kant, perhaps somewhat naïvely, thought he saw a moral law, Mallarmé must have perceived a poetical imperative—poetics." Furthermore, the same stubborn attitude of indifference characterized landscapes and naturalistic novels. "Faith in absolute philosophical truths," wrote Cournot in 1861, "has diminished to such a degree that now the public and the academies are receptive to hardly anything of this kind except works of erudition and historical curiosity." In Europe, as English thought regained its long-lost influence, the logic of Mill, the transformism of Darwin, and the evolutionism of Spencer seemed to outline the natural propensities of the human mind.

JOHN STUART MILL

TWO CONFLICTING and irreconcilable patterns of thought, each with its own salient traits, emerged in England after Coleridge and Carlyle: that of the poet or seer and that of the analyst or interpreter. James Fill tried to transmit to his son John Stuart Mill, born in 1806, the rigorous intellectual discipline of Benthamism, wholly logical and deductive. Young Mill zealously espoused the principles of the school and founded a utilitarian society. Then came the mental crisis detailed in the famous pages of his *Autobiography* (1873): a nagging feeling of inertia which left him indifferent toward the very tasks that had once fired his enthusiasm; he attributed his apathy to the exclusively analytical habits acquired through the training given to him by his father. It was then that he saw the importance of immediate, unreflective feeling. "Ask yourself if you are happy," he wrote, "and thus you will cease to be happy; the only chance is to take as the goal of life, not happiness, but some end outside it." He read Wordsworth, "the poet of unpoetical natures." In 1838 he observed that Bentham's method was excellent but that his knowledge of life was limited: "His method is empirical, but his empiricism has little experience of life." In 1840 he noted the contrast between Bentham and Coleridge, whose insights led him to truths unsuspected by the utilitarians.

Even if Mill retained from his early education a brilliant, clear style of exposition unmarred by oratorical overtones or enthusiasm, it is nevertheless true that the mental crisis recounted in his *Auto-*

biography provided him with a breadth of vision uncommon to the school.

1 *Logic*

The scantiness or insignificance of treatises on logic in relation to other contributions to modern philosophy is noteworthy. Kant's conviction that Aristotle had said the last word on logic was almost universally shared, and Leibniz' outlines of the science, though influential, were never completed. Then suddenly, toward the middle of the nineteenth century, especially in England, there was a complete reversal. In 1826 Whately published his *Elements of Logic*. Making a sharp distinction between logic and epistemology, he held that the practical function of the former was not to discover truth but to reveal the falsity of an argument—for example, by reduction to absurdity. It was also Whately who had the idea of writing *Historic Doubts Relative to Napoleon Bonaparte,* in which he showed that the same arguments that attack the truth of Christianity should cause us to doubt the existence of Napoleon. In 1830 Hershell published his *Discourse on the Study of Natural Philosophy.* In 1837 Whewell's *History of the Inductive Sciences* focused attention on the role of the inventive mind in scientific discovery. Observation through the senses provides only raw data or, at most, empirical laws; the idea that unifies them and provides us with a causal explanation comes from the mind, in the form of a hypothesis; these ideas spring from the keen perception of genius, for which no rule can be substituted; their unifying function is explained by Whewell in terms of the Kantian model of unity produced by an intellectual concept. Attention was shifted to the opposite direction in the case of Augustus de Morgan (*Formal Logic or the Calculus of Inference, Necessary and Probable,* 1847; *Syllabus of a Proposed System of Logic,* 1860) and Boole (*The Mathematical Analysis of Logic,* 1847; *An Analysis of the Laws of Thought,* 1854).

Traditional logic has as its starting point concepts endowed with extension and comprehension. But the theory of concepts, genera, and species did not fit into the representation of the universe which Mill inherited from the empiricism of Hume: a universe in which the given was not concepts but an aggregation or collection of unrelated impressions. Mill's logic consists in taking up the traditional problems of logic one after the other and translating the ordinary solutions into a language which no longer posits the existence of concepts but only of impressions, isolated or connected. Thus the theory of terms, propositions, and reasoning are transformed. A subject—for instance, a body—is merely a certain number of sensations arranged in a certain way; it exists apart from us, and this means that it is a permanent possibility of sensations; like the body, the mind is merely a fabric of inner states or a series of impressions, sensations, thoughts, feelings, and volitions. An abstract proposition such as "A generous person is worthy of honor" contains nothing but phenomena or states of mind followed or accompanied by sensible facts. As for definition, either it teaches us nothing about the thing and enunciates the meaning of a word, or it does not differ from an ordinary proposition.

The syllogism seems to be linked to a theory of concepts, since it is supposed to deduce the particular from the universal. But to an empiricist, the universal premise "All men are mortal" is equivalent to a finite number of determinate experiences ("Peter, Paul, etc., are mortal") and is a memorandum for the mind; from these particular cases which we state summarily, solely for convenience, in a general theorem that we could dispense with if we had a better memory, we infer a similar particular case, "Therefore James is mortal." In the real operation accomplished by the mind, no universal axiom intervenes. Moreover, axioms in their turn fail to go beyond experience, either actual or imaginary. For example, in the axiom "Two straight lines cannot enclose a space," the inconceivability of the contrary, which is proved a priori, is merely the impossibility of imagining that they converge, no matter how far they are extended by the imagination.

Any productive proposition is merely a statement of relations between facts. But this poses a new problem: How are we to determine which of these relations is a law of nature or a connection between cause and effect? Bacon resolved the question by inventing his famous tables, but these tables and Hume's empirical theory of causality differ markedly in inspiration. The tables assume a constant cause-and-effect link between a "nature" observed by us and a "form" sought by us; the relation is hidden from us by the innumerable circumstances that accompany our observations; the tables are a means of eliminating these circumstances. Hume's universe of impressions does not assume knowledge of whether such a relation exists in nature but merely accounts for our belief in this relation by the spontaneous interplay of association and habit. The practical use of Bacon's tables is clearly independent of Hume's theoretical empiricism; whether or not the principle of causality is given an empirical origin, a procedure similar to Bacon's must be adopted if a particular relation of causality is to be revealed—for instance, gravitational variations according to displacements of the earth's surface.

Mill's four methods, which embrace a number of practical procedures for discovering relations of causality that may be formulated as laws, are not related to his empiricism—any more than the rules given by Hume for the same purpose are related to his theory of the principle of causality. Besides, Mill, who was not in any way a physicist, borrowed all the materials of his investigations from Whewell, who was a Kantian, and from Hershell, who had no particular theory of the origin of knowledge. The use of these methods implies a conception of causality on which empiricists and apriorists can agree. Causality is a constant, unconditioned relation between two phenomena, and the nature of this relation is such that the first phenomenon cannot exist without entailing the appearance of the second. Untangling and identifying such relations through observation, therefore, becomes a purely technical problem. This is the role of the four methods: *the method of agreement,* which collects the observations in which the phenomenon under investigation is present and permits the elimination of every circumstance not common to diverse observations; *the method of difference,* which details two groups of observations, those in which the phenomenon is present and those in which it is absent, and permits the elimination of circumstances common to both groups; *the method of concomitant variations,* which indicates the concomitant circumstances that do or do not vary with every variation in the phenomenon and permits the elimination of circumstances that remain constant; finally, *the method of residues,* which permits the elimination a priori of all existing circumstances known through prior inductions to be incapable of producing the effect of which the cause is under investigation (for example, it was through the method of residues that Le Verrier, studying the causes of disturbances which he could not attribute to the attraction of any known body, discovered Neptune). This set of practical directions is to be evaluated by the technician rather than the philosopher; it seems to be a technique for verification and control rather than, as Mills thought, a technique for discovery; furthermore, it does not enable us to identify which of two related phenomena is the cause and which is the effect.

But the empiricist Mill was still faced with a philosophical question: How can we be certain that the apparent permanence of a relation is the sign of a necessary causality, or, putting it another way, that every phenomenon has a cause? Hume had provided a lengthy answer to the question, but Mill failed to take this answer into account, with the result that his solution is completely different. According to Mill, we arrive at the principle of causality through a process of induction similar to that through which we arrive at any universal proposition; induction is distinct from the technical procedure which discovers a constant conjunction or law by elimination; it is Aristotle's process of induction observable in the syllogism; we do not hesitate, beginning with innumerable instances in which we have observed that a fact invariably has a cause, to infer that a new fact will have a cause. Moreover, this act of induction does not attribute an absolute value—any more than in any other universal proposition—to the principle of causality; there may be regions of space and time where facts exist without a cause and where two plus two equals five.

II The Moral Sciences and Ethics

There is a close relationship between the doctrine of the utilitarian empiricists and Mill's treatment of the method of the moral sciences (*Logic,* Book VI). Their method, like Locke's, was strictly deductive; this trait, which seems somewhat paradoxical among "empiricists," is explained when we realize that they stressed, more than anything else, the practical applications of these sciences; they posited permanent motives, such as the pursuit of pleasure, from which they deduced rules of conduct. Mill, in turn, sees deduction as the essential method of the moral sicences; but his concept of deduction, dynamic rather than mathematical, is concerned with the mechanical conjunction—in accordance with a certain law—of causes whose effects are already known. It follows that an individual can foresee the results of his actions—for instance, in politics, when he modifies a constitution. Mill accepts neither the theory of government as a purely human invention, fabrication, or expedient, nor Coleridge's romantic theory of a vital, spontaneous, organic institution. He stresses the influence of the individual and especially of individual beliefs, holding that a person with a belief is a social force equal to several others who have only interests. Mill is himself a liberal, but freedom to him signifies neither the inner deliverance of the romantic nor the economic freedom of the utilitarian. Criticizing the first, he notes that nothing seems more alien or antipathetic to the modern mind than Goethe's ideal of life; that not harmony but a bold, free expansion in every direction is dictated by the needs of modern life and the instincts of the modern mind; and that freedom of action is grounded on a strength of character not subject to the influence of public opinion. As for the second, he feels strongly that unlimited economic freedom is incompatible with true freedom because it does not allow for the just distribution of the fruits of labor. He shows some sympathy for socialism and sees co-operation as a pathway to freedom. He also supports the political enfranchisement of women.

This balance between reason and sentiment is clearly shown in *Utilitarianism* (1863). Here Mills defends the utilitarian against the accusation that he is egotistical, indifferent toward everything except sensory pleasures, indifferent toward the higher pleasures of art and science. In the last analysis, however, this defense is inadequate, for it embraces two contradictory theses. First, Mill argues that the unique motive of human conduct is egotism; if the reverse seems to be true—if a man dedicates his life to helping others without expecting anything in return—the reason is that an altruistic act, which at the outset was a means of satisfying egotism, has ceased to be an end and become a means, through forgetfulness of its motive; thus through transference the amassing of wealth ceases to be a means of enjoyment and becomes an end in itself. Second, Mill tells us that certain pleasures—artistic or intellectual—are of a higher quality than sensory pleasures, and quantitative considerations have no part in determining their value. According to the first of these theses, morality is mediate and acquired; according to the second, moral refinement is primary and essential.

Simple utilitarianism was inimical to Mill's nature. He was also repelled, particularly toward the end of his life, by the complete agnosticism of the utilitarian school. He opposed both dogmatic denial of the supernatural and acceptance of an infinite, omnipotent God. In his posthumous work (*Three Essays on Religion*, 1874), the existence of imperfections in the world caused him (and later William James) to believe in the existence of a finite God.

Bibliography

Texts

Mill, John Stuart. *An Examination of Sir William Hamilton's Philosophy.* Toronto, in preparation.
———. *Auguste Comte and Positivism.* 1865; Ann Arbor, Mich., 1964.
———. *Autobiography,* ed. J. J. Cross. New York, 1924.
———. *Considerations on Representative Government.* 1961; Chicago, 1962.
———. *Essays on Some Unsettled Questions of Political Economy.* 1844.
———. *Ethical Writings,* ed. J. B. Schneewind. New York, 1965.
———. *John Stuart Mill's Philosophy of Scientific Method,* ed. Ernest Nagel. New York, 1950.
———. *On Liberty.* 1859.
———. *Principles of Political Economy.* 2 vols. Ed. J. M. Robson. Toronto, 1965.
———. *Subjection of Women.* 1869.
———. *System of Logic.* 2 vols. 8th ed. 1872.
———. *The Philosophy of John Stuart Mill,* ed. Marshall Cohen. New York, 1961.
———. *Utilitarianism.* 1863.
See also J. S. Mill's own *Bibliography,* ed. M. MacMinn, J. R. Hainds, and J. M. McCrimmon. Evanston, Ill., 1945.

Studies

Anschutz, R. P. *Philosophy of John Stuart Mill.* Oxford, 1953.
Bosanquet, B. *Philosophical Theory of the State.* 1899.
Burns, J. H. "John Stuart Mill and Democracy." *Political Studies* 5 (1957).
Cowling, M. *Mill and Liberalism.* Cambridge, 1963.
Kubitz, O. A. *Development of John Stuart Mill's System of Logic.* Illinois Studies in the Social Sciences, 8. Urbana, Illinois, 1932.
Moore, G. E. *Principia Ethica.* Cambridge, 1903.
Popper, K. *Open Society and Its Enemies.* 2 vols. New ed., Princeton, 1963.
Rees, J. C. *Mill and His Early Critics.* Leicester, 1956.
Ritchie, D. G. *Principles of State Interference.* 1891.
Sabine, G. H. *History of Political Theory,* 3d ed. New York, 1961.
Stephen, Sir Leslie. *English Utilitarians.* Vol. 3. 1900.

TRANSFORMISM, EVOLUTIONISM, AND POSITIVISM

1 *Lamarck and Darwin*

In the eighteenth century and throughout the first part of the nineteenth century, one particularly beguiling idea was that of a natural series embracing all living forms, arranged in such a way that the transition from one to the next could be apprehended intuitively. This notion of the continuity of forms, far from leading directly to the notion of the actual descent of species, is quite distinct from it.

Quite to the contrary, Lamarck (1748–1829) was led to this latter notion, first in his inaugural address of 1800 and later in his *Zoological Philosophy* (1809), by obvious anomalies in natural types of organization.[1] Each type implies a number of definite organs distributed in a definite pattern, for example the vertebrate type implies symmetrically placed eyes, a dentition, paws or feet for locomotion; yet in many instances we find that the organs of vertebrates are distributed differently, that they are atrophied, or that they are missing. Furthermore, each of these anomalies takes a different direction: "The organization of animals, beginning with the most imperfect and continuing through more highly developed forms, offers only an *irregular gradation* embracing a number of deviations

[1] *Philosophie zoologique*, 1809; English translation by Hugh Elliot, 1914.

15

which have no appearance of order in their diversity." Lamarck set out to explain these deviations not by denying their regular gradation, which remains as the normal, spontaneous course of nature, but by interspersing a multitude of vastly different circumstances which tend continually to destroy regularity. These circumstances relating to environment (climate, food, etc.) occasion different needs; these needs and the efforts involved in their satisfaction in turn result in modifications in the organs and even in shifts when the satisfaction of needs makes them necessary. This explains, for example, the asymmetry of the eyes of the flatfish. "Their way of life forced them to swim on their flat sides. . . . In this position they received more light from above than from below; they needed always to be particularly attentive to what was above them, with the result that this need forced one of their eyes to change its location and take the singular position familiar to us in sole, turbot, and the like." Thus Lamarck, in keeping with Sainte-Beuve's remark in his novel *Volupté,* "constructed the world with the smallest possible number of elements and crises and the longest possible duration." Changes become permanent through habit, a conservative force which delineates in bold strokes the forms adumbrated by attempts to satisfy needs. The influence of environment is obvious; it always produces anomalies. As René Berthelot puts it, "far from being the essential cause of evolution, as it is often said to be, the influence of the environment is a disruptive force."

Interestingly enough, it was also the observation of certain anomalies that led Charles Darwin (1809–82) to transformism (*On the Origin of Species,* 1859). His starting point was selection as practiced by breeders intent upon obtaining varieties of animals useful to man. This selection is possible only because, from generation to generation, animals exhibit a host of "accidental variations" of unknown origin. They are beyond the control of the breeder, who can only try to promote and stabilize those which serve his ends. The word "selection" designates a voluntary, reflective procedure.

According to Darwin the procedure followed by breeders is the procedure adopted by nature in producing species; natural selection spontaneously carries out the role of artificial selection. To begin with, natural breeds do in fact evidence a tendency toward variation; through its cumulative effects over a considerable period of time this tendency, though weaker in domesticated breeds, can succeed in producing descendants strikingly different from their ancestors. Furthermore, variations do not follow a predetermined pattern but are truly accidental, each occurring in a completely divergent direction. Finally, according to Darwin, who accepted the Malthusian law and extended it to the whole animal kingdom, the means of subsistence increases much less rapidly than the number of animals; consequently the struggle for existence among men, lugubriously portrayed by Malthus, is also manifested in the animal kingdom. Once these assumptions are granted, the process of natural selection is easily understood. Accidental variations are sometimes advantageous, sometimes disadvantageous in the struggle for life; only animals favored by these variations survive. This is the principle of the survival of the fittest, which has as a corollary the perpetual creation of new species characterized by new means of adaptation. This is the true origin of species, of which the human species is no exception (*The Descent of Man, 1871*). Man's distinctive characteristics—his intellectual development, his moral faculties, even his religion—are considered by Darwin to be useful biological variations, preserved just because they are useful.

The so-called stability of species is an illusion due either to the slowness of their transformations or to a characteristic decline of evolution in the period through which we are now passing. This slowness, moreover, is relative to our method of reckoning time. Just as the Copernican system tore down the walls of the world, transformism opens a perspective on time, of which historical duration, accessible to tradition, is but a minute part; the views of transformism are confirmed by geology and paleontology.

The spirit of Darwinism is quite different from the spirit of Lamarckism. Darwin assumes that variations are isolated, unexplainable phenomena, whereas Lamarck assumes that they are traceable to an inner need and are made permanent by use. It follows that Darwinism is essentially mechanistic, considering only the result of accidents that intervene in the life of animals and excluding any finalism. The same trait reappears in Spencer's evolutionism.

Darwinism, when applied to mental, moral, and social functions, introduced a new concept of man. Problems relating to genesis and origin, which previously had been neglected in favor of structural problems or relegated to the twilight zones of metaphysics or religion, now seemed susceptible of a positive solution, at least in principle. The causes that gave birth to these functions do not differ from those observed to be operative all around us, and we need only imagine their cumulative effects over a considerable period of time to explain the most complex forms. Furthermore, and this is an even more important change, these functions do not seem to be meaningful in themselves but only in relation to their adaptive role in a given environment. Thus a biological significance was conferred on the mind in its entirety. In *The Expression of the Emotions in Man and Animals* (1872), Darwin laid the basis for a transformistic psychology and tried to discover the outlines of adapted acts in the major movements associated with an emotion. Concerning the transformistic explanation of moral sentiments, noteworthy contributions include the works of Paul Rée (*The Origin of Moral Sentiments*, 1877; *The Development of Conscience*, 1885), which served as one of the points of departure of Nietzsche's meditations. Selection, according to him, has the effect of attenuating the altruistic feelings that man inherited from animals and strengthening his egotistical feelings.

II Herbert Spencer and Evolutionism

Herbert Spencer's theory of evolution was most influential, not only in England but throughout the world, during the period extending from 1860 to 1890. In conjunction with Darwin's transformism, it had a profound influence on the spirit of philosophy.

Spencer (1820–1903), trained for the profession of engineering, turned first, between 1842 and 1850, to political and economic issues. The spirit of individualism and the signs of hostility reflected in his first articles for *The Nonconformist* (republished as a pamphlet, *The Proper Sphere of Government,* 1843) became permanent traits of his doctrine. The idea of evolution first came to light in his essays and in the first part of *The Principles of Psychology,* which he published in 1852, before Darwin published his *Origin of Species* (1859). But it was in 1860 that he conceived the plan for a comprehensive work that he executed fully and to the letter, without changing any of his ideas or deviating from the outline—*The Synthetic Principles of Psychology,* which includes *First Principles* (1862), *Principles of Biology* (1864–67), *Principles of Psychology* (two volumes, 1870–72), *Principles of Sociology* (1876–96), and *Principles of Ethics* (1879–92). In addition, he wrote essays on diverse subjects, notably on *The Classification of the Sciences* (1864) and *Education* (1861). His *Autobiography* (1904) shows clearly the ethical character of his work: absolute certainty concerning principles once they have been discovered; strict, dogmatic adherence to these principles without ever juxtaposing them or comparing them (he said that it was always impossible for him to read a book written from a point of view alien to his own); a critical curiosity, constantly rekindled, concerning details that might contribute to the betterment of human life; finally, an unflinching spirit of nonconformity, which instinctively casts doubt on any established authority or custom, whether the matter at issue be funeral ceremonies, courtly parades, or academic titles.

Spencer formulated one metaphysical doctrine which, by origin and inspiration, is independent of his evolutionism: his theory of the Unknowable, in which he adopts for his own purposes arguments advanced by Hamilton and Mansel. Like Hamilton, he sees this doctrine as a means of reconciling religion and science. He differs from Hamilton, however, in assuming that the notion of the unknowable is not purely negative. After every positive characteristic that makes an object knowable has been eliminated, he reasons, there remains a common substratum, absolute Being, which is the object of an indefinite consciousness—an unknown and un-knowable absolute force, which manifests itself in two distinct guises. On the one hand, it defines science and makes it independent of religion; reality, subject to the law of evolution, is in the domain of science; religion, completely and forever satisfied by the doctrine of the Unknowable, has no bearing on anything outside its own domain (and this includes society and ethics). On the other hand, however, the Unknowable also denotes the essence of things, the Force of which reality, subject to the law of evolution, is a mani-festation. There is in this view of the Unknowable something reminiscent of the Kantian noumenon described in the *Critique of Pure Reason*. Spencer is a realist who believes that our sensible knowledge is the symbol of unknowable things. Matter is irreduci-ble to facts of consciousness, contrary to the Berkeleian traditions perpetuated by Mill. This second view of the Unknowable springs from necessities inherent in Spencer's doctrine of evolution, which cannot dispense with the idea of a permanent force.

This evolutionist is neither a historian nor a biologist. He at-tributes only a slight role to the disciplines that provide the im-mediate explanation of development and growth. The notions of development and evolution, prevalent especially in Germany from Leibniz to Hegel, were inseparable from the intuitive awareness of a life reflected in organic beings, in history, and, on a deeper plane, in religion. Spencer was a physicist or rather an engineer, accustomed to meditate on conditions governing the maintenance of an equilibrium; he seeks supports in cosmogonies—for instance, in Laplace's nebular hypothesis, which relies solely on the laws of mechanics, or in transformism, which allows the environment to act mechanically on an inert organism. In this way he formu-lated a universal theory of evolution involving only material changes governed by the laws of mechanics. Evolution is defined as an integration of matter and a concomitant dissipation of motion in the course of which matter passes from an indefinite and in-coherent homogeneity to a definite and coherent heterogeneity and the retained motion undergoes a parallel transformation. A homogenous nebula, for example, through the simple dispersion of heat, produced the solar system with all its heterogeneity. The word "coherent" might seem to allow a trace of finality to subsist in his theory, but even this trace disappears when we recall that, according to Spencer, it simply expresses the effect of the conservation of force, which thus proves to be the sole principle. Moreover, this effect can be offset by an opposite effect, dissolution or passage from heterogeneity to homogeneity. From the mechanistic point of view the two facts are by nature the same; as in a machine which reverses its direction at regular intervals, first one, then the other predominates.

Spencer erred, it has been said, in deducing the principle of evolution from the law of the Persistence of Force. To accept his deduction and show the universality of his theory, we would have to resolve the opposite problem posed by every previous theory of evolution. In these theories the dynamic or vital force is the prime reality, and the mechanical force is the term to be explained; from Heraclitus to Plotinus, from Leibniz to Hegel, the problem is posed, and it is resolved by making the mechanical force a secondary reality or even an illusion. Here, on the contrary, the object is to fit biological, psychological, moral, and social evolution into a theory embracing only mechanical actions. Such an undertaking is possible only through the use of metaphors and artificial analogies. Thus in psychology, where matter and motion in the strict sense no longer intervene, we would begin, like Hume, by reducing consciousness to a mosaic of primary elements; but in analysis we would go beyond sensations and discover that they may be decomposed into elementary "shocks," each of which corresponds to one of the vibrations into which the physicist decomposes sensible qualities. This means that our subject matter is truly mental; its "integration" depends on successive combinations and recombinations which yield compounds characterized by progressively higher degrees of integration and heterogeneity. These are designated by the names of the different operations of the mind: sensations, images, concepts, judgments, reasonings; the laws of association that unite these combinations are the aspect assumed, with respect to the facts of consciousness, by the universal law of evolution. Similarly, in sociology well-known social facts, such as increase in the density of population in towns coupled with a more perfect division of labor, can be classed as an integration of matter with a corresponding manifestation of heterogeneity if the individuals that constitute society can be compared to matter.

Besides, Spencer's theory is perhaps not so purely mechanical as we might assume at first glance. If the first part of his formulation (integration and dissipation of motion) applies more readily to matter, the second part (passage from homogeneity to heterogeneity) finds more natural application in speaking of facts of a higher order—biological, moral, or social phenomena—such as the division of labor. Spencer sought, perhaps in vain, to unify both parts of his formulation.

Spencer adopted the essential notion of Darwinian transformism, the notion of the survival of the fittest, which governs the evolution of species, and drew from it consequences of utmost importance not only in biology but also in psychology, ethics, and politics. Mental and moral superiority depends on progressive improvements and refinements in an animal's adaptation to its environment. Good, if all moral side issues are disregarded, depends on adjustment to environmental conditions. This definition subsumes and explains that of the utilitarians, since pleasure is an accompaniment of the equilibrium between an organism and its environment. The very laws of nature spontaneously direct the organism toward its own good. It is possible to conceive of an absolute morality in which the end would be attained, and man, his evolution completed, would not have to choose between good and evil. This absolute morality would be matched by a perfect social state not unlike that suggested by societies of animals, such as ants, which have reached the end of their evolution. Then consciousness itself, which accompanies hesitation or reaction in the process of finding stability, would disappear.

Can Spencerian naturalism, closely tied to Darwinism, be reconciled with Spencer's own theory of evolution? The idea of an environment is totally alien to the inner development of organisms as this inner development is reflected in their evolution. Nor is there the slightest proof that progessive heterogeneity is the variation which best adapts an organism to its environment; on the contrary, increasing complexity may make the organism more fragile and vulnerable, and it continues indefinitely to create new states of disequilibrium.

But Spencer's fundamental trait, his individualism, fitted in perfectly with Darwinism and evolutionism. Through Darwinism he acquired a faith in nature which made him condemn any human intervention aimed at blocking the effects of the law of the survival of the fittest, such as charity or any kind of intervention designed to enable the individual to escape the natural consequences of his acts. The law of evolution, on the other hand, taught him that, in a society, functions become more and more specialized and are exercised by distinct organs. Consequently the function of government is to prevent acts of aggression; to go beyond this function is to go against nature.

Spencer's doctrine is fashioned from heterogeneous, loosely connected elements, yet it manifests a powerful attraction. He tried to discover, not the substance, but the rhythm of the universe. What appealed strongly to the next generation was the hope of giving to this rhythm a "scientific" explanation in terms of the ordinary laws of mechanics.

III *Positivists and Evolutionists in England*

Positivism in the strict sense predominated from 1850 to 1880. The object was, as G. H. Lewes expressed it, to rid philosophy of all its "metampirical" elements, not for social or practical reasons such as those advanced in the eighteenth century and at the beginning of the nineteenth century, but simply in order to attain the ideal of a scientifically correct body of knowledge. Lewes popularized the philosophy of positivism in England (*Comte's Philosophy of the Sciences*, 1853) and wrote a *Biographical History of Philosophy* (1845–46) which had the approval of Comte himself. His *Problems of Life and Mind* (1874–79) provides a good illustration of the spirit of positivism; one of the philosophical problems that he undertook to solve was that of the relation between consciousness and the organism. He solved it by viewing the physical process and the mental process as two aspects of a single reality.

Thomas Huxley (*Zoological Evidences as to Man's Place in Nature*, 1863; *Collected Essays*, 1894; *Life and Letters*, published by his son in 1900) gave a clear, precise statement of the independence of scientific knowledge as opposed to any metaphysical hypothesis whatsover. The fundamental axiom of speculative philosophy, according to him, is that materialism and spiritualism are two opposite poles of the same absurdity, the absurdity of imagining that we know anything at all about the mind or matter. Even the universality of principles such as the law of causality is in no way imposed by science; it is enough that the act of belief causing us to take the past as our guide in predicting the future is justified by its fruits; but we are never allowed to go beyond the field of verification. Nor does morality depend on any universal creed; it depends on a strong belief in a natural order in which the consequence of immorality is social disorganization.

In other instances positivism tended to draw support not so much from the sciences as from pure, immediate experience. W. K. Clifford's theory of "mind-stuff" (*Lectures and Essays*, 1879) is a good case in point. All reality is mind-stuff. Parts of this mind-stuff can unite; we then have a consciousness and a mind; several minds may coincide partially by virtue of the common portion of mind-stuff that they unite; that is why we have partial knowledge of the consciousness of others. Clifford calls this consciousness the "eject." Finally, psychic matter which is not integrated into consciousness remains continuous with the eject, and awareness of this continuity is a "cosmic emotion," the basis of religious sentiment. From these views Clifford deduced the existence of a "social conscience" or "tribal self," a life common to mankind which governs each man.

According to him, from the dawn of history and from the depths of each soul, the face of our father Man looks at us, watches us with the fire of an eternal youth, and says, "Before Jehovah, I am." His thoughts are similar to those expressed in Renan's positivism which is no longer exactly that of the positive sciences.

The same trait appears in W. W. Reade's *The Martyrdom of Man* (1872). If we consider the life of a single atom, he reasons, everything seems to be cruelty and confusion; but when we consider mankind as a person, we see it become nobler and nobler, more and more divine.

Spencerian evolutionism, influenced by the humanitarianism of Comte, shed its close ties with hedonistic utilitarianism. For instance, Leslie Stephen (*Science of Ethics*, 1882) attempted to wed evolutionary theory to ethics; the true end of individual morality is not happiness but the health, power, and vitality of the social body; the computation of pleasure, which depends on a momentary impression, does not necessarily coincide with this end.

By contrast, in other instances the notion of evolution rapidly lost the purely mechanical interpretation assigned to it by Spencer. In the writings of John Fiske, for example (*Darwinism and Other Essays*, 1879; *The Destiny of Man Viewed in the Light of His Origin*, 1884) appears the idea that evolution hides an immanent finality since it tends toward the development of intelligence and morality, and that through experience we gain knowledge of an immanent God who is the soul of the world. Joseph Le Conte (*Evolution and Its Relation to Religious Thought*, 1888) also viewed nature as the life of God and the human spirit as a particle of divine energy. George Romanes (*A Candid Examination of Theism*, 1878) is typical of thinkers who moved from the Darwinian notion of adaptation to the notion of an intelligent finality, which alone explains the concurrence of circumstances that preserve life.

A short time later, Benjamin Kidd (*Social Evolution*, 1894) separated evolutionism and individualism. Like the old utilitarians, Kidd held that the intellect is a scheming faculty which always serves the interests of the individual. Darwinism taught him that progress is possible only through a process of natural selection which acts in the interests of the race and often sacrifices the interests of the individual. From this he concludes that progress is possible only through the intervention of a powerful irrational force that restrains individual selfishness imposed by reason—religion. Far from interfering with the results of the struggle for life, the altruism advocated by religion tends to favor this struggle by erasing class distinctions and putting all men on an equal footing.

iv *Émile Littré and Positivism*

Referring in *Auguste Comte and Positivism* (1865) to the simplistic notion of relegating theological problems to the past, J. S. Mill accused Comte of never leaving any questions open. Positivism, as developed by Émile Littré (1801–81), accepts Comte's negations as an established fact. "The immutability of natural laws as opposed to theology, which introduced supernatural interventions, the limited speculative world as opposed to metaphysics, which studied the infinite and the absolute—such is the dual basis from which positive philosophy draws its support."[2] Through his articles in the journal *Le National* (1844; 1849–51) Littré did much to spread a doctrine which accepted the positive sciences as evidence of intellectual and social stability, which linked conservatism and the spirit of progress, and which recognized the necessity of predicating social reform on intellectual reform.[3] Littré based his positive faith on the law of the three states; in the positive state the knowing subject is reduced to its logical and formal conditions; any content is on the side of the object.[4] Littré accepted Comte's table of the sciences but added political economy, philosophical psychology in so far as it studies the conditions of knowledge (criticism), and finally ethics, aesthetics, and psychology.[5]

[2] *Conservation, révolution et positivisme*, 1852.
[3] Cf. also *La science au point de vue philosophique*, 1873; *Fragments de Philosophie positive et de Sociologie contemporaine*, 1876.
[4] *Auguste Comte et le Positivisme*, 1863; 3d edition, 1877, p. 656.
[5] *Ibid.*, p. 659.

Littré was not willing, however, to accept the religion of humanity instituted by Comte at the end of his life. Comte found a firm adherent to this religion in the person of Pierre Laffitte (1823–1903), who spread the doctrine through his teaching at the Collège de France (*Great Types of Mankind*, 1875; *Course in First Philosophy*, 1889). The positivist school, in the strict sense of the word, never ceased to support the religion of humanity, which flourished in some foreign countries, notably Brazil.

During the period that followed, the biologist and philosopher Félix le Dantec (1869–1917) combined the positive spirit with Lamarckian evolutionism. According to him, however, belief in determinism does not imply stable prevision of the future. "Things are determined, that is certain, there are no exceptions to natural laws, and we are all puppets subject to these laws; but there are too many strings, and no one can hold all of them at the same time; that is why no one can foresee the future." [6] That is why his positivism is especially critical; to him the moral and intellectual propensities of mankind are simply acquired characteristics transmitted through heredity; even belief in natural laws is a purely human belief, and reality escapes us completely. Among his numerous works are the *New Theory of Life* (1896), *Atheism* (1907), *Against Metaphysics* (1912), and *Egotism, the Sole Basis of Any Society* (1911).

An important development of the positivist spirit occurred in Italy between 1850 and 1890 under the combined influence of Auguste Comte, Häckel, and Spencer. Especially noteworthy is Robert Ardigo (1828–1920), who, in eleven volumes of philosophical writings published between 1869 and 1917, devoted many studies to Kant, Comte, and Spencer. The ninth volume contains two studies of particular importance: "Idealism in speculative philosophy and realism in positive philosophy" and "The perenniality of positivism."

Italian positivism was applied by Ardigo himself, but more especially by Ferri and Lombroso, to the juridical problem and particularly to penal law. If crimes are determined by abnormal phys-

---

[6] *Les limites du connaissable*, 1903, p. 184.

ical conditions, Lombroso observed, the conception of responsibility and punishment should be modified (*The Criminal Man*, 1876; English translation, 1895).

v *Ernest Renan*

"Capricious mobility of the will, strength and tenacity of the intellect" are the two traits, according to P. Lasserre, which are combined in the great Breton thinkers—Abelard, Lamennais, Chateaubriand, and finally Renan (1823–92)—who find their natural place not in centuries obsessed by the notion of organization, such as the eighteenth or nineteenth centuries, but in an era such as the twelfth or thirteenth centuries, "when the disturbances that shook old ideas and institutions as a result of the influx of a vast body of new knowledge and new arrangements affecting mankind were accompanied by a surge of piety encompassing these same ideas and institutions." [7]

We seek in vain to find a stable, coherent doctrine in the writings of any of these great Bretons. All of them had an exquisite sense of spiritual values and scorn for whatever binds the spirit to material interests; all of them searched for a positive reality pure enough to be the depository and organ of Mind. Their restless quest could lead either to despair or to ironic disenchantment. Renan's training led him at first to believe that he had found it in the Catholic faith, but he changed his views as soon as historical criticism revealed to him the emptiness of tradition. Late in 1848, after he had become intimate with the chemist Marcellin Berthelot, he wrote *The Future of Science*, published in 1890. Science became for him what religion had been. "Science alone," he wrote, "will give to humanity that without which it cannot live: a symbol and a law." But how and why? The explanation is that Renan was concerned primarily with history and philology and was at the moment strongly influenced by Hegel and Herder, whom he had just read. In his judgment, philology is the science of spiritual things; it

[7] *Un Conflit religieux au XII⁰ siècle* (Paris, 1930), p. 85.

acquaints man with his development, making him conscious of the unconscious spontaneity that has guided him; scholars and thinkers are the intellectual elite who reveal to man what is best in himself; and since Christianity is the supreme spiritual religion, the investigation of the origins of Christianity is the first task imposed upon the historian.

The situation is paradoxical and almost beyond apprehension. Following a circular course, Renan arrived at religion, which must have seemed illusory to him, since it assumes the miraculous intervention of God and miracles are impossible. The history of religion must be, as it was in the eighteenth century, the history of illusion and deception. Yet religion, especially the Christian religion, saves man from vulgarity; its absolute truth is of little consequence. We should act, he wrote toward the end of his life (*Philosophical Examination of Conscience,* 1889), as if God and the soul existed. Religion is one of a number of hypotheses which, like ether or electric, luminous, caloric, and nervous fluids, or even the atom, we treat as symbols or convenient means of explaining facts, and which we reserve for this purpose.

There seems to be a conflict between Renan's intellectual consciousness, which adopts the methods of the positive sciences, and his romantic aspirations. There is no truth, he says in *Philosophical Dialogues* (1876), that does not proceed immediately or otherwise from a laboratory or library, for all our knowledge comes to us through the study of nature and history. Only history is conceived, following Hegel, as a kind of spiritual revelation in mankind. Consequently positivism and spirituality are united in the study of history.

Yet Renan did not always follow in the footsteps of the Hegelians and neo-Hegelians. David Strauss had considered the life of Jesus to be a myth spontaneously invented in the earliest Christian communities. Renan, tempted at first to follow him,[8] later turned resolutely away from Strauss; his *Life of Jesus* (1863) is one of the first attempts to probe the historical background and individuality

[8] Cf. Jean Pommier, *Renan et Strasbourg* (Paris, 1926), chap. 5.

of Jesus, "that incomparable man." On the whole, Renan substituted the influence of the individualities of the elite—St. Paul, who saved the new religion from the narrowness of the Jewish ritualism, the prophets who discovered in Judea the religion of pure justice, without dogmas or rites—for the inner dialectic which, according to the Hegelians, governs history. Renan considered the elite circle of scholars, thinkers, and religious men to be the sole depository of spiritual values; all his political opinions are dominated by his concern for the preservation of the elite. Sometimes, abandoning all hope of realizing justice for mankind as a whole (cf. *Caliban* and *Philosophical Dialogues*), he dreamed that the elite might impose its will on the masses through terror, using the prodigious tools provided by science; and in *Intellectual and Moral Reform* (1872) he proposed an aristocratic constitution which would substitute government by the elite for democracy. It seems that Renan became increasingly aware of the risks to which the human mind was exposed by our industrial and egalitarian civilization, but his only reaction was dreamy contemplation of the past or ironic resignation.

VI *Hippolyte Taine*

Hippolyte Taine (1828–93), after meditating on the works of Spinoza, Condillac, and Hegel, arrived at a concept of intelligibility that seems at first glance to be somewhat alien to the positivist preoccupations prevalent around 1850. In his *History of English Literature* (1864) he commended the German metaphysicists for having understood "that there are simple notions, that is, indecomposable abstracts, that from their combinations the rest are engendered, and that the rules governing their unions and mutual contradictions are elemental laws of the universe." [9] He also sanctioned the analysis of Condillac, who tried to discover in sensation the simple element which, in a modified form, would produce each of the human faculties, as well as Spinoza's *Ethics* and unique substance, the source of all realities. On the other hand, few men have

---

[9] *Histoire de la littérature anglaise*, V, 1864; edition of 1878, p. 412.

had a more acute sense of the infinite complexity of the data of experience, "this magnificent world in motion, this tumultuous chaos of interpenetrating events, this infinitely varied and multiple life that never stops. For we are overwhelmed on all sides by the infinitude of time and space; we find ourselves hurled into this monstruous universe like a shell at the edge of a beach or an ant at the bottom of an embankment." [10] The contrast between this rich, refined sensitivity and the imperative demand for intelligibility is at the heart of the philosophical problem, according to Taine, and it gives to his style the kind of inner tension or striving which sometimes culminates in dryness, sometimes dissolves into imagery. English philosophy as reflected in Mill and German philosophy as reflected in Hegel seem to him to be open to criticism because these thinkers isolated the terms of the antithesis. Mill reduced all knowledge to facts and clusters of facts; but a fact "is only a slice arbitrarily cut from the infinite, continuous web of being by my senses or consciousness . . . an arbitrary cluster and at the same time an arbitrary cut, that is, a factitious grouping which separates that which is joined and joins that which is separate." Hegel's "gigantic edifice" crumbled because he maintained that he could deduce circumstances from facts.

To pass from the chaotic world to the world of elements, from the complex to the simple, is the analytical task assigned by Taine to philosophy. It is not easy for us to discern the details of this task. There is in fact a fundamental ambiguity in his analytical procedure. Striving to be faithful to the positivistic principle of deriving all knowledge from experience, Taine rejects any intellectual intuition of essences; consequently his only means of attaining them is through the process of abstraction which isolates the elements in the "factitious groups" at his disposal. Thus an abstraction is a portion, an extract, a constituent; but it must at the same time be a productive, prime property, an essence or a cause from which other properties are deduced. It is difficult to follow Taine here and to understand how a part can produce the whole in which it is

[10] *Ibid.*, pp. 408 and 412.

included; the mathematical example that he borrows from Spinoza (the revolution of a semicircle around its diameter as the generative property of a sphere) is hardly conclusive, for according to Spinoza's own observation, this property is meaningful only if we already possess the concept of a sphere. Taine also compares the procedure of the analyst to that of the zoologist who discerns in an animal a type of organization or a synthesis of characteristics such that each characteristic implies the others.[11] Here abstraction was supposed to culminate in the identification, not of an element, but of a connection. Between the elements which were linked together, however, there was no intelligible relation; furthermore, the connection was known only by virtue of an empirical generalization based on the observation of numerous similar cases without which abstraction would be meaningless.

It was to the sciences of man, and especially to literary criticism, art, and political history, that Taine applied his method. His main concern was not a system but an approach to science based on two procedures: the investigation of connected sequences and the investigation of conditions. "Between a bower in Versailles, a philosophical and theological argument of Malebranche, a precept of Boileau concerning versification, a law of Colbert relating to mortgages, a trite compliment heard in Marly, and a pronouncement of Bossuet on the Kingdom of God, the distance seems infinite and insuperable. These facts appear to be unrelated. They are so dissimilar that we are tempted to judge them at first sight just as they appear to be—that is, isolated and separate; but they share a relation based on the definitions of the groups in which they are included."[12] It is obvious that Taine is here concerned less with interdependent relations such as those associated with a certain arrangement of organic parts than with a common characteristic that might be discovered by abstraction in the most disparate facts associated with seventeenth-century France. Investigation of conditions is in turn the discovery of a stable characteristic that persists through every

[11] *Essais de critique et d'histoire,* 1857; 8th edition, 1900, Preface, p. xxvi.
[12] *Ibid.,* p. 12.

period of history, such as nationality, which is one of the great permanent forces of history.

Taine's doctrine is expounded in his treaties *On Intelligence* (1870). This epoch-making work puts great stress on pathological and physiological investigations. His doctrine is summed up perfectly in these lines: "Wherever we are able to isolate and observe the elements of a compound, we can explain the properties of the compound in terms of the properties of the elements and, from a few general laws, deduce a host of particular laws. That is precisely what we did here; first we went down by degrees to the ultimate elements of knowledge, then we climbed step by step to the simplest and, from there, to the most complex knowledge; each rung of this ladder owes its characteristics to the characteristics manifested by the lower rungs." [13] We see at a glance how pathology, by simplifying phenomena, and neurophysiology, by revealing in detail conditions associated with the data of consciousness, enable us to push analysis beyond the level of consciousness even though direct observation cannot penetrate these highly complex data.

Thus, in the normal state, images seem to us to be internal. This interiority, which suggests that an image is a fact which cannot be reduced to sensation, is due to an "antagonistic reducer," which prevents it from being exteriorized. The reducer consists of the whole complex of sensations inimical to the existence of the object of an image; if the antagonistic reducer is weakened, however, hallucination springs up. An isolated image is no less external than an isolated sensation, and the two are by nature the same.

By virtue of many of its features, mainly its atomism, which resolves psychological phenomena into simple elements, Taine's psychology belongs to the mainstream of English psychology and owes much to Mill and Bain. Its distinctive trait, however, is its explicative claims. Because of the diversity of their arrangements, the identical infinitesimal sensations into which any mental event is finally resolved should produce all the diversity of mental phenomena. Here again, the part should generate the whole.

[13] *De l'intelligence,* 2d edition, II, 429.

This identity of an abstract element and a creative force is the heart of Taine's metaphysics, expressed in a classic passage: "At the supreme summit of things, at the peak of the luminous, inaccessible ether, the eternal axiom is pronounced; and the prolonged reverberation of this creative formula, through its inexhaustible undulations, constitutes the immensity of the universe. Any form, any change, any movement is one of its acts. It subsists in all things and is limited by nothing. Matter and thought, planets and men, masses of suns and the palpitations of an insect, life and death, grief and joy—nothing fails to express it and to express it fully. It fills time and space and remains beyond time and space. . . . Indifferent, immobile, eternal, omnipotent, creative force—no name exhausts it; and when its serene, sublime face is unveiled, every human spirit must fall prostrate, overwhelmed by admiration and horror. Immediately this spirit arises again; sympathetically it possesses the infinity that it contemplates and shares in its grandeur."[14] Here the richness of Taine's images hides the poverty of his concept, just as, in his literary criticism, his vivid portraits of writers— Shakespeare or Carlyle, for example—hide the vagueness and shortcomings of his attempts to explain their works in terms of milieu and race.

VII *Arthur de Gobineau*

Arthur de Gobineau wrote to Tocqueville on November 29, 1856: "If I say that I am a Catholic, it is because I am a Catholic. . . . Of course, I have been a Hegelian philosopher, an atheist. I was never afraid to go to the limit. It is through this last door that I departed from the doctrines that lead to the void and came back to those that have value and density" (*Correspondence with Tocqueville,* 1908). In his *Essay on the Inequality of the Races* (4 vols., 1853–55), he lays a physical, realistic basis for the idea of the superiority of the Nordic and Germanic races, which Hegelianism grounded on an idealistic dialectic. By itself race confers a physical and moral su-

[14] *Les Philosophes français du XIX⁰ siècle,* 1856, p. 371.

periority on men; civilization which seeks to make all men alike and humanism which posits an underlying identity of spirits are signs of decadence, for they favor a mixture of races which will always be to the advantage of the inferior race. Direct experience with Oriental affairs led him to believe that human civilization was impossible. "Much has been said during the past thirty years about civilizing the other peoples of the world, carrying civilization to this or that nation. Even though I look for examples, I do not find that any such result has ever been obtained, either in modern times or in ancient times. . . . When the population of a country is weak numerically speaking, it can of course be civilized, but through the process of elimination or assimilation" (*Three Years in Asia,* 1859). Racial intermingling destroys noble values; intermingling with the Orient, beginning with Alexander, was the true cause of the abasement of Greco-Roman civilization.

Gobineau, compaining that he was unknown in his own country, wrote in 1856: "Must I wait for my opinions to be translated from English or German and brought back to France?" It was in Germany, in fact, especially after Nietzsche, that he found fame and success.

VIII *Ernst Haeckel*

The image of the world that appears in *The Riddle of the Universe* (1899), written by Ernst Haeckel (1834–1919), professor of zoology at the University of Jena in 1865, recalls the most ancient philosophers of Ionia. Infinite space; time without a beginning or an end; everywhere matter animated by an incessant universal motion, which periodically reintroduces evolutions involving a condensation of matter producing numberless little centers at each point where it occurs; the destruction of these bodies by collision, accompanied by the production of huge quantities of heat, which are vital forces for new formations—these, with the exception of a few items borrowed from thermodynamics, are the notions that might be found in the fragmentary writings of the pre-Socratics.

This "pyknotic monism," which ignored all the questions which had been posed by philosophers since the sixth century B.C., was in reality a weapon to use against the traditional doctrine of the dualism of mind and body, whose advocates were opposed to the spread of Darwinian transformism. After the *Origin of Species* (1859), Haeckel had written his *General Morphology* (1866) and, before *The Descent of Man* (1871), had published his *History of Creation* (1868). In both the *History of Creation* and the *Evolution of Man* (1874), he applied transformism to the origin of man. The monism of *The Riddle of the Universe* was intended to nullify, in the general explanation of the world, God, freedom, and immortality, the beliefs that remained as fundamental obstacles to this new doctrine: man is nothing but an aggregate of matter and energy.

Then Haeckel's monism took an unexpected turn in *The Miracle of Life* (1904), and he became even more animistic than the Ionians. In his view everything, even crude matter, possesses life in different degrees; God is identical with the world. Religion is knowledge of the true and the good—that is, the laws of nature—and respect for them. From sociability, which is a vital condition of human nature, he deduces the evangelical precept, "Thou shalt love thy neighbor as thyself." Monism is one of the last attempts to base the religious and social life of man on simple knowledge of natural laws. In spite of the foundation of the Deutsche Monistenbund in Munich in 1906 and the support provided by an international congress held in 1912, dogmatic and whimsical treatment of scientific facts undermined the success of the movement, which finally was absorbed in the general trends associated with freethinking radicalism.

IX *Positivism in Germany*

German thinkers of vastly different persuasions[15] agree in proclaiming the emptiness of philosophical preoccupations in Germany in 1880, when there was only orthodox Kantianism reduced to a critique of metaphysics or the trite positivism of Ernst Laas (1837–

---

[15] *Philosophie der Gegenwart*. For example, Natorp, I, 2; Drews, V, 70.

85). In the opinion of Laas, the whole history of philosophical thought is dominated by collision of two doctrines which he identifies as Platonism on the one hand and positivism on the other (*Idealism and Positivism,* 1879). Platonism is the realm of realized concepts, innate ideas, spiritualism, final causes; it is a system which adopts deduction as its sole procedure, reduces all knowledge or action to absolute principles, tries to find their suprasensory, intemporal origin, assumes a spontaneity alien to the mechanism of nature, and directs life toward a supraterrestrial eternity; it is the doctrine of Plato, Aristotle, Descartes, Leibniz, Kant, Schelling, Hegel—the doctrine of error and illusion. Positivism is the doctrine that assumes a correlation between subject and object; an object exists only by virtue of the content of consciousness, and a subject is the stage or substratum of the object; it asserts the perpetual variability of the objects of perception; finally, it assumes that knowledge is identical with sensation. Here we recognize the three assertions made by Protagoras in Plato's Theaetetus; Laas is in fact much closer to Plato than to Auguste Comte. Thus Laas introduces into Platonism (in a manner not unlike that adopted by Nietzsche in *The Will to Power*), along with the vulgar belief in a world that exists in itself, the scientific image of the universal mechanism; this world was obtained by eliminating from reality all of the non-social content of experience, feelings, voluntary acts, memories; the residue is the world of knowledge—a fictive supposition.

In his system of ethics Laas avoids any contact with "Platonism" by defining moral values in terms of social interest. His social morality was adopted by T. Zeigler (*History of Ethics,* 1886) and F. Jodel (*History of Ethics,* 1906–12). Like Comte, Jodel insisted on reinterpreting and retaining religious precepts. "The ideal within us," he wrote, "and our faith in our ability to realize the ideal. . . . Faith does not mean union with supernatural powers but the living certainty that, in the course of history, man becomes God."

Dühring wrote a *Critical History of Philosophy* (1869) designed to emancipate his readers from philosophy itself. Feuerbach and Comte, according to him, are the only authentic thinkers of the nineteenth century; philosophy is a spiritual reformation directed, like Nietzsche's, against the pessimism of Schopenhauer, against Christianity which makes man a slave, and against Judaism. Yet he does not view the world as a materialistic mechanism. Everywhere he sees a beginning, limits, finitude: the vital is distinct from the mechanical; life had a beginning; the law of numbers rules out the assumption of infinitely large and infinitely small quantities. In his theory of a finite world, godless, uncreated, and devoid of freedom, we find an opposition not only to all theism but also to all continuist evolutionism.

x *Richard Avenarius and Ernst Mach*

The second half of the nineteenth century exhibits a characteristic which had long been the exception: physicists and biologists turned to philosophy and tried to find for their own sciences new approaches and new solutions to problems. Their conceptions are related to legalism, an idea that Comte borrowed from the physics of Fourier. For example, the physicist Mayer, who discovered the law of the conservation of energy, thought that the physicist's task was finished when he had completely described a phenomenon (*Observations on the Mechanical Equivalent of Heat,* 1850). Similarly Rankine (*Outlines of the Science of Energetics,* 1855) opposed descriptive physics, the only true science, to explicative physics. Generally speaking, thermodynamics, which describes universal processes of change, favors such a view.

The philosophical consequences of this view are discussed by Avenarius, professor at Zurich in 1877, in his *Critique of Pure Experience* (1888-90). His empiriocriticism is an attempt to adhere to the facts—not by any means to an immediate experience in the Bergsonian sense, but rather to the general circumstances relating to a subject's knowledge. For instance, the biologist considers an organism in relation to its environment. He considers the enunciations of the subject (E) and the changes in its central nervous system (C); he knows that these changes are conditioned by an environment which acts either as a source of nourishment (S) or as raw material for its instruction and stimulation (R). Now we know the different values of E depend on changes in C, and that these changes are sometimes a function of $R[f(R)]$, sometimes a function of $S[f(S)]$. Biology also teaches us that $f(R)$ and $f(S)$ are contrary processes, that is, that exhaustion produced by excitation is offset by nutrition; whenever $f(R)$ and $f(S)$ are out of balance, there is a tendency toward destruction; whenever they are brought into balance, there is a reverse tendency toward conservation. The optimal condition, perfect balance, is never realized because of changes originating in the environment; any series of oscillations that promotes conservation assures the continuity of the living organism.

Some of the elements of the environment (R) reappear constantly, whereas others are accidental and inconstant. As the brain develops, it becomes more easily stimulated by the constant elements and less easily stimulated by the accidental elements; it follows that the values of E actually depend almost solely on the constant elements; instead of a continuous flow of impressions, there is an ever-present environment—the physical environment of terrestrial things, the social environment of mankind; familiarity with habitual stimulants produces a feeling of security; the world is no longer a problem for us; the enigma issues from a feeling of nonfamiliarity; therefore knowledge tends to nullify this feeling, to achieve homogeneity or "a heterotic minimum."

Thus, according to Avenarius, the insoluble problems of criticism vanish. They all depend on Schopenhauer's dictum, "Things are my representation." Then the object is to find out how we reach a reality that is not ourselves. This precept in turn issues from a procedure that Avenarius calls *introjection*. A man begins by introducing into his equals the sensations and perceptions of things he himself knows. Afterwards the thing experienced is separated from the perception his equal has of it, for the real world and a reflection of this world is in his equal—an outer world made of things and an inner world made of perceptions. Then the man carries out the same operation for himself, separating reality from the phenomenon that is in him. This gives rise to a subjectivism which all theories of knowledge try in vain to overcome. Empiriocriticism takes place before introjection and shows the coordination of the thing and the ego by virtue of the same principle in experience. The values of E—the enunciations that follow the action of the environment (R and S) on the brain—are things as well as thoughts; they are things when they depend on conditions outside the organism, thoughts in the opposite case.[16]

Empiriocriticism is one of the greatest efforts ever made to avoid the critical problem. The work of Ernst Mach, professor of physics (1867), then of philosophy (1875) at Vienna (*The Science of Mechanics,* 1883; *Contributions to the Analysis of Sensations,* 1906; *Space and Geometry,* 1905) is directed toward the same end even though it draws less support from biology than from the method of physics. The essential point is that physics dispenses with the concept of causality and uses the mathematical concept of function which links the variation of one phenomenon to that of another. Along with the concept of cause, three other concepts are found to be useless: the concept of substance (replaced by a relatively stable sum of sensible qualities), the concept of a thing in itself, and the concept of the self, which is simply a complex made up of the body and memories and emotions associated with it. Thus it is possible for us to give a complete description of the world of experience through sensations and the functions that unite them; there is no gap between the physical and the psychic. A color is a physical reality when we consider its connection with other physical phenomena; it is a psychic reality when we apprehend its relation to the retina.

The rule governing this description, in science, is linked to a law derived from biology—the law of economy. In economics, for example, capital is considered to be an instrument or an accumulation of work through which we achieve freedom from work; in

---

[16] Cf. H. Delacroix, "Avenarius, Esquisse de l'empiriocriticisme," *Revue de Métaphysique,* 1897.

the same way, scientific laws are intended to free us from an infinitude of experiences. Thus if we know the angle of incidence, the refractive index and the laws of refraction which enable us to calculate the angle of refraction and free us from the task of measuring it directly. Mathematics itself is but a set of procedures for shortening calculations.

This conception of science as the economics of thought is linked to the legalism of thermodynamics. It is not surprising, then, to find them together in the writings of the chemist Wilhelm Ostwald (*Lectures on Natural Philosophy*, 1902). This energeticist, who held that modes of energy are subject to the laws of thermodynamics in matter, in the soul, and even in civilization as well as in heat and light, also considered laws to be instruments for providing us with foresight and eliminating the need for constant recourse to experience. The sole aim of philosophy is to facilitate the work of specialists.

Theodor Ziehen, professor of psychiatry at Berlin, undertook a description of reality which, like that of Avenarius, was designed to eliminate the duality of the physical and the psychic. In *Theory of Knowledge* (1912) and *Textbook in Logic* (1920) he separates sensations and representations. In a sensation, however, he identifies two "components": a "reduced sensation," which obeys natural laws and constitutes what is vulgarly called the object—for example, the determinations of place and space studied by the physicist—and the additional remnant, which constitutes what is commonly called a sensation. Psychology studies the second of these—the component which is subject to modifications independently of the first component (for instance, modifications due to changes in distance or perspective). Ziehen finds the same composition in representation; in memory, for example, the components are the "objective" events which we recall. This is about as far as we could go in the direction of accepting reality passively, describing it, naming it, and refusing to raise any questions.

From this viewpoint the difference between idealism and realism, which once seemed to be of utmost importance, disappears, and the idealism of Schuppe's *Cognitive Theory of Logic* (1878) and *Outline of Pure Logic* (1894) almost coincides with the realism of Avenarius. Of course Schuppe considers the self or consciousness to be irreducible to a complex of states of consciousness, and he assumes that any reality may be the content of consciousness, since the existence of things which are not in consciousness depends on the possibility of their being seen under certain conditions. Only this consciousness is to him merely a theater or a receptacle since he refuses to acknowledge the existence of any kind of mental functions or activities. Thus his position would become identical with that of Mach of Avenarius if his "immanentism" did not pose a supplementary difficulty arising from the individuality of consciousness, which leads him to solipsism. Schuppe avoids this situation only by formulating a kind of Berkeleian hypothesis of an abstract self, common to all individuals; space and time become objective and universal because they depend on the universal self and therefore are independent of a particular self. The self plays such a minor role that Schuppe's doctrine caused Schubert-Soldern (*Human Happiness and the Social Question,* 1896) to accept a "solipsism of the theory of knowledge," which eliminates the self completely and preserves only the continuous flow of states of consciousness.

XI *Wilhelm Wundt*

The works of Wilhelm Wundt, published for the most part in 1874 and 1890, are the low-water mark of strictly philisophical preoccupations in German philosophy. Wundt (1832–1920), professor at Leipzig in 1875, began with physics and came to philosophy by way of experimental psychology; his thought always proceeded by addition rather than development, and his writings are more remarkable for their breadth than for their depth. Early in his career he initiated laboratory research in psychology; his *Principles of Physiological Psychology* (1874, 6th edition, 1908–11) contains, in particular, research concerning reaction time, following the method of Helmholtz, with whom he had worked as an assistant. The time that elapses between the application of a stimulus and our reaction differs according to our psychological state (attention, distraction, emotion, and so on), and Wundt assumed that by measuring it he could characterize some of these states. Psychophysical parallelism is accepted, at least as a working hypothesis, as the basis for this procedure, since what is measured is invariably the duration of a nervous process of which one part (the one that takes place in the cerebral centers) is assumed to coincide with the duration of a psychological phenomenon.

His *Logic* (1880–83, 4th edition, 1919–21) is merely an extension of his psychology. It is grounded on the distinction between passive association, in which representations are given free play, and active apperception, which "develops the correlations of individual representations into new representations." To Wundt apperception is a psychic act *sui generis*, accompanied by a feeling of tension and producing a greater distinction in our representations. Logical thought begins only when apperception produces syntheses. Psychological synthesis has this distinctive trait: its product is always more than the sum of the elements it contains. It follows that a logical concept, contrary to what has been assumed, is not a simple extraction of the common elements in a series of representations but a "synthesis accomplished by the active apperception of an individual preponderant representation [the one linked to the name] and a series of dependent representations." Thus Wundt is concerned more with the logical life of the mind than with logical relations in themselves. In this context, one of the most curious points in his work is the explanation of the psychological origin of Aristotelian logic on the basis of the theory of displacement (*Verschiebung*). There are in fact many judgments in which the predicate belongs to a category different from the subject—for example, when it designates a state or a quality (verb or adjective); Aristotle recognized only concepts of objects and the relations of subsumption; consequently he gave in to the tendency, characteristic of logical thought, constantly to increase the concepts of objects; beginning with a small number of concepts of objects provided by sensible intuition, thought transforms all concepts into concepts of objects, as we see in languages in which substantives were first adjectives and adjectives originally had the meaning of verbs; thus all concepts become comparable to each other, and formal logic can take shape.

Ethics (1886, 4th edition, 1912) is a system of "ethics of facts." It consists for the most part of an analysis of the moral motives operative at the present time and of the investigation of the general points of view to which they are subordinate. According to Wundt, an action is judged good or bad depending on whether it promotes or hinders the free development of spiritual forces; this development is the ultimate aim of human society.

In *System of Philosophy* (1889, 4th edition, 1919) Wundt considers the task of philosophy to be "the reunion of our knowledge of particulars into an intuitive apprehension of the world and life which satisfies the requirements of reason and the needs of the soul." He further defines philosophy as "the universal science which must draw together into a coherent system knowledge obtained through special sciences and reduce to their principles the universal suppositions used in the sciences." The coherence of the universe, the certainty that the principle of reason necessitates a unified totality of which experience reveals only parts—such is the only characteristic, purely formal, attributed to philosophy. To provide content for this form, Wundt again uses psychology: the only activity given to us immediately is the exercise of our will; if we are acted upon by another being, we can represent this being to ourselves only as will and any evolution only as being due to the reciprocal influence of different wills. Thus the influence of one will on another awakens in the second will the activity which is representation: will and representation, here as in Leibniz, are the attributes of being. In Wundt, however, these attributes account in full for substance; his psychology, of which metaphysics is an extension, is in fact *actualistic;* in the soul nothing is real except actual processes. This explains his hostility to monadology; his volitional units can be joined in a synthesis to form a vaster unit. This theory of the production of beings by synthesis also makes Wundt completely hostile to the emanationist image of the universe; the idea of "creative resultants" is perhaps the most valuable idea in his metaphysics.

But to Wundt metaphysics was merely an interlude, and in *The Psychology of Nations* (*Völkerpsychologie,* 1904, 2 vols.; 3d edition in 10 vols., 1911–20), he devoted his energies to another extension of psychology, to radical psychology, which deals with the great permanent classes of the manifestations of collective psychology—language, art, myth, religion, society, law, civilization. It is the synthesis of every science of man developed during the nineteenth century. His study of language is the study of the evolution of language from primitive mimicry to its final employment in the manipulation of abstract ideas. Myth derives from a peculiarity of apperception belonging to simple consciousness; it is "the apperception that animates things." Art has as its aim neither the production of the beautiful, nor aesthetic pleasure, nor a contemplative arrangement; it is the expression of life in its totality, with its seriousness and its gaiety, its sublimity and its baseness, its disjointedness and its harmony; but what produces a work of art is life apprehended in a personal institution.

Bibliography

I

Studies

Cannon, H. G. *Lamarck and Modern Genetics.* New York, 1960.
Gillispie, C. C. "The Formation of Lamarck's Evolutionary Theory." *Archives internationales d'histoire des sciences* 35 (1956).
———. "Lamarck and Darwin in the History of Science." *American Scientist* 46 (1958).
Landrieu, Marcel. *Lamarck.* Paris, 1909.
Packard, A. S. *Lamarck, The Founder of Evolution.* New York, 1901.
Russell, E. S. *Form and Function.* Cambridge, 1916.
Wilkie, J. S. "Buffon, Lamarck and Darwin." In *Darwin's Biological Work,* ed. P. R. Bell. Cambridge, 1959.

II

Texts

Spencer, Herbert. *Essays on Education.* London, 1861.
———. *First Principles.* London, 1862. 6th ed. Reissued 1937.
———. *Principles of Biology,* 2 vols. London, 1864–67.
———. *Principles of Psychology.* 2 vols. 2d ed. London, 1870–72.
———. *Principles of Sociology.* 3 vols. London, 1876–96.
———. *Principles of Ethics.* 2 vols. London, 1879–93.
———. *Man versus the State.* London, 1884.
———. *Autobiography.* London, 1904.
———. *The Study of Sociology,* with introduction by Talcott Parsons. Ann Arbor, Mich., 1961.

Studies

Asirvatham, E. *Herbert Spencer's Theory of Social Justice.* New York, 1936.
Bowne, B. P. *The Philosophy of Herbert Spencer.* New York, 1874.
Diaconide, E. *Étude critique sur la sociologie de Herbert Spencer.* Paris, 1938.
Duncan, David. *Life and Letters of Herbert Spencer.* 2 vols. New York, 1908.
Elliot, Hugh. *Herbert Spencer.* New York, 1917.
Hudson, W. H. *An Introduction to the Philosophy of Herbert Spencer.* 2d ed. London, 1904.

Rumney, Judah. *Herbert Spencer's Sociology.* London, 1934.
Taylor, A. E. *Herbert Spencer.* New York, 1928.

III

Texts

Clifford, W. *The Common Sense of the Exact Sciences,* ed. Karl Pearson. London, 1885. New York, 1955.
———. *Lectures and Essays,* ed. F. Pollock. 2 vols. London, 1879.
———. *Mathematical Papers,* ed. H. J. Smith. London, 1882.

Studies

Eddington, A. S. *The Nature of the Physical World.* Cambridge, 1929.
Fullerton, George S. *A System of Metaphysics.* New York, 1914.

V

Texts

Renan, Ernest. *Averroes et l'averroïsme.* Paris, 1852.
———. *Essais de morale et de critique.* Paris, 1859.
———. *The Life of Jesus,* trans. C. E. Wilbour. New York, 1864.
———. *Questions contemporaines.* Paris, 1868.
———. *Dialogues et fragments philosophiques.* Paris, 1876.
———. *Recollections of My Youth,* trans. C. B. Pitman. Boston and New York, 1929.
———. *The Future of Science,* trans. A. Vandam and C. Pitman. London, 1891.

VI

Texts

Taine, Hippolyte. *Essais de critique et d'histoire.* Paris, 1858.
———. *History of English Literature,* trans. H. van Laun. 2 vols. Edinburgh, 1873.
———. *Nouveaux Essais de critique et d'histoire.* Paris, 1865.
———. *The Philosophy of Art,* trans. J. Durand. New York, 1865.
———. *Intelligence,* trans. T. D. Hayes. 2 vols. London, 1871.
———. *Les Origines de la France contemporaine.* 5 vols. Paris, 1876–1893.
———. *Derniers Essais de critique et d'histoire.* Paris, 1894.

XI

Texts

Wundt, Wilhelm. "Things Experienced and Perceived, Autobiography." Stuttgart, 1920.

———. *Wilhelm Wundts Werk, ein Verzeichnis seiner sämtlichen Schriften* ("Wilhelm Wundt's Work, A List of His Complete Writings"), ed. Eleonore Wundt. Munich, 1926.

Studies

Boring, E. G. *A History of Experimental Psychology*. 2d ed. New York, 1950.

Peters, R. S. ed. *Brett's History of Psychology*. London, 1953.

Peterson, Peter. *Wilhelm Wundt und seine Zeit*. Stuttgart, 1925.

A William Wundt Archive. The Psychological Institute of the University of Leipzig.

RELIGIOUS PHILOSOPHY

IN THE FIRST half of the nineteenth century religious philosophy, when not led astray into the vague religiosity of Schleiermacher, had tended toward the elaboration of extensive dogmas concerning the real or toward a comprehensive interpretation of the philosophy of history. The fideist movement signaled a change: religious thought became at once more dogmatic and more internal; acceptance of dogma was accompanied by reflection on the inner faith that caused it to be accepted by a religious soul. Here, too, the positive spirit reigned supreme.

1 Cardinal Newman and Religious Thought in England

Benthamism, with its purely rational authority, is not very remote in spirit from the dry, unemotional, authoritarian religion typified at mid-century by Pusey. Just as utilitarianism was declining, religious formalism was harshly attacked by the members of the Oxford Movement, led by John Henry Newman (1801–90). Newman's doctrine is an apologetic of the Christian religion and more especially of the Roman Catholic Church in which, after his conversion, he became a cardinal. At the heart of his apologetic is an irrationalism which then found numerous expressions—in Coleridge, Carlyle, and, in one respect at least, in Renouvier in France. Its point of departure is the impossibility or producing "real assent" through pure logical inference. By assent he means a state of ac-

49

quiescence, untroubled by any doubt, with a concrete and individual reality; one which helps us to live, moves us, causes us to act; one no less receptive to beauty and heroism than to truth. Whereas rational inference leads us to a probability covering a rather wide range, there are no more degrees in positive assent than in comprehensive representation among the Stoics; whereas logical inference is governed by definite conditions and can be transmitted, assent is an unconditional, purely personal act which engages the whole self. As Pascal contrasted the mathematical mind and the discriminating mind, Newman contrasts the logician and the true reasoner, who takes as his premises the total experience of life.

That assent as defined here is realized in religious belief and that the sole religious belief which entails assent is found in Catholicism are the apologetic components of Newman's work. To believe, according to him, is to accept a doctrine as true because God says it is true. Faith is a principle of action, and action does not allow time for carrying out detailed investigatons; whereas reason is grounded on obvious proof, faith is influenced by presumption. Happiness predicated on obedience and subordination, the essence of sin in insubordination, strength of conviction linked to traditional customs which we should have resisted before they were acquired, immediate awareness of the necessity of redemption—these traits all involve assent but have their full strength only in Catholicism (*A Grammar of Assent*, 1870).

W. C. Ward (*Ideal of a Christian Church*, 1844) evidences the same spirit of resistance to a Protestantism which to him seemed dull, trite, lifeless, and spiritless. F. D. Maurice (*Theological Essays*, 1853; *Lectures of Social Morality*, 1870) also saw religion as a way of life rather than knowledge, and this caused him to oppose scholastic discussions of theology as well as the critical study of Biblical texts, which were written to inspire prayers rather than definitions. At this time the development of religious ideas in England was scarcely affected by criticism of the Old Testament and the Gospels, even though such criticism had played a very important role in Germany and France; it was not until 1860 that three authors—

Benjamin Jowett, Baden Powell, and Mark Pattison—in a volume titled *Essays and Reviews,* published the results of critical studies. The same need for a living religion prompted Seeley in *Ecce Homo* (1865) to advocate a pure evangelism which renounced the whole intermediary tradition and went back to the personality of Jesus. With more originality and authority, the poet Matthew Arnold (*God and the Bible,* 1875) made a distinction between his conception of religion and historical Christianity: religion should be a firsthand affair, a verifiable experience, but the Christian faith is the product of both the material imagination of the Apocalypse and metaphysical reasonings unintelligible to almost everyone. The immediate religious experience is the certainty that justice, the law of our being, is at the same time the law of the world; yet this precept, which is almost Stoic, is not reduced to morality; the Stoics saw it only as the logical pursuit of human happiness; Jesus and St. Paul added the sense of a divine mission.

II *Pierre Leroux*

Pierre Leroux (1797–1871) was a harsh judge of ecclesiastical philosophy, the philosophy "of immobility and apathy, of fact and the status quo," and "of men dispossessed of both traditions and ideals. They were mere scholars, but they dealt with philosophical matters. They said they were philosophers and believed they were philosophers, and they called themselves eclectics; but eclecticism was a product of the Napoleonic normal school, which ignored the eighteenth century in its entirety, except for Condillac and Reid, and concentrated on training rhetoricians and dialecticians." As Lerminier wrote in *Philosophical Letters Addressed to a Berliner,* the eclectic "has the characteristic of never having been able to discover and sense philosophical reality, but must have it translated, revealed, systematized; then he understands it, borrows it, and expounds it."[1] He criticizes eclecticism less for its doctrine and method than for its spiritual attitude; philosophy becomes a special

---

[1] *Réfutation de l'Éclectisme* (1839), pp. 51, 71–72.

sphere of knowledge and loses contact with social life; psychology is taught to students in normal schools just as differential calculus is taught to students in polytechnical schools. This attitude is reflected in Jouffroy's doctrine, which separates everything that life unites—God from the universe, mankind from nature, men from mankind, individuals from society, and finally, in man, ideas from feelings.

Instead, according to Leroux, philosophy should follow the course of mankind and express the life of man through all its stages. "It is the science of life . . . and should provide definitions or expositions of life consonant with the true revelations of art, politics, science, and industry during each period." Philosophy never assumes the definitive character possible for geometry, since the latter deals with abstractions; philosophy recovers its vigor as humanity progresses, for "thought and the other powers that exist in mankind are, by the same token, creative and fertile." Pure thought does not exist in isolation in an empyrean but takes shape through contact with reality and molds reality in turn through continual action and reaction. But since "any progress either in knowledge of external nature or in the organization of the collective life of mankind necessitates progress in metaphysics," philosophy does not differ essentially from religion if religion is assumed to be progressive. The sole difference is accounted for by the origin of philosophical thought, which is collective when adopted by mankind and "infused, so to speak, into individuals" and individual when the individual aspires to a systematization which, perhaps in the future, will be incarnated in mankind. Thus Leroux reserves a place for Messiahs alongside collective evaluation.

That these ideas are traceable to Saint-Simon as well as to Hegel is obvious. Still, Leroux does not adopt Saint-Simon's distinction between critical or negative epoch and organic epoch; for any negation involves and implies a potential affirmation; mankind always constructs and never destroys. But what is to be done about this philosophy which, during the seventeenth and eighteenth centuries, dealt almost exclusively with the problem of the origin of knowledge

—the so-called critical problem? Leroux has a specious theory on this point: the aberrant development of philosophy issues from the form taken by the Christian religion; it became rigid and used condemnations to stifle any discussion that could cast doubt on its conclusions; the result was that philosophy deserted religion to concentrate on the "psychological" problem.

The spirit of the period found its optimal expression in the joy of being delivered from shackles that forced the mind to examine the origin and value of knowledge. The philosophy of Leroux embraces both the condemnation of everything that immobilizes and stifles and the affirmation, in very general terms, of the reciprocal internality of the parts of the real world. For example, if soul is limited to intelligence, the result is Platonism and with it the despotism of science; if it is limited to sensation and passion, the result is Hobbes's system, in which the passionate brute can be restrained only by the despotism of the state: if it is limited to sentiment as in Rousseau, the result is the necessity of a social contract which annihilates the individual. The truth is that any particle of reality is explained and justified only by its relation to the whole; by the "mutual solidarity" of all living beings, he means a "communion" rather than the purely external relation suggested by the word.

Thus social institutions, property, native land, and family are justified. It is only through these intermediaries that man can commune with the Whole for which he was made: property, to the extent that it is an instrument of labor, unites him with nature; his native land introduces him to a historical tradition, which belongs in turn to a larger history, the history of mankind; his family provides him with a name, a character, a personality. If these institutions cease to be simple intermediaries between the individual and the infinite—if they choose to exist for themselves and for the individual who isolates himself in his egotism—then property becomes capital, which threatens labor; the family, a means of maintaining hereditary privileges and patriotism, becomes an instrument of war and domination. Leroux directs all his efforts toward correcting these abuses, toward replacing these institutions in the life of mankind; his socialism is merely the means of making the benefits of property available to everyone. On June 15, 1848, as a member of the National Assembly, he delivered an address in which he urged that Algeria become a testing ground for socialism. "Let the people try," he said, "for they have this right. . . . Otherwise you are going to be obliged to seal the swarm in the hive, and then what is observed in the life of bees will be observed in human society: war, implacable war. . . . How can you contain something that wishes to emerge, something that divine law wishes to emerge?" Thus, as these institutions are reformed in keeping with their spirit, they are made into instruments of deliverance.

Through them the individual is linked to humanity. But what is the nature of this link? It is based not on charity or on love actually addressed to a God separated from man rather than to man himself, but on solidarity, which makes the individual feel that he is nothing without humanity from which he draws his life and support. Though his temperament is very different, the ideas expressed by Leroux on this point are very close to those of Auguste Comte: "The civilized egotist thinks that he can know and feel by himself. Fool! He has knowledge and feeling only through humanity and for humanity." Humanity is continued in each of us, and we continue in later humanity. The continuity of mankind is in fact not very different from the continuity of an individual life, in which memory discards the details and retains only the essentials; physical, intellectual, and moral heredity is the memory of mankind.

III   *Jean Reynaud*

Several earlier studies such as "The Infinity of the Heavens," in the *Revue Encyclopédique* (on Bonnet, Cuvier, paleontology, theory of the earth, Condorcet, Pascal, St. Paul, Zoroaster, Origen, Druidism) in the *New Encyclopedia* (*Encyclopédie nouvelle*), which Reynaud and Leroux founded in 1838 in an attempt to revive Diderot's enterprise, had prepared the ground for *Earth and Heaven*. Born at Lyons, Jean Reynaud (1806–63) attended the École Polytechnique, worked as an engineer in Corsica, and became a convert to Saint-Simonianism before meeting Enfantin in Paris in 1830. He broke with Enfantin a year later, however, claiming that the doctrine abolished freedom and human dignity and worsened the plight of women because of its immorality.

His preoccupations are quite remote from those of the Saint-Simonians and even of Leroux, and are in fact much closer to the illuminism of Ballanche. He is concerned with the individual destiny of each soul, not the destiny of mankind as a whole. Nor does he believe in the panaceas of the Saint-Simonians or the Fourierists for curing the ills of mankind; it is in a superterrestrial destiny that each soul must be improved. Our life is itself the continuation of an earlier life whose faults it expiates, but it lays the basis for another life which will come about somewhere in the infinitude of the celestial regions; from globe to globe the soul, which is never actually disincarnate (Reynaud believes, with Leibniz and Bonnet, in an indissoluble link between soul and body), is forever advancing, from ordeal to ordeal, toward a state of perfection which it will never reach; there is no heaven or hell, in the theological sense, no man damned without hope of forgiveness or forever blessed, his task accomplished; there is only an endless series of habitations through which the soul moves in its perpetual advance.

The Christian solution—the creation of souls—which he rejects, seems to him to have engendered revolutionary ideas. "It seems to me," he says to the theologians, "that the time has come when the theory of inequalities is imperiously demanded in the name of public order. . . . But do you not see that if the utopia of the egalitarians flourishes and becomes ever more threatening, it is just because your belief has given birth to it and sustains it?"

IV *Charles Secrétan*

The teachings of Charles Secrétan (1815–95), professor at Lausanne, are aimed at two kinds of excesses: the excesses of rationalistic theologians and those of authoritarian doctrines, or the optimism "of preachers and so-called liberals" who eventually become pantheists and the fideism of those who rely on pure authority.[2] Midway between the two, Secrétan establishes the notion of "Christian reason." His attitude is typical of that associated with the religious movement known in Switzerland as "The Awakening."

His *Philosophy of Freedom* (1848–49) is a philosophical sermon on Christianity. We must separate "pagan reason from Christian reason," he says. "On the one hand, reason can understand Christianity only through the influence and power of Christianity itself; on the other hand, the understanding of Christianity is one part of the work of our recovery [here he means the restoration of man after the Fall] and cannot be disavowed. . . . We must therefore achieve an understanding of the principal doctrines of Chritsianity, which we associate with the philosophy of history, since they are, strictly speaking, its heart and substance. We do not think that natural reason would have predicted these things [the Fall and redemption] before the event, but we think that Christian reason should try to understand them, following the event and its proclamation in the church, and that it will and can succeed in the endeavor."

This metaphysics, which is an interpretation of Christian doctrine, is designed only to serve as an introduction to ethics. Consequently it is shaped not by any externally imposed dogma but by this end. It has to justify human freedom and the existence of a higher principle which can serve as a standard.

Under the name of pantheism Secrétan includes any doctrine that sees finite beings as the necessary consequence of an absolute necessarily positing itself. Like Jacobi, he considers pantheism to be the rational expression of the unity of being and finds traces of it in many theologians. All those who see God as an intrinsically necessary being are forced to attribute to him an equally necessary influence. "When we start from the necessary we never arrive at the contingent." We can escape pantheism only by assuming that God is absolute freedom. "Free with regard to his own freedom," says Secrétan in language reminiscent of Plotinus', he is only what he wishes to be, he is everything he wishes to be, he is everything he wishes to be because this is what he wishes to be. . . . The idea of a naturally perfect being is contradictory, for such a perfect being would be less perfect than a being that freely procured perfection for itself." [3]

It follows that metaphysics is in essence only a history of the acts which depend on absolute freedom. First, creation, a wholly free production having no substance except the divine will which posits it: that God is not incarnate in the divine will—that no splitting occurs—is the "miracle" which makes possible the independence of his creation. God does not create because of a desire for glory or because of any inherent desire, for this would make creation necessary. He wills the creation of man not for himself but for man, because of his love for man; he wills man as an end and therefore wills man's freedom. "God produces a living being which produces itself; that is what we must understand." Man produced himself. Indeterminate at the very beginning, he could strive, like an angel, to be godlike; he could turn against God, like the devil; or he could try to shape his own life independently of God. Man chose the latter course and brought about the Fall. Outside of pantheism, the Fall is the only possible reconciliation of the actual state of the world and the existence of a loving God. Furthermore, since the evil that weighs on men from birth is universally shared, mankind is one and has sinned through a single decision; indeed, it is not the existence of moral evil that proves the Fall but the fact that it is willfully imposed. Because God is his source, man wills his own annihilation when he wills his independence from God; but man is saved from annihilation by the absolute nature of God's will and is helped by a restorative power to emerge from his state of contradiction and suffering. The history of all humanity is the history of the restoration of primitive unity and the love of God for man.

The dissociation of mankind into distinct individuals is both the result of the Fall and the key to restoration. Countless numbers of successive generations in reality constitute a single being, and this

[3] *Ibid.*, II, 16.

unity has its decisive proof in the law of charity, which identifies us with others. Individuation makes continuous evolution possible and provides a means of restoration. Its principle is divine grace, which responds to the wishes of mankind by creating distinct individuals, each of whom might be said to represent a degree of being or an aspect of humanity and therefore a means of progress. As such the individual has an absolute worth and is immortal. In the idea of curative becoming—much more so than in his central notion of Liberty—we can see the influence of Schelling's teachings on Secrétan. Progress leads to "the perfect individual"—to Christ, in whom the restorative power and humanity are united; in him and by union with him, human nature is transformed, and this transformation is salvation. The death of Christ is not an act of expiation in which Christ substitutes himself for mankind; it is an example.

Here Secrétan finds a contrast between the idea of personal salvation and the idea of the salvation of all mankind. The union of the two ideas is accomplished for him by the concept of the church as "the absolute organism" in which all contribute, each in his own way, to the attainment of the same goal. The individual is saved only with mankind as a whole and in mankind as a whole.

Secrétan showed some indifference toward metaphysics. "I have built systems," he wrote, "which I have carelessly discarded." His metaphysics was, in fact, merely an introduction to ethics, which, along with social action, later became his main concern. Ethics, according to him, is the realization of freedom through the conquest of nature, which is the subject matter of economics, and the formation of states, which, born of despotism, become the guarantee of freedom of action. Furthermore, he does not have in mind the realization of freedom in the way prescribed by Kant. In his view, the substance of an obligation cannot be deduced from its form, and Kant made a great mistake when he drew a sharp distinction between speculation and practice. Indeed, "the will is at the heart of the intellect; reason, separated from will, is always formal." Reason is the perception of necessary relations and cannot be the basis of moral order. But effective reason is a synthesis of will and intellect; "it is the same reason which, theoretically, finds expression in the necessity to believe and, practically, in the obligation to act." Experience provides relations of solidarity between the individual and the species, giving rise to the obligation to which all other obligations are traceable—that of realizing the whole, which is charity.[4]

v *Jules Lequier*

At the very time when determinism was the reigning doctrine— the doctrine brilliantly asserted later through the influence of Darwin, Spencer, and Taine—Jules Lequier (1814–62), a solitary Breton and a friend of Renouvier at the École Polytechnique (Renouvier published some of his writings, all of which were uncompleted), penned these lines: "This hideous dogma of necessity cannot be demonstrated; it is a chimera which in its bowels conceals absolute doubt. It vanishes in the face of careful methodical examination, like phantoms formed by a mixture of light and shadow, which inspire terror only where there is fear and are dispelled by the hand that touches them."[5] Determinists are speculative thinkers for whom only externals exist. They conceive only of actions on things, as a machine is acted upon. Opposing them are the spiritualists, who claim that they can apprehend freedom through an inner experience; but awareness of an absence of coercion is not a proof of their claim. Experience would be conclusive only if the actions of an individual consciousness proved different on two or more occasions under identical circumstances, and this would obviously be impossible. But neither can outward signs be trusted, for obvious proofs may be illusory.

Lequier's *Search for a First Truth* (1925) was radically new in that it introduced freedom as an indispensable condition of the search for truth, a "*positive* condition, that is, a means of knowledge" (p. 141). Freedom is found only in meditation which searches for a

---

[4] J. Duproix, *Ch. Secrétan et la philosophie kantienne* (Paris, 1900), pp. 15, 36.
[5] *La Recherche d'une première vérité*, ed. Dugas, 1925, p. 134.

first truth, truth which is self-sufficient and safe from any doubt. Lequier first follows the course of Descartes in his meditation, reaching complete doubt or the vanity of any affirmation, yet his tone is quite different. "A forced doubt! An unnatural doubt, a violent, imaginary state, the exasperation of a greedy, unreasonable mind, which nothing can satisfy" (p. 104). He is almost ready to give up when, taking up the ancient aporia of the *Meno,* he describes "the impossibility of reaching knowledge except through knowledge itself" (p. 160); then, by a sudden reversal, he seizes upon a more profound requirement governing the investigation of truth—freedom: "How can I take a step in this investigation, even a groping step, except by means of the free movement of my thought? How can I make plans for an investigation, set a goal, break with habit and prejudices, try to insure my independence and sincerity . . . if my thoughts are prepared, produced, pursued in an order beyond my control, in such a manner that I can do nothing, each of those thoughts being obliged at each instant to be precisely what it is and being unable not to be what it is." Freedom, then, is the power to dispose of our thoughts, to confer on them an order that is not of natural necessity. But this is the very answer to the investigation of truth: the first truth is freedom. It is discovered by a process that Lequier himself compares to algebraic analysis. The question (What is the first truth?) has rectified itself and become the knowledge sought; it has produced the answer—that is, the knowledge which is discovered (p. 107). The mistake was in trying to discover something—for example, an outer sign—which would entail the affirmation of truth, "but it [the search itself] is an act of freedom that confirms freedom."

To understand Lequier clearly, we must consider briefly the moral atmosphere (quite different from that of Renouvier) in which he fashioned his idea of freedom. A fervent Catholic and an assiduous reader of the Bible and the Fathers, particularly St. Paul and St. Augustine, he practiced intense meditation constantly, juxtaposing freedom and the dogmas of creation, the omnipotence of God, and especially predestination. Never did his meditation lead him to a precise doctrine of any sort. Feverishly he reexamined theological themes but never succeeded in finding the point of coincidence of all these themes. Our freedom is a creation of ourselves; to be free is "to do, not to become, but to do and, in doing, produce ourselves" (p. 143). But how can the omnipotence of God be reconciled with this view? "To create a being strictly independent of him, a truly free being, a person—what an undertaking! . . . It required all his cunning, and the feat of strength responsible for the completion of this masterpiece is beyond comprehension! . . . The human person, a being capable of doing something without God! Awful wonder! Man deliberates and God waits." If freedom is indeed real, duration must also have a reality distinct from eternity. Lequier refers in a note to the "reality of succession," and he adds this commentary: "Considered from the point of view of their being, things really are successive"; therefore God must "see them reaching being successively, with the result that something similar to succession is introduced into God." Thus Lequier—and later, under his influence, Renouvier and James—tended to organize a theory of God around the notion of freedom. He still had to deal, however, with the dogma of predestination. The astounding dialogue between one of the elect and one of the damned fails to shed much light on the way in which Lequier intended to reconcile the dogma of predestination and the real freedom of human actions. The dialogue does show, however, that freedom is not conscious of itself or the results of its actions, and that man therefore is more readily subject to the judgment of God. "God reads man's heart more readily than man himself; . . . man is kept in a state of humility by the feeling of his own ignorance if particular acts are rfee." By his free act "each man introduces into the history of the world something which can never fail thereafter to be a part of it. The man who is the author of a particular act forgets it . . . but God has seen it. . . . What do we know about what is possible or impossible with respect to each of our acts in the future, and I am speaking of even the least of them? . . . How our own being escapes us, especially as it spreads farther and farther!" (p. 148; 298). Freedom, according to Lequier (whose views are quite different here from Fichte's), leaves us in profound ignorance of ourselves and our destiny.

Bibliography

I

Texts

Newman, John Henry. *Two Essays on Biblical and on Ecclesiastical Miracles.* New York, 1924.
——. *An Essay in Aid of a Grammar of Assent,* ed. C. F. Harrold. New York, 1947.
——. *The Idea of a University,* ed. C. F. Harrold. New York, 1947.
——. *Essays and Sketches,* ed. C. F. Harrold. 3 vols. New York, 1947.
——. *Apologia Pro Vita Sua,* ed. C. F. Harrold. New York, 1949.
——. *An Essay on the Development of Christian Doctrine,* ed. C. F. Harrold. New York, 1949.
——. *Sermons and Discourses,* ed. C. F. Harrold. 2 vols. New York, 1949.
——. *The Letters and Diaries of John Henry Newman,* ed. C. S. Dessain. New York, 1961——; to be published in 30 vols.

Studies

Benard, E. D. *A Preface to Newman's Theology.* St. Louis, 1945.
Boekraad, A. J. *The Personal Conquest of Truth According to J. H. Newman.* Louvain, 1955.
——. *The Argument from Conscience to the Existence of God according to J. H. Newman.* Louvain, 1961.
Bouyer, Louis. *Newman: His Life and Spirituality.* New York, 1958.
Collins, James. *Philosophical Readings in Cardinal Newman.* Chicago, 1961.
Culler, A. D. *The Imperial Intellect: A Study of Newman's Educational Ideal.* New Haven, 1955.
Walgrave, J.-H. *Newman the Theologian.* New York, 1960.
Ward, Wilfrid. *The Life of John Henry Cardinal Newman.* 2 vols. New York, 1912.

V

Texts

Lequier, Jules. *Œuvres Complètes,* ed. Jean Grenier. Neuchâtel, 1952.

63

THE CRITICAL MOVEMENT

THE FAILURE of the vast metaphysical systems of the first half of the century was offset not only by the emergence of an enlightened positivism and the development of religious thought but by a return to the critical attitude initiated by Kantianism.

1 *Charles Renouvier*

The critical movement had its prelude in France with Charles Renouvier (1815-1903). Born like Comte at Montpellier, he was associated, after his arrival in Paris in 1831, with the Saint-Simonians. Comte was his tutor at the École Polytechnique, which he entered in 1834, and it was there that he met Lequier. His first works were handbooks of philosophy, ancient (1842) and modern (1844), then an article on philosophy for Pierre Leroux's *New Encyclopedia*. The revolution of 1848 caused him to write *The Republican Handbook* (1848) and *The Communal and Central Organization of the Republic* (1851) as well as a number of articles for the *Feuille du Peuple*. The coup d'état of December 1851 forced him to confine himself to religious and philosophical speculation. His critical philosophy is developed in his *Essays in General Criticism* (1854-64; I, *General Analysis of Knowledge;* II, *Man;* III, *The Principles of Nature;* IV, *Introduction to the Analytical Philosophy of History*). *Uchrony* (1857) and *Science of Ethics* (1869) belong to the same

64

period. From 1872 to 1889 he wrote a great number of articles for the *Critique Philosophique,* which was supplemented (1878–85) by the *Critique Religieuse.* The last issues contain his *Outline of a Systematic Classification of Philosophical Doctrines* (later published in two volumes, 1885–86). After 1891 the *Critique* was replaced by the *Année Philosophique,* edited by F. Pillon. His last works were *The Analytical Philosophy of History* (4 vols., 1896–98), *The New Monadology* (in collaboration with Prat, 1899), *Dilemmas of Pure Metaphysics* (1901), and *Personalism* (1903). He had established ties of friendship with Secrétan, and their correspondence between 1868 and 1891 was published in 1910.

Renouvier's doctrine marks a break with the great unified systems constructed at the beginning of the nineteenth century. He became the declared enemy of any doctrine that considered the moral life of man to be a necessary, though fleeting, manifestation of a universal law of reality. Scientific determinism, historical fatalism, mysticism, materialism, evolutionism—all these doctrines are the same from his point of view, for they absorb and annihilate the individual.

Renouvier's philosophical theories, like his intuition of the world, are related to three parallel themes, which sometimes converge but remain distinct by origin and nature. The first theme is the law of numbers, derived from his reflections on the infinitesimal calculus, dating from his first mathematical studies at the École Polytechnique. Mathematicians—Cauchy for example—had demonstrated the impossibility of an infinite number in the realm of the abstract. The law of numbers states that by virtue of this impossibility, any real group must be finite.

The second theme is freedom. After meditating on the arguments of his friend Lequier, he saw that free will was the root not only of moral life but also of intellectual life and that no certainty was ever attainable without it.

The third theme is idealistic relativism, derived from Kant and from Auguste Comte. Only phenomena are assumed to have any real existence, and each phenomenon is relative in that it can be understood only as a component or a compound in relation to another given phenomenon.

There is no essential connection between these three themes. The doctrine of the finite may be perfectly consonant with the denial of free will, for the law of numbers states that a series of phenomena can be traced back to a starting point, not that this beginning must be a free act; it might be pure chance. The doctrine of the finite is even less closely linked to relativism. Whereas Kant thought that the laws of mind required an indefinite regression into phenomena, Comte refused to study the problem; furthermore, in its ancient forms (Aristotle's finite world and Epicurus' theory of the atom) the doctrine of the finite is inseparable from realistic absolutism. Finally, relativism is perfectly compatible with the denial of free will. With Kant as with Comte, relativism assumes a rigid determinism of phenomena and may even be incompatible with the affirmation of free will if a free act is an absolute beginning, unrelated to that which precedes.

To understand Renouvier's philosophical theories we must examine more closely the notion of the independence of points of departure and the difficulty of reconciling the doctrine of the finite with relativism. The doctrine of the finite generally assumes an effective or at least a possible determination of reality, ranging from the infinitely large to the infinitely small, from the world to the atom. But the positive sciences show clearly that it is not possible for us to start from the idea of a world conceived as a whole or from an ultimate, indivisible element; and idealistic relativism gives proof of its acceptance of this fact by reducing any reality to a relation. Renouvier could support both the doctrine of the finite and relativism only by assuming on the one hand that total synthesis, in itself at least, is something finished and completed (the doctrine of the finite) but that, on the other hand, it is inaccessible to knowledge (relativism); in other words, we can know neither the number of elements in the world nor the extension and duration of the world even though duration, extension, and number are in themselves determinate; such knowledge, unattainable through direct, empirical evaluation, could be accomplished only if there were a law of maximum and of minimum for the diverse cosmic quantities; but there is no such law. Similar arguments prove the impossibility of arriving at a complete listing of the hierarchy of species from the highest to the lowest, a comprehensive theory of cosmic evolution, or a synthesis of causal series going back to first causes or a synthesis according to the ends and their sequence, and of passing from our limited states of consciousness to a total consciousness or a totality of consciousness embracing all phenomena. Renouvier is willing to accept the doctrine of the finite, but he rejects the world of Aristotle and the Scholastics as well as their cosmogony, which penetrates to the radical source of things and apprehends the universal cause and the universal end; that is reality *a parte foris,* seen from without, and we apprehend it only *a parte intus.*

Now we understand these three fundamental themes even if their interrelatedness in the mind of Renouvier is not yet clear.

Let us also note that each theme is grounded on distinct evidence. Proof of the law of numbers derives from the principle of contradiction of which it is but one form. Numbers exist only by virtue of the act of counting; the existence of an infinite number would assume both a complete synthesis, since the number exists, and an incomplete synthesis, since it is infinite.

The proof of freedom, borrowed in its entirety from Lequier, is of a different kind. Immediate experience and a priori proof, like their opposite—determinism—simply do not exist: we sense the necessity of choosing between freedom and determinism even in the absence of any intellectual motives that link us to one side rather than the other, but we still need to reflect on the motives underlying the necessity of choosing. If I declare positively that necessity exists, my affirmation is either true or false. If it is true, the certainty that I have of it is a necessary fact, but the certainty that another person may have of freedom is equally necessary and not open to choice, since both convictions are equally necessary; consequently I am forced to doubt. If my affirmation is false, I am in error in making it; furthermore, I remain in doubt. If I declare positively that freedom exists, my affirmation is equally true or false. If it is false, I am doubtlessly in error, but through it I gain many practical advantages —for example, belief in moral responsibility and confidence in a future which depends partly on my choice. Finally, if it is true, truth lies on the same side as practical advantage. I am therefore persuaded by logical motives to choose a world in which men are truly free—that is, capable before all else of making decisions through reflection.

For Renouvier's third thesis, relativism, we can find no particular proof. It is a common state of mind, the product of the positive sciences; it is also the state of mind typical of positivism and of Kantianism.

Where can we find the link between these themes? Only in a certain belief concerning moral destiny, a belief which seeks to find rational motives and supports in them but which at the same time sustains them and provides them with a true foundation. It sustains them all. First, the law of numbers: proof of the law of numbers by the principle of contradiction falls so far short of being convincing that Renouvier himself, at the outset of his career when he was writing the *Handbook of Modern Philosophy,* was at once, as a mathematician, a believer in the impossibility of infinite numbers and, as a philosopher, a supporter of the doctrine of the infinite and of the Hegelian thesis of the identity of contradictories. The reason is that the law of numbers deals with the principle of contradiction, not in its abstract form, but in its application to reality. In Renouvier's thinking the thesis of the reality of this principle relates not to a clear proof but to a belief and an option. Toward the end of his career, in *The Analytical Philosophy of History* (IV, 434–35), he explained with utmost clearness how, after the Hegelianism of the *Handbooks,* he believed himself obliged to choose between the Hegelian principle of the identity of contradictories and the unrestricted application of the principle of contradiction, and how he chose the second because the first offered no safeguard against mystical metaphysics with all its eccentricities (there were many such eccentricities around 1850). It would seem, then, that the views of two recent interpreters of Renouvier should be combined and his doctrine of the finite ascribed both to his mathematical speculations and to his belief in a moral destiny.

From what has been said it is clear that the theme of freedom is tied to the same belief. This is also true of phenomenalistic relativism. In Renouvier we find nothing comparable to Kant's transcendental deduction, which demonstrates categories in accordance with the principle of the possibility of experience. Instead, there are simple, general facts "proposed to belief as essential forms of reality." The contrary of relativism, which is absolutism and belief in things in themselves and substance, is opposed to our moral beliefs because it leads to pantheism—that is, to the denial of a free, responsible person.

Thus the two parts of Renouvier's system—the doctrine of the finite, freedom, and relativism on one hand and moral beliefs on the other—are interdependent, each supporting the other in a circular pattern characteristic of his thought. To be sure, the doctrine of the finite and relativism are not postulates of morality in the Kantian sense of the word—that is, affirmations which are inaccessible to theoretical reasoning and derive their value from moral necessity alone; they are, on the contrary, theses which are perfectly rational in themselves, independently of moral considerations, even though they derive the full measure of their certainty from the vision of a universe in which moral life is possible. Such is the origin of Renouvier's somewhat ambiguous notion of rational belief, grounded on the mutual support provided for each other by reason and belief. In his view this belief, rational and reflective, is distinct from spontaneous beliefs due to "a confused state of mind, a rash, subjective impulse by which any arbitrarily imagined relation whatsoever is declared to be a real one," as in hallucination, belief in prophecies and miracles, or sleepwalking.

Renouvier's world has a two-sided characteristic which makes it equally favorable to science and belief. Consisting of representations or phenomena, it is accessible to science, which studies the laws or constant relations of phenomena, expressible as functions. Renouvier shares Comte's opinion of science or even surpasses him in his "general critique," which investigates the most general relations or categories. On the other hand, a representation contains, as correlative terms, a representative element and an element that is represented (in Kantian terms, a subject and an object), of which the synthesis is consciousness or an individual; consequently the world is a world of consciousnesses. The category of personality, a synthesis of self and nonself, outranks all other categories: first those that define the constant structure of the world—position, succession, quality; then those that describe the general laws of change—becoming, causality, finality.

This interpenetration of the theoretical and the practical finally persuaded Renouvier to divide all known systems of philosophy into two classes. The first of these, under the pretext of satisfying theoretical considerations, makes moral life impossible; the second satisfies both theory and practice. On one hand are those systems of philosophy that maintain the infinite, necessity, substance, things in themselves, historical fatalism, and pantheism; on the other, those maintaining the finite, freedom, phenomenalism, and theism. There are no grounds for reconciling the two classes; they are the two horns of a dilemma, and one must choose between them. Reason "as pure intelligence," impersonal reason, is incapable of making this choice: "Intellectualism has led philosophy astray. . . . What is needed is reason in a higher sense—reason inseparable from belief."

One basic belief dominates Renouvier's option, and that is belief in the moral destiny of the individual. This idea, expressed in his *Last Conversations,* is fundamental: "A philosopher does not believe in death." Everything in Renouvier's universe is built around the destiny, not of humanity itself as with Auguste Comte, but of the individual. It was this moral individualism that caused him to write *The Republican Handbook* (1848), in which he demanded for each citizen an economic status appropriate to the development of moral life, and to reject vigorously the idea of the inevitability of progress, which sacrifices the individual to humanity.

Hence his theology. For him God is not a substance or an absolute but the moral order itself, the assurance that there is in the universe a law of justice which requires each individual to accomplish his duty. He refuses to see God other than in his relation to the phenomenal world, and he attributes to God only infinity of moral perfection, which is indivisible. At the beginning of his career, under the influence of his friend Louis Ménard, the author of *Reveries of a Pagan Mystic*,[1] he was even inclined strongly toward polytheism because of its moral superiority to a national, exclusive monotheism, such as that of the Jews.

The notion of justice is precise and definite enough to serve as the basis for a science of morality constructed, as in mathematics, with concepts. Pure ethics is the definition of the rule of reason that a free moral agent, in isolation or united with others, should impose on his passions; the pure rule of justice implies ownership of wealth derived from the labor that each agent imposes upon himself as a duty, and creates between agents a relation of debtor and ceditor, depending on the relative size of the contribution of each to the common task. An ideal society, defined by justice, is a "society of peace": credits and debits are always in balance, each individual is obliged to contribute as much labor as he is authorized to expect from others, and the permanence of this state is assured.

But to pure ethics must be added practical ethics, which shows how ideal precepts are to be applied to the actual state of man and society. Renouvier defines this state as a "state of war"—a diffuse state characterized by the exploitation of one man by another and mutual distrust among associates. The state of war justifies the right of self-defense; one of the most effective instruments of self-defense is private property, which is legitimate in a state of war. Communism is nothing less than universal serfdom; the abuses of private property ought simply to be limited by the establishment of a progressive tax. Renouvier, whose socialistic tendencies were

---

[1] Cf. their correspondence, published by A. Peyre, *Revue de Métaphysique*, January 1932.

unmistakable in 1848, later expounded a program identical to that of the French radicals.

The existing state, which is the state of war, poses a problem distinct from the practical problem—the ancient problem of evil. The existing state, which is not the normal state, has its source in a vice inherent in every moral agent in whom egotistical passions dominate reason. It is as if man were tainted at birth as a result of what theologians call the Fall. His state cannot, however, be due to the first cause of the world, identical with moral order, but must be due to the decision of free will that Kant called radical sin.

This theodicy, which explains evil by free will and the Fall, led Renouvier to certain hypotheses concerning the origin, history, and end of mankind. Inspired by Christian beliefs, these hypotheses propose to the imagination a likely description of man's destiny—one which clearly expresses moral beliefs even if it is not objectively exact. Renouvier imagines a primitive human society, perfect and just, living in a natural environment that freely submits to his will. The Fall was possible, for man is free; it must have originated in the prevalence of egotistical passions, but more likely still, in the experiment that man, by his own free will, chose to make. The result was a titanic state of war, all the more violent in proportion to man's greater physical powers. The destruction of the primitive world ended in the formation of the nebula and the present solar system, with the result that the life of historical humanity is erected on the ruins of the primitive world—a disjointed world of conflicting forces. But mankind is composed of the very individuals who brought about the fall of the primitive world; the individual preexists this life and will survive it. Renouvier shared Leibniz' belief in the indissolubility of the individual or monad, which contains a material germ that can produce a new organism when conditions are favorable. His monadology is that of Leibniz, but without the doctrine of the infinite, for he was naturally inclined to accept a doctrine that reduced substance to a law of succession of its states and to a being similar to a consciousness, and denied transitive causality in favor of preestablished harmony. The free human will, just as it caused the Fall, will in the future be the author of mankind's restoration and of standards for establishing the rule of justice in a natural environment restored to its primitive state. What distinguishes this eschatology from the commonplace utopias of the middle of the nineteenth century is that it is "astronomical." It assumes the return of the solar system to the state of a nebula and, in this vast era, physical, moral, and social changes beyond imagination. Such are the general features of his doctrine of *personalism,* in which nature exists only in relation to the person, the substantial element of reality, in which only risk or initiative exists, and in which there is nothing that resembles a necessary law governing the evolution of humanity. This is what he has to say about it in his *Last Conversations:* "Nothing indicates that personalism can be, for the philosophers of today and tomorrow, anything but an object of curiosity. The utopia of *progress* has blindfolded all thinkers. They fail to see evil or to feel injustice."

All his life Renouvier strongly resisted belief in the inevitability of progress, still dominant when he opposed to the philosophy of history a "Uchrony." In this historical outline he imagines the development of European society not as it was but as it might have been if Christianity had failed and there had been no Middle Ages (in his view Christianity was responsible for the medieval system). Later, his concept of the evolution of the physical world echoed Spencer's evolutionistic naturalism.

From roughly 1870 to 1900 Renouvier's ideas exercised a profound influence on philosophical thought. Pillon popularized his teachings. L. Prat, who collaborated with him on *The New Monadology,* wrote *The Notion of Substance: Historical and Critical Investigations* (1905), a work on certain cardinal points of his system. Victor Brochard (1848–1907), before he became one of the most remarkable historians of ancient philosophy, had written his work *On Error* (1879) under the inspiration of Renouvier. The main point of Brochard's theory is that error does not differ essentially from truth. "Truth is simply a confirmed hypothesis, error a refuted hypothesis." In short, truth and error are defined by a process of verification that is undertaken voluntarily. In *Belief and Reality* (1889) Lionel Dauriac (1847–1923) tried to define a general critique which would be a critique of inner feelings and will as well as of knowledge. Jean Jacques Gourd (1859–1909), the Genevan philosopher, was influenced by Renouvier's phenomenalism (*The Phenomenon*, 1883; *The Three Dialectics*, 1897), but he found an irreducible duality in the phenomenon itself: on one hand an element accessible to science thanks to causality and stability, and on the other an element of difference, instability, or absoluteness inaccessible to scientific knowledge; beside a law, creativity; beside a rule of justice, sacrifice; beside the coordination of the beautiful, the sublime. These "illegalities" are related to discontinuities which Renouvier's critique introduces into the phenomenon and, according to Gourd, to a religious interpretation of reality.

As Brochard stressed the limitations of rational evidence and the role of will in judgment, Louis Liard (1846–1917), in *Positive Science and Metaphysics* (1879), stresses the impossibility of changing positive science into a metaphysic, as naturalism does, and the role of moral belief in affirmations concerning reality. The absolute is the good or perfection which moral life causes us to recognize in advance as its necessary condition. There is in Liard's doctrine much of the Kantian method of the postulates of practical reason.

The doctrine of the finite expounded by F. Evellin (1836–1909) in *Infinity and Quantity* (1880) and later in *Pure Reason and the Antinomies* (1907), unlike Renouvier's, is not subordinated to belief. Here we find no true dilemma of the finite and the infinite, for only the finite proves to be demonstrable, and, in the Kantian antinomy, the infinitary antitheses are not logically conclusive. The concept of an infinite quantity, ostensibly used by mathematicians, is merely an illusion born of the imagination. So-called continua, even real space and time, are made of indivisibles. This doctrine of the finite is linked to spiritualism: a continuum, by its indefinite divisibility, assumes the disappearance of any stable being; only the doctrine of the finite explains the existence of being endowed with spontaneity, intelligence, and freedom.

11 *German Neo-Kantianism*

Each chapter of O. Liebmann's *Kant and His Followers* (1865)
ends with the reminder, almost a refrain, "Thus one must return to
Kant." The dominant element in the return to Kant, which was
at the same time a reaction against the speculative philosophy of
the post-Kantians, seems to be the appeal of relativism, which
stresses the dependence of objects with respect to the conditions of
the human consciousness. Human thoughts, human representations,
comparison of the conditions of knowledge and the conditions of
visual images, complete agnosticism concerning things in themselves
—these are the principal features found in the work of Liebmann
himself (*Analysis of Reality,* 1876; *Thoughts and Established Facts,*
1882–89). Here Kantianism seems to have merged with the school
of Feuerbach.

We would not be wholly justified in making Helmholtz, the
famous physicist and author of the great work on *Physiological
Optics* (1856–66), a forerunner of neo-Kantianism in Germany. He
did, of course, write: "To require a representation to convey the
nature of the thing represented without modification and to be
true in an absolute sense would be to require an effect to be fully
independent of the nature of the object on which it is produced,
and this is a flagrant contradiction. Consequently our human representations and the representations of any intelligent being whatsoever are all images of objects, essentially dependent on the nature
of the consciousness that represents them." But this relativism, quite
commonplace, is so untypical of Kantian philosophy that it treats
representations as symbols or signs which we use on one hand to
direct our actions and on the other to conclude, on the basis of the
law of causality, that external objects actually exist. Furthermore,
Helmholtz was persuaded by his works on non-Euclidean geome-
tries to assert the possibility of spaces different from ours and to
reject the apriorism of the transcendental aesthetic. "The Kantian
proof of the a priori origin of geometric axioms, based on the notion

that no spatial relation different from them can be represented in intuition, is insufficient, for the reason given is inexact." Helmholtz was in fact trying to free Kant's system from a contradiction by denying the a priori origin of axioms considered to be a residue of metaphysical speculation and by making geometry the first of the sciences of nature.

The reduction of all knowledge to phenomena, the subjectivity of forms and categories, the impossibility of any metaphysics, our inability through inward observation to identify the soul—all these are features that Lange borrowed from Kantianism. His interpretations of these features, however, sometimes sets him apart from his model. Like Helmholtz he claims to see the justification of Kantianism in the physiology of the senses; he attributes to categories the same subjectivity as to the forms of sensibility and vaguely ascribes them to our psychophysical organization, without retaining any trace of the transcendental deduction; he sees materialism as the necessary successor to metaphysics as a science, for this system "satisfies the tendency of reason to seek unity while rising as little as possible above reality" (*History of Materialism,* 1866; 9th edition, 1908). He also criticizes Kant's use of the thing in itself; its existence is in no way proved; our mind is simply constructed in such a way that it is led to the concept of a problematic term as the cause of phenomena. Thus nothing in Lange corresponds to Kant's practical reason: he substitutes for Kant's intelligible world predicated on practical reason the creations of religion and metaphysics, and he ascribes their worth wholly to the spiritual elevation that emanates from them.

Alois Riehl was one of the most staunch supporters of the view that philosophy should be reduced to a theory of knowledge and should abandon metaphysics (*Philosophical Criticism and Its Importance in Positive Science,* 1876–87). His Kantianism is limited to *The Critique of Pure Reason*; with but few changes, he accepts apriorism, which grounds principles on the possibility of experience, but contributes something new—a comparison of the a priori proof and the social proof. Thus, he reasons, if the reality of the outer world is given to us immediately by sensation, an even more important proof is the social proof, drawn from the community of experience which we share with others. By the same token, he interprets the formation of experience, through the interaction of a priori concepts and sensations, as a social fact and not simply an individual one. These sociological considerations brought him closer to a new interpretation of Kantian apriorism, the interpretation found in Durkheim.

III *English Idealism*

J. H. Stirling's intention in introducing Hegelian philosophy to England (*The Secret of Hegel*, 1865) was wholly consonant with the revolt against rationalism manifested in England between 1850 and 1880. Naturalism, economic individualism, social materialism were his enemies, and Hegel's concrete universal, which reveals lower degrees of reality in all these doctrines, was his weapon. But it was Thomas Hill Green (1836–82) who constructed the idealistic Anglo-American doctrine, inspired by Kant, which today finds expression in the writings of Bradley, Bosanquet, Josiah Royce, and M'Taggart.

Green's idealism, notwithstanding borrowings, differs strikingly from Kantian idealism in spirit and intention. Green is not troubled by the critical problem and does not take into account the close ties between critical thought and the positive sciences. His neo-Kantianism, coming after German and French neo-Kantianism, is also of a different nature and directed, from the outset, toward the refutation of empiricism, atheism, and hedonism. By virtue of a single principle, his doctrine of idealism reintroduced mind into knowledge, God into the universe, and ethics into conduct.

Empiricism, according to Green's interpretation of Hume, eliminates mental operations from knowledge by reducing the mind to an aggregation of states of consciousness, with the result that notions which seem to establish a relation between these elements—substance and causality, for example—are merely illegal fictions. The ideal of knowledge would be to dispense with these fictions, but this would amount to declaring knowledge impossible, since to know is to relate. Consequently, as Kant insisted, beyond the succession of events there must be a principle of unity, completely stable and unique, which constructs objects of knowledge by fashioning sensations into organic wholes.

From this principle of the unity of *self*-consciousness Green tries to deduce spiritualism, theism, and moral philosophy. First, spiritualism: contrary to the teachings of evolution, mind cannot be the result of an unintelligent mechanism; nature, far from being capable of engendering mind, implies its existence and is real only for knowledge, for an immaterial and immutable self beyond time and space. Next, theism: the empirical theory of isolated sensations is closely linked to the Spencerian and Hamiltonian theory of the unknowable Absolute. The first theory makes one sensation completely independent of another, just as the second makes the Absolute completely independent of anything else. Both theories are equally false, and the second is contradictory, since to say that the unknowable is, is to know something about it (an argument that seems to derive from Plato's *Parmenides*). The first theory must be rejected because each sensation, partial and incomplete in itself, is related to other sensations and consequently to a total system of thought relations which embraces all sensations. Nothing is isolated or excluded from the system: reality or truth is the concrete universal implied by every part, but this universal exists through the universal consciousness or God, who therefore is a postulate of any element of knowledge. It follows that, for man, God is not an object, a thing, or another being apart from him; human consciousness does not differ essentially from divine consciousness; the finite element in man, his organic system, is the vehicle of an eternal consciousness.

Finally, ethics derives from the same principle. Our own self is related to the universal self; morality is tied to our success in identifying ourselves with the universal principle, an end attainable through the satisfaction, not of any particular desire, but only of our whole nature. In this advancement toward the realization of universal perfection, the individual finds support rather than resistance in social institutions. Green's idealism therefore manifests conservative tendencies in politics. Any form of authority, because it surpasses the individual in scope, is in effect divine, and we do not under any crcumstances have the right to impose our individual good on an institution. Green's aversion to individualism, then prevalent in England, may provide the hidden key to his whole doctrine.

IV *Antoine Cournot*

Antoine Cournot (1801–77) was an inspector general of public instruction in France. He was one of the first men to study critically the fundamental notions of the sciences. From Kant and Comte he inherited the idea of the relativity of knowledge and of the impossibility of our ever grasping the essence of things. Nevertheless, his first work was on the *Theory of Chance and Probability* (1843). The certainty of any knowledge, according to his *Theory,* appears as a limiting point on a scale of the different degrees of probability. Cournot's distinctive contribution was in likening probability to relativity in his *Essay on the Foundations of Knowledge* (2 vols., 1851). In physics, a hypothesis—for example, Kepler's elliptical orbit, which includes the observed positions of a planet—is accepted because it enables us logically to connect observed facts. Theories are probable in so far as they satisfy this condition in the simplest possible way. We can come closer and closer to reality; the immediate perception that gold is yellow, for instance, is further from reality than the knowledge of the physicist who associates this yellow color with the characteristic color of gold and the effect of the reflection of light on its surface, and the physicist is still closer to reality if he can connect the optical properites of gold with its molecular structure. Even though we cannot grasp absolute reality, "it is within our power to rise from an order of phenomenal and relative realities to an order of higher realities and in this way

gradually penetrate to the very heart of the reality of phenomena."
Consequently Cournot's theory of probability is quite different
from Kant's theory of relativity, in which concepts take on a wholly
different meaning. Cournot recognizes degrees of relativity; in his
view a certain law, such as the law of universal attraction, is closer
than any other law to the essence of things (*Treatise*, p. 186).
Kantianism, on the other hand, recognizes no degrees of relativity,
since one uniform cause—the sensible character of our intuitive
apprehension of space and time—governs all our knowledge. To
disprove the subjectivity of space and time, Cournot uses arguments
drawn from his theory of probability: if these notions were merely
subjective illusions, "how could chance possibly account for the fact
that phenomena known to us are linked together in accordance
with simple laws that imply the objective existence of time and
space? For instance, the Newtonian law, which provides us with
an admirable explanation of astronomical phenomena, implies the
existence, outside the human mind, of time, space, and geometric
relations" (*Essay*, sec. 142).

Furthermore, Cournot's theory of categories, though parallel to
Kant's theory, is wholly different in spirit. This theory is elaborated
in his *Treatise on the Interdependence of Fundamental Ideas in the
Sciences and in History* as well as in *Reflections on the Course of
Ideas and Events in Modern Times* (1872; 2d ed., 1934) and *Materialism, Vitalism, and Rationalism* (1875). The subject of this
Treatise is precisely stated in the *Essay* (sec. 124): "On one hand
we have the idea of a certain subordination among different categories embracing the phenomena of nature, among scientific theories associated with the explanation of each category; on the other
hand, we understand that, in passing from one category to another,
we may find solutions of continuity that relate not merely to an
actual imperfection in our knowledge and methods but to the necessary intervention of new principles, which subsequently provide explanations [for example, the notion of affinity, which must be introduced because chemical phenomena cannot be explained through
the principles of mechanics alone]. . . . Now that the sciences have

developed to a degree unknown to the ancients, we should determine a posteriori and by more observation the primitive ideas or conceptions to which we constantly turn in order to understand and explain natural phenomena and which ought thereafter to be imposed on us by the very nature of things or by conditions inherent in our intellectual constitution."

Categories, which Cournot in his *Treatise* prefers to call *fundamental ideas,* owe their existence not to some intrinsic power but to several wholly distinct and independent sources: experience, deduction, which reduces a new notion to simpler notions, the needs of the imagination (which are, for example, the source of the atomic theory), the harmony that a notion establishes between the facts governed by it and between itself and the fundamental notions of contiguous sciences. In short, a fundamental idea asks "to be judged by its works, that is, by the order and coherence that it introduces into the system of our knowledge, or by the confusion it creates and the conflicts it incites" (*Essay,* sec. 135). For example, we can apply the notion of substance, derived from our awareness of our own personal identity, to ponderable phenomena, since experience shows us that weight is a permanent element in chemical decompositions, but not (according to Cournot who does not accept the theory of fluids) to the interpretation of imponderable phenomena such as light.

Cournot's method makes him receptive to the lines of demarcation drawn between mathematics and mechanics, cosmology and physics, the physical and the vital, the vital and the social, not because of any knowledge of the reality of corresponding essences but because of the necessity of introducing new fundamental ideas at each of these degrees. His attitude on this point, though related to that of Comte, who also supported the irreducibility of the sciences, differs from it considerably, for he is no dogmatist but a probabilist who studies each case separately. Thus (sec. 152), it is advantageous to extend a mechanical principle such as the conservation of energy to physics in its entirety; on the other hand, according to Cournot (sec. 156), the atomistic hypothesis fails by far to express the essence of things, even though it accommodates many experiences and habits of mind, "because it is incapable of grouping known facts systematically and leading us to the discovery of unknown facts." The result is that Cournot grounds the irreducibility of one notion to another, not on the impossibility of deducing the first from the second, but on the complication entailed by the deduction. Applied mechanics, therefore (sec. 128), might be grounded on celestial mechanics or the mechanics of central forces; but this approach entails the use of such complicated hypotheses that it is better for us to introduce a whole new category, that of traction or work.

If we now consider the concatenation of fundamental ideas from mathematics through the life sciences to the social sciences, we note that these ideas are grouped according to a principle of "symmetrical polarity." Whereas the median region, the region of life, is dark and beyond our powers of intuition and representation, the extreme regions reveal the clear ideas of order and form—on one hand in mathematics, and on the other in the most advanced social states, in which civilization tends "to substitute the calculated or calculable for the living organism, reason for instinct, the fixity of arithmetic and logical combinations for the movement of life" (*Treatise*, sec. 212). The chain of ideas, instead of proceeding from the mathematical to the vital, turns back toward mathematics. In the very beginning society depends on the vital—for example, race—but it later adheres to rational norms independent of time and place; in the same way, in a particular human being the contrast between the extreme biological complication of the conditions that govern human thought and the extreme simplicity of the laws apprehended by thought is so great that there can be no cause-and-effect relation between life and intelligence. Whereas imagination and passions are inexplicable without life, "logic has not the slightest need of physiological prolegomena." "Progressive civilization is not the triumph of mind over matter but rather the triumph of the rational, general principles of things over the energy and distinctive qualities of the living organism, and this entails many advantages as well as many disadvantages" (sec. 330). The Roman Empire and China (as Cournot imagined it), in which history was reduced to journalism, prefigure the final phase of humanity: no life, no heroes, no saints, no great personalities, but only a mechanism of sure duration.

Cournot's probabilism rules out the supposition that the fundamental ideas of the sciences exhaust reality, and leads to transrationalism. Man can understand himself philosophically only within the context of the universal order; he has, however, a personal destiny, which is revealed to him by religion but which does not enter into the universal order and cannot be understood *ex analogia universi,* since the religious life cannot be compared with anything else. In his transrationalism Cournot remains faithful to the spirit of his doctrine: one "fundamental idea" cannot claim the right to serve as our model in interpreting others; Nature, which is conceived by reason, cannot exclude the supernatural, which is necessitated by man's religious feelings.

BIBLIOGRAPHY

I

Texts

Renouvier, Charles. *Essais de critique générale.* 4 vols. Paris, 1854–64.
———. *Science de la morale.* 2 vols. Paris, 1869.
———. *Uchronie, l'utopie dans l'histoire.* Paris, 1876.
———. *Esquisse d'une classification systématique des doctrines philosophiques.* 2 vols. Paris, 1885–86.
———. *Philosophique analytique de l'histoire.* Paris, 1896–97.
———. *Le Personnalisme.* Paris, 1903.

III

Texts

Green, Thomas Hill. *The Works of Thomas Hill Green,* ed. R. L. Nettleship. 3 vols. London, 1885–88.

Studies

Lamont, W. D. *Introduction to Green's Moral Philosophy.* London, 1934.
Milne, A. J. M. *The Social Philosophy of English Idealism.* London, 1962.
Pucelle, J. *La Nature et l'esprit dans la philosophie de T. H. Green.* 2 vols. Louvain, 1961–65.
Richter, M. *The Politics of Conscience: T. H. Green and His Times.* London, 1964.

IV

Texts

Cournot, Antoine Augustin. *Mémoire sur le mouvement d'un corps rigide soutenu par un plan fixe.* Paris, 1829.
———. *Researches into the Mathematical Principles of the Theory of Wealth,* trans. N. I. Bacon. Economic Classics series. London, 1877.
———. *Traité élémentaire de la théorie des fonctions et du calcul infinitésimal.* 2 vols. 2d ed. Paris, 1841.

———. *Exposition de la théorie des chances et des probabilités.* Paris, 1843.

———. *De l'origine et des limites de la correspondance entre l'algèbre et la géometrie.* Paris, 1847.

———. *An Essay on the Foundations of Our Knowledge,* trans. Merritt H. Moore. New York, 1956.

———. *Traité de l'enchaînement des idées fondamentales dans les sciences et dans l'histoire.* 3d ed. Paris, 1922.

———. *Principes de la théorie des richesses.* Paris, 1863.

———. *Des Institutions d'instruction publique en France.* Paris, 1864.

———. *Considérations sur la marche des idées et des événements dans les temps modernes.* 2 vols. Paris, 1934.

———. *Matérialisme, vitalisme, rationalisme: Études sur l'emploi des données de la science en philosophie.* Paris, 1875, 1923.

———. *Revue sommaire des doctrines économiques.* Paris, 1877.

———. *Souvenirs: 1760 à 1860.* Paris, 1913.

METAPHYSICS

NOTWITHSTANDING THE collision of positivism and criticism, metaphysics did not disappear during the period under consideration, but it did undergo a transformation, becoming more analytical and more reflective. "Ramshackle houses," as Taine said of Hegel, "are not reconstructed."

1 *Gustav Fechner*

The cultivation of the philosophy of nature had almost disappeared in Germany by the middle of the nineteenth century, when Gustav Fechner (1801–87) took up its principal themes in *Nanna or the Inner Life of Plants* (1848) and *Zendavesta or the Little Book of Life After Death* (1851). According to Fechner, plants have souls, and the earth has a universal soul of which the souls of all terrestrial creatures are parts; the stars are heavenly angels, and their souls are to God as our souls are to the soul of the earth. But these random speculations lack the dialectical structure of early nineteenth-century philosophies of nature; they bear a closer resemblance to the myths of Comte or Jean Reynaud and remind us of Plotinus and Spinoza. The image of the production of lower souls by the higher soul that contains them is like a psychological interpretation of Spinozism: the souls of terrestrial creatures are to the earth's soul as the images or thoughts that arise in us are to our souls, and it is by inner reflection that we learn the nature of God. "If we examine our own consciousness—which can be measured in no other way—do we not find that it is an active progression from the past to the present and the future? Does it not join the remote and the immediate? Does it not fuse a thousand diversities into an indivisible unity? The law of the world is a unity endowed with the same properties, except that they belong to it in an unlimited way" (*Zendavesta,* 2d edition, 1901, p. 117). Another such image also reminds us of Plotinus: there is in the world but one consciousness, God's; each consciousness, seemingly distinct, has a threshold above which only a limited portion of divine consciousness protrudes; the soul is elevated in proportion as the threshold is lowered; in God alone there is no longer any threshold, and consciousness is total; thus discontinuity between souls is only apparent. Opposing both Kantianism and epistemology, this metaphysics was offered as a total revelation—a "daylight vision" in contrast to a "nocturnal vision" of things in themselves—and was sympathetically received at the beginning of the twentieth century, particularly by men like William James, even though it had at first passed almost unnoticed. In physics also, Fechner opposed Kant and Hegel, for he was not a dynamist but a mechanist and an atomist in the sense that he saw mechanism only as the expression or organ of mind.

The precise, positive character of his investigations sets his *Elements of Psychophysics* (1860) apart from his metaphysical musings. Following E. H. Weber, who, in 1846, had experimented with the relation between stimulation and sensation,[1] Fechner formulated his law, which states that the intensity of a sensation is proportional to the logarithm of the stimulus.[2]

II *Rudolf Lotze*

Rudolf Lotze (1817–81), professor at Göttingen and Berlin, turned against Kantianism and Hegelianism and in a certain sense restored the system of Leibniz. Even in his *Metaphysics* (1841) he

---

[1] Wagner, *Handwörterbuch der Physiologie,* art. on *Tastsinn.*
[2] Cf. G. Séailles, "La philosophie de Fechner," *Revue philosophique,* 1925.

adopted a "theological idealism," in which the theory of categories, which concern only the possible and cannot explain the appearance of any phenomenon, is contrasted with the Good, which is the true substance of the world. In his *Medical Psychology* (1859) he used the unity of the self to demonstrate the spirituality of the soul. While he acknowledges the interaction of body and soul, he does not assume that either of them has any influence on the other; transitive causality is impossible, for it would be tantamount to realizing, as a thing, the influence of a cause that is transferred to a patient, and to separating, contrary to the maxim of logic, attributes from substances. Reciprocal action is possible only between parts that belong to one whole. "Pluralism has to lead to a monism, through which an action which appears to be transitive is changed into an immanent action. . . . This action only appears to involve two finite beings; in truth, the absolute acts upon itself." His theory of local signs is an application of these ideas to the problem of perception: an object cannot influence the knowing subject in such a way that its attributes will be detached from it and transferred to the subject; external influences are only signals bidding the soul to produce inner states in accordance with immutable laws.

The *Microcosmos* (1856–64) was intended to be equivalent, in the science of man, to Alexander von Humboldt's *Cosmos* in the science of nature. Here he deals with body and soul, with man and history, and collects many positive data. His overall intention is to draw together the results of science that apparently lead to a godless nature, or idealism. The Leibnizian method, which subordinates the mechanism of nature to a spiritual reality, must be adopted, for the world of space and time is only a phenomenon. In his conception of spirit he is rigidly monadistic and refuses to accept Fechner's view that some souls can contain inferior souls; for the same reason, he is not pantheistic but theistic. A personal God answers the soul's desire. "Its desire to conceive as real the highest being of which it is allowed to have a presentiment cannot be satisfied in any other form but that of a personality. . . . True reality, which is and should be, is not matter and still less the

[Hegelian] Idea, but is the living, personal spirit of God and the world of personal spirits created by him: that is the place of the good and of goods" (*Microcosmos*, III, 559–616). Lotze acknowledges three superposed realities: the prevalance of universal and necessary laws governing every possible reality; singular realities or facts that cannot be deduced from the possible and are known to us through perception; and the specific plan of the world or prevalence of values that give unity to our intuition of the world.

He tried to reestablish the equilibrium of the different parts of philosophy, shattered for more than a century. In his *System of Philosophy* (1874–79) he seeks a "pure logic," completely independent of psychology. The psychological act must be separated from the content of thought; logic considers only the validity of this content. Pure logic has its source in Plato, whose Ideas Aristotle wrongly interpreted as things existing in themselves, whereas they have no existence except that of a value. He also tries to separate metaphysics from the theory of knowledge, to which philosophy then was being reduced.

III   *Africano Spir*

Africano Spir (1837–90), a Russian by origin, lived first in Germany, then in Geneva. The summation of his doctrine is found in these words: "We must of necessity choose between two goals—true knowledge or a metaphysical explanation of that which exists. If we choose the first goal, we can succeed in acquiring knowledge of things as they are, in understanding the fundamental law of thought, the basis of morality and religion. But then we must renounce the metaphysical explanation of things, for we see that there is an absolute opposition between the normal and the abnormal, and consequently that it is absolutely impossible for us to deduce the latter from the former." [3]

Here we have two theses: the possibility of laying a foundation for morality and religion, and the impossibility of finding a meta-

[3] "Essais de philosophie critique," *Revue de Métaphysique,* 1895, p. 129.

physical explanation of things. Let us begin by considering the second thesis: "A true essence cannot deny itself, as Hegel claimed, and become its own opposite; an object's denial of itself is rather proof that it does not have a normal mode of being, that it contains elements alien to its true essence." The norm is the principle of identity, and the normal being is one identical to itself. This Spir states with the conviction of a new Parmenides. It would be completely illogical for us to attribute being to that which changes, to becoming, to the composite; most metaphysicists have had the illusion of deducing conditioned becoming from the Absolute by way of creation or emanation, but such a derivation is contradictory. Spir holds that on this point he is following the thought of Kant, who demonstrated the impossibility of passing from phenomena to being and whose thought was distorted by post-Kantians.

It is true that becoming (this world of public opinion, as Parmenides said) resembles reality. With Hume and Mill, Spir shows becoming in the act of slowing down or reappearing, as if it wished to resemble substance; simultaneity and spontaneity in the grouping of several sensations can produce the illusion of substance, just as our psychic states are organized as wholes which produce the illusion of a permanent self. Thus the abnormal can subsist only "to the extent that, through a systematically organized deception, it succeeds in disguising its contradictory nature and takes on the appearance of substance; in this way it testifies against itself and in favor of the Norm." [4]

But the radical opposition between the Absolute and the abnormal rules out anything other than an illusory reconciliation, and this brings us to the first of the two theses: knowledge of this irreducible duality lays the foundation for a religious and moral life. This life is essentially a liberation, in which the self renounces its abnormal individuality, transcends itself, and is identified, beyond consciousness (which still implies composition and becoming), with the Absolute. Renunciation of egotism, abnegation of self—such is the means of participating in the eternity of true existence.

[4] G. Huan, *Essai sur le dualisme de Spir* (Paris, 1913), p. 47.

IV *Eduard von Hartmann*

In 1869 Eduard von Hartmann (1842–1906) published *The Philosophy of the Unconscious*, a work which served as the basis for his numerous studies relating to ethics, the philosophy of religions, political and social questions, and finally the theory of knowledge (*Theory of Categories*, 1896) and metaphysics (*History of Metaphysics*, 1899–1900).

He combines in his theory so many elements borrowed from divergent sources—Hegel, Schopenhauer, the "positive philosophy" of Schelling, Leibnizian individualism, the natural sciences—that his intuitive apprehension of the world exhibits little coherence. His point of departure seems to be the observation of living beings and, above all, of their organic functions and instincts; these instincts imply an intelligence superior by far to ours with respect to its knowledge, skill, and speed in making decisions, but which nevertheless is without consciousness; thus life reveals to us an intelligent unconscious endowed with will. This unconscious is in no sense a lower degree of consciousness; it has nothing in common with the unconscious facts which are assumed by psychologists to be preserved in the memory as images. Hartmann rejects all such facts and assumes that what is preserved in the memory is an organic state. In contrast to the unconscious, consciousness proves to be divided and diluted; in a human organism there are doubtless several distinct centers of consciousness outside the one associated with the brain; there are probably consciousnesses not only in animals and plants but even in molecules.

Hartmann therefore is led "by induction" to separate the notion of mind from the notion of consciousness. Beside the conscious mind there is an unconscious mind whose superiority is revealed to us in the organic functions, in artistic inspiration, and in the "categorical functions," which, as Kant realized, inform experience prior to any consciousness. Hartmann, generalizing, believes that he has found in the unconscious a principle that in some respects plays the role of God and in others the role of the Schopenhauerian will. As the creator of the world, the unconscious acted in an irrational manner, as pure will, without intelligence; this emergence of being is not related to any end. But as the unconscious is also intelligence, there is in the created world a finality extending not only to the structure of things (as we see in an organism) but also to the course of the world. The course of the world compensates for the irrationality of its existence by the final tendency toward nonbeing and destruction. As in Schopenhauer, consciousness, with its diverse degrees ranging all the way to man, is one means of attaining this final annihilation.

We can easily discern in Hartmann's doctrine a system imbued by pessimism quite different from that of Schopenhauer and much closer to the theosophy of Schelling. Hartmann's God is a God who needs to be saved and who, initially pure will or pure creative force, is saved by the intelligent principle that introduces into creation consciousness, which atones for imperfection. Thus Hartmann rediscovered, perhaps unwittingly, a myth from the distant past. His antipathy toward the personal God of Christianity, toward optimism and the "trivial deism" of liberal Protestantism, his fondness for an impersonal God who "alone is capable of saving us because he alone is capable of being in us and we in him"— these are the natural reactions of such a state of mind. One of Hartmann's disciples, A. Drews, who denied the historical existence of Jesus (*The Myth of Christ* 1910–11), rightly called attention to traditionally German traits in this religious doctrine, and L. Zeigler who defined this doctrine as "the process of deliverance of the unconscious mind of the world in the consciousness of man," fully agrees with Drews. Drews traced the theistic fallacy to the Cartesian *Cogito*, which identifies being with consciousness. This is the gist of rationalism, and even of English empiricism and the psychology of Wundt and Dilthey. They deny the existence of soul and equate the content of inner experience with the totality of the given.

v *Spiritualism in France*

Spiritualism traceable to Cousin, and liberal opposition under the Second Empire, have an affinity which is particularly evident in the career of Jules Simon (1814–96), who refused in 1851 to take the oath required of professors. In *Natural Religion* (1856), *Liberty of Conscience* (1857), *Political Liberty* (1859), and *Civil Liberty* (1859) he defends the same ideas as the publicist Édouard Laboulaye in *The Liberal Party* (3d edition, 1863) against a reaction which claimed to draw support from a French tradition. One of the points of departure of the movement had been Alexis de Tocqueville's *Democracy in America* (1835), which defended political liberties even against the leveling egalitarianism of democracy. In several other works—*The Worker* (1863) and *The School* (1864), for example—Jules Simon essayed the practical application of his political principles.

In keeping with the Cousinian tradition, the spiritualism of this period was reflected in the history of philosophy. *The Dictionary of the Philosophical Sciences*, under the direction of Adolphe Franck (1809–93), Chaignet's (1819–90) *Psychology of the Greeks*, Simon's *History of the School of Alexandria* (1844–45), Vacherot's *Critical History of the School of Alexandria* (1846–51), the studies of Charles de Rémusat (1797–1875) and especially of Hauréau concerning the Middle Ages, F. Bouillier's *History of Cartesianism*—these are some of the principal historical works of the school. To them must be added T. H. Martin's remarkable *Commentary on the Timaeus*, which attempts to draw together the history of philosophy and the history of the sciences.

The principle of eclecticism, however, was either abandoned or given a new interpretation. Étienne Vacherot (1809–97), in *Metaphysics and Science* (1858) as well as in *The New Spiritualism* (1884), combats a philosophy which would leave to common sense the task of choosing between systems. In addition, he brings out the irreducible opposition between them and identifies the three sources of knowledge: imagination, consciousness, and reason. Imagination uses sensible things as a model in picturing reality to itself and leads us to materialism; consciousness, by revealing us to ourselves as active being and persuading us to picture the essence of reality to ourselves as energy, leads us to a spiritualistic dynamism; reason, the faculty of principles, guides us toward an idealism such as that of Spinoza, who finds in things the necessary development of an indefinite power. There is no possibility of reconciling the three tendencies or of choosing one of them at the expense of the other two. In Vacherot we find an eclecticism of a wholly different kind, based on the distinction between the domain of existence and the domain of the ideal. The conditions of existence, in so far as we can determine them, are such that only finite beings, such as those represented by the imagination, can exist; existence is compatible with infinite perfection and, in direct contrast to the ontological proof, Vacherot finds in the perfection of God a reason for refusing to concede his existence. Perfection, in return, belongs to the realm of the ideal which, as such, gives existence its meaning and direction. In certain respects his doctrine resembles Renan's doctrine, which also derives from meditation on Hegelian philosophy and which E. Caro, a member of the same school, tried to refute in *The Idea of God* (1864), criticism of Vacherot, Renan, and Taine.

Paul Janet (1823–99) remained more faithful to Cousinian eclecticism, in which he saw not only a mechanical choice involving the common elements of all doctrines but also an application in philosophy of the objective method, which had succeeded in establishing harmony in the sciences in general (*Victor Cousin and His Work*, 1885). Philosophy is not grounded on any intuitive apprehension of the absolute, and it is doubtless through self-reflection that one finds the absolute, one's own self, and God; it does, however, involve knowledge of the absolute, which is wholly human and progresses only as the positive sciences evolve. A book like *Final Causes* (1877) draws its substance entirely from the sciences.

Paul Janet's moral philosophy (*Ethics,* 1874) is characteristic of his eclecticism: Aristotle's eudaemonism is carefully reconciled with Kant's rigorism; accomplishment of duty is simply the development of human nature toward its perfection; perfect being is at once our sovereign and our ideal. Paul Janet's last work, *Psychology and Metaphysics* (1897), develops the essential theme of Cousinian spiritualism, the apprehension of metaphysical realities through self-reflection and introspection.

VI   *Spiritualistic Positivism: Ravaisson, Lachelier, and Boutroux*

In 1867, when metaphysics was universally discredited, Jean Ravaisson (1813–1900), in his *Report concerning Philosophy in France in the Nineteenth Century,* foresaw the formation of "a spiritualistic realism or positivism having as its generative principle the mind's inner awareness of an existence that it recognizes as the source and support of all other existences, which is nothing except its activity." Lachelier, Boutroux, and Bergson proved that he was right by continuing the movement initiated in 1838 by his thesis *On Habit.* The characteristic trait of this movement, setting it apart from Cartesian spiritualism, is the significance it attaches to the idea of life. To reduce life to a mechanism, like Descartes, was to separate soul from matter and assert a dualism which broke the continuity of reality; this dualism had been attacked in the eighteenth century by the animism of Stahl and the vitalism of the school of Montpellier, which Ravaisson valued highly; and the last teachings of Schelling, under whom Ravaisson had studied in Munich, had as their principal theme the close connection between nature and spirit; consequently it must have been Schelling's "positive philosophy" rather than Comte's which, because it contrasted realism and the theory of contingency with Hegelian idealism, suggested to Ravaisson the idea of a "realism and spiritualistic positivism."

Unlike Schelling, however, Ravaisson was not inclined by temperament to create great metaphysical frescoes; instead, he tried to penetrate consciousness and to discover the continuity of spirit and matter in one precise, circumscribed fact—habit. Distinct consciousness implies a certain gap, filled by reflection, between the idea of an end and its realization. In habit, an intelligent but unconscious act, this gap diminishes, then disappears. "Reflection, which crosses and measures distances between contraries or spheres of oppositions, is gradually replaced by immediate comprehension, in which nothing separates the subject from its object in thought. . . . Habit is more and more a *substantial idea*. Obscure comprehension, which through habit takes the place of reflection, or that immediate comprehension in which object and subject are fused, is a *real* intuition in which the real and the ideal, being and thought, blend" (Baruzi edition, pp. 36–37). Through habit we discover what nature is: "Thus in the depths of the soul, as well as in this lower world, which it animates and which is distinct from it, we discover as the limit to which the progression of habit reduces activity, the unreflective spontaneity of desire, the impersonality of nature" (p. 54). It follows that Nature is not a blind, mechanical power but is inherent in a desire which perceives its object immediately and is therefore joined to Liberty. "In everything the Necessity of nature is the chain fashioned by Liberty, but it is an active, living chain—the necessity of desire, love, and grace" (p. 59).

Before his thesis on habit, Ravaisson had prepared a monograph on Aristotle which was later given definitive form in his *Essay on the Metaphysics of Aristotle* (1837–46). His interpretation, dominated by the criticism that Aristotle himself made of the Platonic theory of Ideas, performs a valuable service in explaining the movement and life of Nature by the desire that thrusts Nature toward Intelligence, a veritable reality and not an empty abstraction like an *Idea*. Moreover (in the manner of Schelling at the beginning of *The Philosophy of Mythology*), he sees Aristotelianism as an introduction to Christianity. From the outside Aristotle merely unites potential and actual, matter and thought; for nature's desire to attain a Good which is unaware of nature, Christianity substitutes the condescending Love of God for his creature; consequently the real and the ideal, potential and actual, become solidary and inseparable even though they remain distinct.

"True philosophy will investigate the nature of Love."[5] The mistake of Kant and the Scottish philosophers was in using only intellect or the faculty of abstract concepts, in thinking that experience, whether internal or external, can give us direct access only to facts. Through intense reflection such as that practiced by Maine de Biran we can discover the substance of the soul, which, though first revealed as will and effort, involves a tendency and a desire that imply an awareness of an incipient union with the good. This union is simply love, which constitutes the true substance of the soul.

Ravaisson's meditations on art (cf. *Venus de Milo,* 1862) also lead him to discover, beneath the rigidity of forms, everything that constitutes their inner harmony and unity: beneath beauty, grace; beneath a flexible line, the undulating, serpentine movement of which it is the mark; beneath forms, their music. "To learn to draw is to learn to discover the melody created by forms. For vocal music and singing are the most expressive elements that the world contains. Thus we should give first place to learning music in order to become aware of what things are saying.[6] A universal harmony like divine grace spreading through things—such is the innermost being of nature.

Jules Lachelier (1832–1918) introduced the notion of a reflective method into French philosophy. It is rather difficult for us to find in his published works the meaning and especially the distinctive nature of a doctrine which was elaborated mainly in his teaching at the École Normale. Some of its traits are known through G. Séailles' work, *The Philosophy of J. Lachelier* (1920). Lachelier was dissatisfied with the associationist empiricism which seemed to him to lead to skepticism, but he was equally dissatisfied with the eclecticism then prevalent at the University of Paris. Eclecticism, in effect, posits "on one hand thought with its own inner determina-

---

[5] Unpublished work. Quoted by J. Baruzi in the introduction to his edition of *De l'Habitude* (Paris, 1927), p. xxvi.

[6] Unpublished work. Quoted by J. Baruzi, p. xxv.

tions and on the other an object of which thought is only the image, but which consciousness neither penetrates nor envelops." This means giving in to the skeptic's every demand, for it is absurd and contradictory to think that one's thought can emerge from itself and think of something that is alien to it. There is certainty only if reality is in thought itself.

It was through contact with Kant that this took definite shape in Lachelier's thinking, but its features were quite distinct from those exhibited by the model. Kant makes a distinction between the possibility of experience, which is the source of a constituent judgment such as the principle of causality, and the possibility of conceiving objects once they are constituted, which accounts for a reflective judgment such as the principle of finality. Lachelier does not make this distinction. "If the conditions of the existence of things are the sole conditions of the possibility of thought," he writes, "we can determine these conditions absolutely a priori, for they result from the very nature of the mind." In the *Foundation of Induction* (1871) he demonstrates the principle of causality as well as universal mechanism by using the arguments of the *Transcendental Analytic,* and he demonstrates the principle of finality by following, roughly, the *Critique of Judgment;* he attaches the same value, however, to both principles.

This divergence is characteristic: the trend of thought in *The Foundation of Induction* contrasts sharply with that of the *Critiques.* Between the principle of causality and the principle of finality Lachelier sees a distinction quite different from the Kantian one—the distinction between the abstract or the poor reality of mechanism, and the concrete or the rich reality of tendency and aspiration. In his view thought, even more than the condition of the objectivity of the world, is a thrust toward the Good and toward fulness of being; consequently, it posits mechanism not as constituting reality but as a limit to be surpassed.

It should not surprise us, therefore, to find that Lachelier preferred the synthetic method employed in his *Psychology and Metaphysics* (1885) to the Kantian method of analyzing the conditions of experience. It was much more appropriate for demonstrating the identity of the laws of thought and the laws of being. *The Foundation of Induction* shows clearly that the world is governed by a law, but not that it depends on thought or that thought has an absolute, independent existence. We can be sure of its existence only if we see it engender its objects by a synthetic operation. "Absolute existence can be demonstrated only directly, through discovery of the operation by means of which thought posits itself and ascribes to itself principles of action."[7] The idea of being or of truth posits and asserts itself even if we deny its existence; for then we are asserting that it is true that the idea does not exist; our assertion, constantly springing up again, is symbolized by time, in which an instant appears infinitely—the first dimension or length—and finally by mechanical necessity, in which one homogeneous element determines the next. By a second act it creates the heterogeneous diversity of sensation, intensive quantity, which spreads through the second dimension of space—width—while the totality of its degrees constitutes a will to live, an attempt to reach a goal. Finally, by a spontaneous operation thought reflects on itself as the source of being and becomes sovereign liberty, which is conscious of itself and of which nature with its necessity and finality is but a moment.

The foregoing statements, though far from complete, reveal the differences between the spirit of Lachelier's dialectic and that of the post-Kantians. Each act of consciousness is not attached to the preceding act by any necessity, analytical or synthetical; one act cannot produce or foresee another and is related to it only in the sense that the general trend of consciousness is toward absolute liberty.

Thus consciousness in its striving cannot be satisfied with the formal absolute that philosophy discovers. "The highest question of philosophy, more religious in fact than philosophical, is passage from the formal absolute to the real, living absolute, from the idea of God to God. If the syllogism miscarries, let faith run the risk; let the ontological argument yield to the wager" (*Note on Pascal's Wager*). The living God of the Christian faith, which is Lachelier's

[7] Cf. É. Boutroux, *Nouvelles études d'histoire de la philosophie*, p. 23.

faith, is the extreme consequence of this dialectic. As with Plotinus, our true interiority is always higher than the transient forms in which we place it, for it is in our resemblance to the living God, who is our reality and the only true reality. Our moral activity is but the symbol of this resemblance. "Certain acts," said Lachelier in his lectures, "can acquire an absolute value insofar as they represent symbolically the absolute essence of things, . . . on one hand the absolute unity of the human soul notwithstanding the diversity of its faculties, and on the other the absolute unity of souls notwithstanding the diversity of persons; . . . to reject everything which impedes consciousness and freedom . . . and to reduce whenever possible the diversity of human souls to the unity of souls in God" [8] are the fundamental maxims of a moral philosophy which gives first place to charity. That is why Lachelier bases conduct, and even political conduct, on forces that transcend the individual—particularly tradition, inasmuch as laws become dissociated from lawmakers with the passage of time and tend, like logic, to become impersonal; he is hostile to democracy, which is derived from a common will, uncertain and capricious; in short, stability or communion in any form is for him the symbol of rationality. For reasons easily perceived, the notion of symbol has the leading role in Lachelier's philosophical speculations, especially, it would seem, in his "unwritten" speculations. Has not symbolism always been the only means of justifying the finite in a doctrine which attributes true existence only to the infinite?

His influence and most of his writings place Émile Boutroux (1845–1921) in the twentieth century, but he published his fundamental work on *The Contingency of the Laws of Nature* in 1874 (complemented by *The Idea of Natural Law,* 1895), shortly after *The Foundation of Induction.* After 1850, Spencer, Büchner, and many others had developed and popularized the conception of the world that Renouvier calls scientism—that of a tissue of phenomena interconnected by rigorous laws; denying finality and the freedom it implies, they claimed to draw support for their conception from

[8] Quoted by G. Séailles, *La philosophie de Lachelier,* pp. 124–25.

the requirements of scientific knowledge. Boutroux' great innovation, and the reason for the enormous significance of his work, was to leave aside the results or so-called results of the sciences and to try to determine, solely through analysis of scientific work, "whether this category of necessary connection, inherent in the intellect, actually reappears in things themselves. . . . If we found that the world manifested a certain degree of truly irreducible contingency, we would have grounds for thinking that the laws of nature are inadequate in themselves and have their reason in the causes that dominate them; thus the point of view of the intellect would not be the definitive point of view in our knowledge of things" (2d edition, 1895, pp. 4–5).

Boutroux devotes particular attention to the laws of conservation, on which determinism, especially, is grounded. Conservation of vital energy, the law of equivalence of heat, laws of organic connections and correlations, the law of psychophysical parallelism, the law of permanence governing amounts of psychic energy: for each degree of being studied by the mechanical, physical, vital, and psychological sciences, these laws seem to be principles which exclude any contingency. But in the first place, there are as many laws as there are degrees of being, and on the hierarchy of degrees ranging from the least perfect to the most perfect, a higher degree is contingent in relation to a lower degree; this contingency or irreducibility is a positive datum—the one that provided Comte with a point of departure for his classification. But that is not all. These laws of conservation pose a problem which, though it has diverse applications, remains identical in its general form: Is the permanence of a given quantity necessary? In mechanics the principle of conservation of energy does not show us that energy contains any metaphysical essence transcending experience; it is expressed, not in things, but in a finite system of mechanical elements known through experience; furthermore, that two successive states are in a strict sense equal cannot be verified; finally, permanence is permanence through change and therefore implies a change which it does not explain. Similar observations could be made for every degree of being, but it should be noted that contingency becomes progressively greater at each degree. For example, at the level of life we notice not only that vital energy is something that can hardly be measured, inasmuch as it implies an idea of quality that resists number, but also that transformations of living beings involve a historical factor or variability which is perfection or decadence. The possibility of our finding such a principle of conservation in consciousness would be even less, for the higher we climb, the more "the law tends to approximate the fact. Hence the conservation of the whole no longer determines the acts of the individual; it depends on them. The individual, once he alone has become the whole class to which the law applies, is its master. He makes it into a tool, and he envisions a state in which he would thus be, at every instant of his existence, equal to the law" (p. 130).

Thus positivity, correctly understood, agrees with spirituality. We must not be deceived by the deductive character assumed by science when it is complete; necessity is in the consequence, not in the principle. It is therefore "the value of the positive sciences" (p. 139) that Boutroux formally calls in question; these sciences select only the stable, permanent aspects of being; "still to be investigated is its creative source." In this investigation, experience must not be abandoned but extended, for only data useful in induction and the establishment of a law are retained in the sciences, while the historical aspect—and this includes every aspect of being relating to actions which are unpredictable and beyond deduction—is omitted. Inductive knowledge, however, fails to explain contingency. A complete, perfect explanation can be found only in morality or inclination toward the good. "God is the very being whose creative activity we feel in our inmost depths in the midst of our efforts to draw nearer to him," and the whole hierarchy of beings appears to us as a set of conditions and a means of attaining freedom, which grows slowly at the expense of physical fatality.

The studies in the history of philosophy undertaken by Boutroux are closely related to his doctrine. His Latin thesis (*De veritatibus aeternis apud Cartesium,* 1874) dealt with Descartes' concept of contingency and its crucial role in God's actions. His introduction to the translation of the first volume of Éduard Zeller's *Philosophy of the Greeks* (1877) provided him with an opportunity to show, with Zeller and against Hegel (as well as the eclectics), the contingency of historical progress, which is a history of reason. The explanation is that reason, instead of trying to explain things scientifically, encompasses man in his entirety—including his religion, his ethics, and his art. This reason, which encompasses the whole man, is shown in action in the great systems, particularly those of Aristotle, Leibniz, and Kant (cf., in addition to his *Studies* [1897] and *New Studies in the History of Philosophy* [1927], *The Philosophy of Kant* [1926], and *Studies in the History of German Philosophy* [1927]). Thus it was natural for him to focus his attention on discordances which seem to introduce contradiction even into the human mind: science and religion, which had been the underlying theme of his first book, appear in the title of one of his last published works (*Science and Religion in Contemporary Philosophy,* 1908); previously in *Pascal* (1900) and *Psychology of Mysticism* (1902), and subsequently in *William James* (1911), he gave proof of the unity of his preoccupations. Is it true that the scientific spirit issued from the reaction of reason against the religious spirit and that its triumph and the disappearance of the religious spirit are but one and the same thing? Put in its simplest terms, that is the question he raises (*Science,* p. 345). A reconciliation, according to him, can come neither from reciprocal concessions nor from impositional limits but only from a thorough investigation of the facts. There can be no question, in religion, of imposing any restrictions on the scientific spirit and democracy; religion needs only to free itself from the political forms and texts in which it has been imprisoned, to be returned to itself, to become what it is in essence—worship of God in spirit and in truth. Eclectic spiritualism saw tolerance as the philosopher's normal attitude toward religion. In the spiritualism of Boutroux, "the principle of tolerance is an ill-conceived notion, the expression of a disdainful act of condescension" (p. 392). We must go beyond tolerance to love. "In his appraisal of others, the religious man gives first place, not to the traits through which they resemble him, but to the traits through which they differ from him."

Bibliography

II

Texts

Lotze, H. *Allgemeine Pathologie und Therapie als mechanische Naturwissenschaften.* Leipzig, 1842.

————. *Medizinische Psychologie oder Physiologie der Seele.* Leipzig, 1852.

————. *Mikrokosmus.* 3 vols. Leipzig, 1856–64.

————. *Microcosmus,* trans. E. Hamilton and E. E. C. Jones. 2 vols. Edinburgh, 1885–86.

————. *Die Geschichte der Aesthetik in Deutschland.* Munich, 1868.

————. *Lotze's System of Philosophy,* ed. Bernard Bosanquet. Oxford, 1884.

————. *Kleine Schriften,* ed. D. Peipers. 3 vols. Leipzig, 1885–91.

Studies

Hartmann, Karl Robert Eduard von. *Lotzes Philosophie.* Leipzig, 1888.

Jones, Henry. *A Critical Account of the Philosophy of Lotze.* Glasgow, 1895.

Schmidt-Japing, J. W. *Lotzes Religionsphilosophie in ihrer Entwicklung.* . . . Göttingen, 1925.

Thomas, E. E. *Lotze's Theory of Reality.* London, 1921.

Wentscher, Max. *H. Lotze. Lotzes Leben und Werke.* Vol. 1. Heidelberg, 1913.

FRIEDRICH NIETZSCHE

WHEN FRIEDRICH NIETZSCHE (1844–1900) and his friend Ervin Rohde, the author of *Psyche,* were attending the universities of Bonn and Leipzig (1864–69), philology, on account of its methods and results, was considered the key to German culture. Nietzsche was soon diverted from this study by his intimate knowledge of the work of Schopenhauer and the latter's clear, direct vision of things and men. "A scholar can never become a philosopher," he wrote in *Untimely Meditations* (1873–75). "One who lets books and the notions, opinions, and things of the past come between him and objects, who in the broad sense is born for history, will never see objects for the first time." He charged Hegelian philosophy with being the source of this "Philistine culture," of which David Strauss seemed to him to be a typical representative. Hegel had announced that the end of time was approaching. "The belief that one is a latecomer is truly paralyzing and apt to provoke moodiness," Nietzsche wrote, "but when through a bold reversal such a belief begins to defy the direction and aim of everything that has happened up to this time, as if learned trifles were equal to a realization of universal history, then this belief seems terrible and destructive."

But it was his philological studies that caused him to meditate on Greece and to discover "the reality of an antihistorical culture and yet, or perhaps consequently, an unspeakably rich and fertile culture." His reflections on this culture and his interpretation, in terms of Schopenhauer's philosophy, of the lyrical drama of his friend Richard Wagner resulted in *The Birth of Tragedy from the Spirit of Music,* a work written just before the war of 1870 and published in 1872; the edition of 1886 is subtitled "Hellenism and Pessimism." According to Nietzsche, classical criticism (which began with Winckelmann) is familiar with only one aspect of Greek art, the plastic art of Apollo, god of form; this is the art of balance, of measure, of knowledge and mastery of self; it is associated with serene, impassive contemplation in the midst of a world of sorrows. "The real world is covered by a veil, and a new world, clearer, more intelligible, and yet more spectral is constantly emerging and changing before our eyes." Opposing Apollinian contemplation is the ecstasy of Dionysius, which is knowledge of the unity of Will, the pessimistic view of things according to Schopenhauer. In Greek tragedy the chorus represents Dionysius' companion, who "shudders at the thought of the misfortunes that will strike the hero and has a presentiment of higher and infinitely more powerful joy." He shudders because the excess of misfortunes rules out Apollinian contemplation, but this very excess leads him to seize its cause in the will to live and to find calm in its denial. This is the theme of the *Tristan* of Wagner, whose lyrical drama, according to Nietzsche, is a revival of Greek tragedy; this drama "leads from the world of semblance to the limits where it creates itself and seeks again to take refuge in the one true reality."

1 *Criticism of Higher Values*

This gloomy, hopeless metaphysics did not endure. It discovered the psychological and physiological reasons for the negation of the will to live in a diminution and weakening of the vital instinct; pessimism was a symptom of degeneracy. Nietzsche quarreled with Wagner. Like Schopenhauer, he turned to the French moralists— La Rochefoucauld, Pascal, and all the writers of the eighteenth century. In *Human, All-Too-Human* (1878) and *The Wanderer and*

His Shadow (1880) he shows how essential moral feelings—pity, self-contempt, altruism—arise through a false antiscientific explanation of his actions and feelings. Morality is an "autotomy": for example, if a soldier hopes to fall on the battlefield, the reason is that he has more love for *some part of himself*—an idea, a desire, a creature—than for *some other part of himself* and that as a consequence he divides his being, sacrificing one part of it to the other" (p. 92). The mistake is in believing that one can emerge from oneself.

In 1879 Nietzsche, in ill-health, resigned his professorship at the University of Basel. He lived in Rome, Genoa, Nice, and Sils in the Engadine before his wandering life, ever more solitary, came to an end in 1889, when he suffered an attack of general paralysis. During this ten-year period he wrote the impassioned books in which his thought, avoiding systematic development, usually was concentrated in the form of aphorisms but occasionally diffused, as in *Thus Spoke Zarathustra* (1883-92), in the form of striking images like those of the Romantic prophets. The sole problem to which he devoted his attention was the problem of modern culture. A culture lives on beliefs and values, but the values on which the life of modern man depends—Christianity, pessimism, science, rationalism, ethics of duty, democracy, socialism—are all symptoms of decay, of a life which is becoming impoverished and extinct. Nietzsche's work was an attempt to reverse the current. His twofold task was to destroy existing values by showing that their true source is in weariness of living and to effect a transmutation of values by giving first place to the will to power, to everything that affirms the upsurge and fullness of life.

The most easily understood part of his work is his implacable critique. Although it did not seem to go beyond the limits of eighteenth-century philosophy in *Human, All-Too-Human*, Nietzsche's critique changed radically when he dealt at length with the evil that in *The Will to Power* is called European nihilism. His aim is no longer to trace the origin of ethics to egotism but to discover in a thoroughgoing physiological decline the origin of the common attitude which takes the form of pity in the religious man, objectivity in the scholar, egalitarianism in the socialist. In *The Dawn* (1881) he counters Rousseau's paradox, "This deplorable civilization is the cause of our bad morality" with a paradox of his own. "Our good morality is the cause of this deplorable civilization," he writes. "Our social conceptions of good and evil, weak and effeminate, by exerting an enormous influence on our bodies and spirits, have finally weakened all bodies and spirits and crushed the true pillars of a strong civilization—independent, self-sufficient, unprejudiced men." In *The Gay Science* (1882) appears what might be called Nietzsche's pragmatism, the idea of vital mistakes on which our knowledge of truth is grounded: our belief, for example, in objects and bodies; our logic derived from "the inclination to treat similar things as if they were equal"; finally, our category of cause and effect, inasmuch as "an intellect which saw cause and effect as a continuity or stream of events and not, in our fashion, as an arbitrary parcelling out would deny the idea of cause and effect and all conditionality."

It is in *Beyond Good and Evil* (1886) more than in any other work, however, that we find his harshest critique of values. His analysis of the philosopher, the freethinker, the religious man, the scientist, the patriot, the nobleman leads him in each instance to determine the ascending or descending vitality which is the substance of the judgments made by each of them concerning the real. The sentiment of cruelty, for example, is at the heart of any higher culture; it produces the sad voluptuousness of tragedy, like the sacrifice of reason in Pascal, "drawn secretly by his own cruelty, turned against itself." *The Genealogy of Morals* (1887) deals in particular with the problem of asceticism, considered to be the extreme form of which morality and science are often an aspect. "The despiser of all health and power, of everything uncouth, wild, unruly, the delicate man who scorns even more easily than he hates, on whom falls the necessity of waging war against animals of prey, a war of trickery (of spirit) rather than of violence"—this is the definition of the ascetic, in whom we see the birth of the spirituality of science and morality.

These aphoristic writings were oriented toward the critique of fundamental ideas which subsequently took the form of pragmatism and influenced the critical movement in the sciences. They also reflect the moralist's psychological critique, as in this passage concerning the scientist: "Science is today the refuge of any kind of discontent, incredulity, remorse, *despectio sui,* or bad conscience; it is uneasiness prompted by a lack of idealism, grief over the absence of great love, discontent caused by unnatural temperance. . . . The capacity of our most eminent scientists, their uninterrupted application, their brains which seethe night and day, even their technical superiority—everything tends to make them blind to the evidence of certain things" (*Genealogy,* p. 259). Nietzsche felt that he could develop and state his two critiques precisely only by acquiring scientific knowledge that he, at first a philologist, did not possess. We find in *The Will to Power,* a posthumous book which is actually a collection of outlines for a work first conceived in 1882 and begun in 1886, the first results of this systematic approach, which was to lead to the elaboration of many ideas adumbrated in *Twilight of the Idols* (1889). He appears at this time to be violently opposed to the great Spencerian and Darwinian systems with their idea of inexorable, mechanical progress. The struggle for existence "ends unfortunately in a manner contrary to that which the school of Darwin might desire, contrary to that which one might dare, perhaps, desire of it: I mean to the detriment of the strong, the privileged, the happy exceptions. Species do not grow toward perfection, for in the end the weak always become masters of the strong—because they are more numerous and also because they are more cunning." "European nihilism" is the expression he uses in *The Will to Power* to designate this decadence, which began with Socrates and Plato, "this universal aberration of mankind as it turns away from its fundamental instincts"; all higher judgments, all those who have become masters of mankind are reduced to judgments of physiologically exhausted beings." Any ideal, any statement of an end that is not in existence is a condemnation of existence, bearing witness to an abatement of vitality.

II *The Transmutation of Values: The Superman*

All his books seem to Nietzsche himself to be steps toward recovery. "Be absolutely personal without using the first person—be a kind of memory" is typical of the maxims which he sets down for himself. The transmutation of values has its source, in fact, not in reflection and analysis but in the simple affirmation of power, which simply is, and does not have to be justified; the men of the Italian Renaissance, with their *"virtu* divested of morality," and Napoleon are typical of undomesticated individuals whom Carlyle and Emerson wrongly tried to justify as representatives of an idea. So this transmutation naturally takes the form of a prophetic announcement in *Thus Spoke Zarathustra* and in the posthumous work *Ecce homo* (1908). The superman predicted by Zarathustra is not the consummation of the human type. Nietzsche's idea of the last man is similar to Cournot's: having organized everything in such a way as to eliminate all risks, he is ultimately satisfied with his bland happiness. But "man is something that must be overcome, a bridge and not an end." The superman is characterized by his love of risk and danger; the will to power is inseparable from the will to live; life flourishes only by tying itself down to its environment. How is the complete poem of Zarathustra to be interpreted if not as an account of the risks incurred by the hero—the risks to which our civilization exposes the emerging superman, which his generosity makes more dangerous, and which he finally overcomes? First of all, it is the myth of the eternal recurrence, of the indefinite return of the same cycle of events, proposed by Schopenhauer as an idea dreadful enough to justify pessimism and disgust for a life whose terrors must be relived. Zarathustra first experiences this disgust, then not only accepts the myth but makes it his own: Is not the eternal recurrence deliverance from servitude to ends, the boundless and joyous affirmation of an existence justified solely by this very affirmation, and the subjugation of existence to a definite and limited form, which is the ultimate expression of power? The eternal recurrence exemplifies the transmutation of values, the Yes which is opposed to the No. Another temptation is that of "higher men," those about whom the common people say, "Higher men—there are no higher men; we are all equal . . . in the sight of God." Higher men—it is the proclaimer of utter weariness who teaches, "Everything is equal, nothing is worth the effort." These are all types of higher men whose nobility derives from the disgust they feel for men and for themselves: the conscientious in spirit who prefer to know nothing rather than to have partial knowledge of many things and for whom "in true knowledge, there is nothing great, nothing small"; the expiatory or captivating in spirit (Wagner himself), who seek love and suffering; "the ugliest of men," who see a compassionate God as a witness on whom they seek revenge; voluntary beggars, disgusted with "slaves to wealth who know how to reap a profit from every pile of filth, with the gilded, corrupted populace"; and "shadows of Zarathustra," disciples who must guard against surrendering to a narrow faith. The pessimist, the philologist and scholar, the artist, the despiser of wealth—none of them knew how to overcome his own disgust. The superman is not the man to continue their task: "You, higher men, do you believe that I am here to redo well what you have done badly? . . . More and more of the best of your species must perish. . . . Only in this way does man grow in stature."

Thus Nietzsche disassociated himself from the intellectual aristocracy whose nobility contained so many traces of decadence. Even though he was still more opposed to the social and democratic ideal, it is not true that for him the will to power was simple force, brutal and destructive. His last meditations seem, on the contrary, to show that the fulness of life is manifested in a choice, in a precise, rigorous order of the elements it dominates; that "the purification of taste can only be the consequence of a reinforcement of the type," which itself results from a superabundance of power; that "we do not have the great synthetic man whose dissimilar powers are restrained by the same yoke" but only "multifarious man, weak and multifarious man." These last thoughts, published in the second volume of *The Will to Live,* probably opened the door to a new conception of being and life, but at the beginning of the twentieth century Nietzsche's numerous plebeian followers, seeing only his individualism and not the self-mastery and asceticism which make men strong, hardly suspected the importance of this new conception.[1]

III *Jean Marie Guyau*

Jean Marie Guyau (1854–88) was in a sense an immoralist like Nietzsche. The great mistake of the moralists, according to him, was to ignore the unconscious: man is motivated primarily, more so than by a reflective impetus, pleasure, or anything else, by a vital drive rooted in the darkest depths of his being. Activity does, in fact, penetrate his consciousness, but then the danger of analysis is present. "Consciousness can eventually react and gradually, through the clarity of analysis, destroy what the obscure synthesis of heredity had accumulated; it is a dissolving force" (*Morality without Obligation or Sanctions,* 1805). The aim of moral philosophy is to reestablish harmony between reflection and spontaneity by offering a thorough justification of spontaneity. It can do so because "the most intensive and the most extensive life" unites egotism and altruism. Like Nietzsche, Guyau sees that life is prodigality and waste, and that egotism is therefore a mutilation of life; it is our power, our vital energy, that determines our duty.

Aesthetics, like ethics, discovers its principles in life itself. The beautiful is that which increases our vitality, and that is why—according to *Art from the Sociological Point of View* (1889)—an aesthetic emotion is a social one. Art tries to elevate an individual life in order to make it coincide with universal life. Moral and

---

[1] Cf. concerning Nietzsche's influence, Geneviève Blanquis, *Nietzsche en France,* 1929.

aesthetic sentiment does not perish for want of a rule that transcends life; by the same token, religious sentiment should subsist after the disappearance of dogma, for all it is is the sentiment permeating this universe of a physical, moral, and social dependence with respect to the universe and the source of life (*The Religion of the Future*, 1887).[2]

[2] Cf. the same author's *Vers d'un philosophe*, 1881; *Éducation et hérédité*, 1830; *Genèse de l'idée de temps*, 1890.

Bibliography

Texts

Nietzsche, Friedrich. *Gesammelte Werke, Musarionausgabe.* 23 vols. Munich, 1920–29.
——. *The Complete Works,* ed. Oscar Levy. 18 vols. Edinburgh and London, 1909–13. Reissued 1964.
——. *The Portable Nietzsche,* trans. and ed. Walter Kaufmann. New York, 1954.
——. *Basic Writings of Nietzsche,* ed. and in part newly translated with notes by Walter Kaufmann. New York, 1966.
——. *The Will to Power,* trans. Walter Kaufmann and R. G. Hollingdale, and edited, with notes, by Walter Kaufmann. New York, 1966.

Studies

Bernoulli, C. A. *Franz Overbeck und Friedrich Nietzsche.* 2 vols. Jena, 1908.
Brinton Crane, *Nietzsche.* New York, 1965.
Danto, Arthur C. *Nietzsche as Philosopher,* New York, 1965.
Hollingdale, R. G. *Nietzsche: The Man and His Philosophy.* Baton Rouge, La., 1965.
Löwith, Karl. *From Hegel to Nietzsche,* trans. by David Green. New York, 1967.
Reichert, H. W., and Schlechta, Karl. *International Nietzsche Bibliography.* Chapel Hill, N.C., 1960.

III

Texts

Guyau, Jean Marie. *La Morale d'Épicure et ses rapports avec les doctrines contemporaines.* Paris, 1878.
——. *La Morale anglaise contemporaine.* Paris, 1879.
——. *Vers d'un philosophe.* Paris, 1881.
——. *Les Problèmes de l'esthétique contemporaine.* Paris, 1884.
——. *Esquisse d'une morale sans obligation ni sanction.* Paris, 1885.
——. *The Non-Religion of the Future.* Reprinted with an introduction by N. M. Glatzer. New York, 1962.
——. *L'Art au point de vue sociologique.* Paris, 1889.
——. *Le Genèse de l'idée de temps.* Paris, 1890.

SECOND PERIOD
1890-1930

THE SPIRITUALISM OF
HENRI BERGSON

1 *The Renewal of Philosophy around 1890*

What were the dominant philosophical opinions around 1880?
First there were only prohibitions, negations, reductions that annihilate being and intellectual or moral values: Spencerian prohibitions, which stop the mind at the gates of the unknowable and claim to eliminate decisively any metaphysical speculation; the negations of Schopenhauerian pessimism, which discloses, at the heart of every existence, the vanity of an identical will to live; the reductions of Taine's philosophy, which traces all mental phenomena to sensation, all sensation to movement, and finally, all material and spiritual realities to a kind of infinitesimal pulsation that recreates itself indefinitely. Against this, with the exception of the dynamic philosophy of Lachelier and Boutroux, we find at most a sparse, emaciated spiritualism, which continued as if in fulfillment of a vow to assert the irreducibility of consciousness and liberty, always based on immediate inward observation.

Intelligence and the concern for objectivity seem to have led to a vision of the universe in which everything that conferred worth and value on real, directly experienced life vanished and was lost. Conscience and morality were as illusory as the "vital deceptions" that philosophy undertook to denounce even though to deprive human frailty of them was extremely dangerous, as Ibsen showed in his dramas and Nietzsche in his philosophy. The extreme consequence of this situation was the mentality of Renan, who passed from a solemn respect for truth that obliged him to denounce these illusions to a superior irony that treated this very obligation as illusory and allowed him to accept untruths through conservatism or simple fear of scandal. Here intelligence devoured itself.

Then, at the end of the nineteenth century and the beginning of the twentieth, there were often violent and disorderly reactions motivated by an instinctive urge to reestablish this equilibrium at any cost. Hence the profoundly irrational character of many doctrines which came to light at that time: Brunetière's famous declarations concerning the failure of science and his return to the Christian faith, the fideist and modernist movement, Barrès' nationalism, and the favor shown in Germany to Gobineau's racial theories are all symptoms of the same spirit. This development and the Romantic movement are not without analogies: rich and obscure, both produced works of great literary beauty, but too often both also were characterized by a lack of sincerity or by imposture. It was too easy for philosophers to yield to the temptation to link philosophy with the interests of a particular group, church, nation, or class and in this way to transform the pursuit of truth into a means of defense or attack.

Thus even today there persists a current of agnosticism which prohibits a choice between emotional and intellectual imperatives. *The Uneasiness of Philosophical Thought* (1905) and *The Unverifiable* (1920) are revealing titles of works in which André Cresson explores the inexorable alternative which forces every philosopher, depending on his temperament, to accept positivism or to find "a means of escaping the deterministic suggestions of the sciences because he judges them to be contrary to the moral needs of the soul." Such agnosticism is nevertheless remote from the doctrines discussed in this and the following chapters, for they deny the necessity of this very alternative.

One of the strongest ramparts of the scientific spirit was the mechanistic theory of life, which, after Darwin, seemed to be indispensable. The resurgence of vitalism, observable particularly in Germany—for example, in Hans Driesch's *Philosophy of the Organic* (2 vols., Leipzig, 1909; 2d edition, 1921)—is indicative of a lively reaction against even this theory. Transplantation, heredity, regeneration, organic action conditioned by the individual's entire past are all positive proofs against the theory that an organism is like a machine. A living organism is an "equipotential" harmonious system—that is, a mass of cells whose organization remains the same even if parts are arbitrarily removed. The notion of life, taken as an absolute, is the basis of many doctrines of our time—for example, the doctrine of the Russian philosopher N. Losski, whose book on *The Intuitive Bases of Knowledge* (1904) supports an organic conception of the world. But all these studies are dominated by the doctrine of Henri Bergson (1859–1941), which offered the inducement of a spiritual conversion and thereby transformed the conditions of philosophical speculation in our own time.

II *The Bergsonian Doctrine*

Distinct from the negative doctrines is the dynamic current of spiritualistic positivism observable in France, as early as 1870, in Lachelier and Boutroux. This same current continues and grows stronger, though in a different way, in the doctrine of Bergson. Boutroux had written at the conclusion of *The Contingency of the Laws of Nature:* "If we abandon the external point of view, which suggests that things are fixed, limited realities, withdraw into our inmost self, and apprehend our being in its source, if it is possible for us to do so, we find that liberty is an infinite power. We sense this power each time we truly act" (p. 156). All negative philosophies originated in the inverse idea that the data of inward experience are identical with those of outward experience: they are calculable quantities, and the psychological reality is reduced to elements interconnected in accordance with precise laws; consciousness deceives us with its array of qualitative differences and its apparent indetermination; freed from this deception, psychology will become a natural science. Bergson's first book, *Time and Free Will: An Essay on the Immediate Data of Consciousness* demonstrates that, if we discard the constructions used in everyday language and later in scientific language to express the data of immediate consciousness—if we apprehend these data directly—we no longer see them as quantities but only as pure qualities; they constitute a qualitative multiplicity rather than a plurality of distinct, countable terms, a continuous progression rather than a succession of distinct events bound by the relation of cause to effect. Here, however, Bergson goes beyond mere repetition of the trite appeal of spiritualism to inner consciousness and shows the reasons that delay our return to immediate data as well as the extreme difficulties posed by our attempt to effect such a return. His doctrine is in the same vein as Berkeley's or Brown's, for his concern is not moral dissipation, which interferes with inner meditation, as in traditional spiritualism, but complications posed by the nature of intelligence. Our intelligence measures, and measurement is impossible outside homogeneous space, since it consists in making one space coincide with another. In measuring time, for example, the physicist takes as a unit of measurement a certain space —the space traversed by a moving body under physically determined conditions. In the same way we try to introduce into our states of consciousness a homogeneity which will allow us to measure them. By resorting to language and giving these states names, we imagine that they are separated from each other, like words; then we imagine that they are arranged one after the other as along a line. This gives rise to difficulties relating to free will. We see motives as distinct events which converge—we liken their convergence to that of several forces applied to the same point—to produce an act, with the result that liberty would imply the addition of another force born of nothing in reality, however, in the progression of a free act, in a decision that grows and ripens along with our whole being, there is nothing that resembles this convergence of distinct forces, which is merely a spatial metaphor. The blunder is in translating time into space, the successive into the simultaneous. Pure duration is not composed of homogeneous parts capable of coinciding but is pure quality, pure progression; it does not flow, indifferent and uniform, like the spatialized time of mechanics, alongside our inner life; it is this very life, considered in its progression, its maturity, and its senescence. "Philosophy is only a conscious, reflective return to the data of intuition." [1] The method first applied in *Time and Free Will* is elaborated in *Matter and Memory* (1896) and *Creative Evolution* (1907). In these works we find no sudden invocation of a particular faculty such as the intuition of the mystics but rather an appeal to reflection to "invert the habitual direction of the activity of thought." [2] That is the course taken by good sense, which, going beyond statements and generalities, seizes the inflection that these must be given if they are to be adapted to new situations which are forever appearing.

The problem of memory offers a particularly good opportunity for the application of this method. No other problem brings us closer to the constructions of associationistic psychology. Each image is seen as a distinct event, which disappears from consciousness, persists as a cerebral deposit, and reemerges through association with another image present to consciousness; recognition and localization of this image are effected through other associative operations. By contrast, it might seem that the Bergsonian conception of mind, as outlined in *Time and Free Will,* only complicates the problem: can the continuity of an integral spiritual life be reconciled with the obvious fragmentation introduced by forgetfulness? The problem of forgetfulness is fundamental in the thinking of men like Bergson, Plotinus, and Ravaisson; furthermore, according to the foreword to *Matter and Memory,* it seems to have been Bergson's point of departure. The difficulty would be insoluble if perception and memory were operations involving pure knowledge; if they introduce discontinuity into the mind, this is an indication that these operations involve something like the divisive intelligence described in *Time and Free Will.* Indeed, mental con-

---

[1] *Matière et Mémoire,* 1896, p. iii.
[2] "Introduction à la Métaphysique," *Revue de Métaphysique,* 1903, p. 27.

tinuity is possible only if the entire past of a consciousness is present to it at each instant of its life; if we were purely contemplative beings, pure spirits, this presence would be complete and indefectible. But we are bodies, that is, a mass of organs which, thanks to the nervous system, must respond to impressions from without by adaptive reactions; our attention, far from having the power to disperse and permeate the depths of the past, is dominated by this circumstance; without an "attentiveness to the present" to guide us constantly in our reactions, life would be impossible; as soon as our attentiveness to the present disappears, in sleep, we are invaded by the images of dreams, which are completely at variance with the existing situation; without a body man would be a perpetual dreamer; the body is the ballast which prevents the mind from going astray. Better still, it is a selector, an instrument which chooses images from the past to enable us to interpret or utilize the present. It is a principle of utility that produces this discontinuity in the memory. "It is not necessary," Plotinus had already remarked, "for us to retain the memory of everything we see." [3]

But this selection of useful images is at variance with the fixity of the mechanism of association. For a given situation memory can occupy different planes; the difference is not in the quantity of images evoked but in the level of consciousness chosen by us. A memory appears between two extreme limits, as an enacted memory or as a dreamed memory. An enacted memory or habitual memory is the repetition of learned movements—for example, the movements of an actor who is performing his role; a dreamed memory or pure memory is the image of a past event with its concrete tonality and its unique character—for example, the image of an earlier performance. Between these two limits are the different intermediate planes between dream and action; on each plane the memory of the past is present in its entirety, but this memory becomes dimmer and more blurred as one comes closer to the "enacted memory." Strictly speaking, certain images are not chosen at the expense of

[3] *Enneads* iv. 3. 11.

others, as if images were distinct entities; instead, an individual consciousness assumes different attitudes as it strays from the present and plunges into the past.

This theory naturally poses numerous problems, notably that of cerebral localizations in aphasia, which, in 1896, seemed clearly to indicate the existence of distinct images in separate regions of the brain. But if aphasic lesions are simply an interruption of nervous conduction from the afferent zone to the efferent zone, the loss of verbal images can be explained without recourse to localization. What has disappeared is not simply the possibility of producing speech but the possibility of reviving verbal images.

Bergson's first two works pose a problem which is resolved in *Creative Evolution*: What is the nature of this intelligence which unceasingly introduces discontinuity into the view we have of things and of ourselves? It was to resolve this question that he studied the nature of life and evolution in general. With respect to intelligence, there are two traditions in Western philosophy. The older and more constant tradition, which treats intelligence as a purely contemplative faculty that penetrates to the eternal essence of beings, has difficulty in accounting for the relations between intelligence and the living being that engenders it. Aristotle introduced it "from without"; Descartes, in turn, made the living being as such an object just like other material beings and therefore a part of the universal mechanism, all of which made the union of soul and body a mystery. According to the second tradition, intelligence is linked to life, but in two very distinct senses, depending on whether we interpret life in the sense of βίος, practical life, or in the sense of ζωή, vital principle. In the first interpretation, the Greek Skeptics teach us that intelligence is not made for theoretical knowledge but for actual practice, that it is a means of living and not of gaining direct access to reality. The same idea appeared earlier in Nietzsche and later in the pragmatists. In the second interpretation, among the neo-Platonists, Life designates a dual movement of procession and conversion—procession, by which it circulates and is diffused, conversion, by which it becomes concentrated and returns toward the Unity from which it derives. Intelligence designates the first phase of procession; it is like a vision which, incapable of embracing things in their unity, breaks them into a multiplicity of details placed side by side; consequently intelligence is produced within the vital process.

It is this second tradition that is rediscovered, and in both of its interpretations, in *Creative Evolution*. Intelligence is treated as a practical function in the second chapter, as a product of the evolution of life in the third; the intimate link between both interpretations accounts for the originality of the doctrine. The essential theme of the second chapter is the identity of *homo faber* and *homo sapiens*: the role of intelligence is first of all to fabricate solid tools to be used on other solids; that is why it can apprehend only discontinuous and inert beings and is unable to understand life in its continuity and progression; drawn naturally to inert matter, it gives rise to a mechanistic physics to which it tries in vain to relate biology; it knows only the relations, forms, and general schemes of objects. But the nature of intelligence presents us with a mysterious paradox: intelligence is designed to fabricate but it seeks after theory; it does not settle down in its objects but is forever overflowing the action it accomplishes, as if "it were searching for something which it is incapable of finding." This is the reverse of the ordinary problem. The object is not to determine how speculative intelligence becomes practical but how intelligence, which is practical, can become speculative. This is not true of the instinct of animals which is also action upon matter, but by means of their organs and without the intermediary of tools. Instinct supposes an intuitive and perfect knowledge of its object, but of this object alone; intelligence has imperfect but progressive knowledge.

The nature and function of intelligence can be illuminated by reflection on the relation between Life and intelligence. Life designates consciousness itself with every possible potentiality. We know it as a force which organizes matter into living beings by accumulating at a single point reservoirs of energy for sudden release. It appears in animal species in the form of an *élan vital* or an impulse toward a more complete life. In plants, animals, and man, this vital force strives to free itself from the matter that it animates and that destroys it in order to rediscover full possession of itself. It has used two means: instinct, which proves unsuccessful because the knowledge to which it clings, though perfect, is scanty; intelligence, which, by contrast, succeeds because it frees the spirit from enslavement to matter and puts it at the disposal of a more perfect intuition. The absurdity of regarding Bergson as a despiser of intelligence is obvious: the truth is that after three centuries during which intelligence was considered to be an absolute of some sort—whether it was exalted in the form of a divine intellect or made the substance of a reality accessible to our knowledge, as in critical philosophy—Bergson, preceded in a certain sense by Schopenhauer, returns to the metaphysical problem of intelligence. He sees in intelligence one reality within a larger reality. In the language of Plotinus, it is a procession which prepares for a conversion; this conversion is religion as it emerges in the saint and mystic.

Instinct leads eventually to the perfect, stable societies of hymenoptera, whereas intelligence culminates in the imperfect and progressive human societies in which morality and religion appear. This subject is dealt with in Bergson's last book, *The Two Sources of Morality and Religion* (1932). Its essential theme is the opposition between moral obligation, as binding as a code, which originates in the social group to which we belong, and the morality of the hero or saint—the morality of Socrates and Isaiah, of brotherhood and the rights of man. It is wrong to interpret the second source as a simple development of the first, as if natural societies like those of bees—closed, hostile toward each other, and conservative—could be enlarged to encompass mankind. To be sure, life favors and preserves the societies it has created by giving man a mythmaking function; the myths and religious rites invented by man have no role except that of preserving social cohesion; this is the origin of "static religion," the religion of "closed societies" and "closed souls." But Life would be swallowed up in stable forms if it did not recover its creative principle in the spirit of the great mystics, who, going back through intuition to the source of all things, reach the fountain of a "dynamic religion," the religion of the prophets and Christ, which produces all of the spiritual impulses that cause man to break out of the restricted circle of social life. Bergsonian morality, which is essentially the philosophy of religion, finally becomes a philosophy of history, not fatalistic and optimistic, but marked by uncertainty and remarkable perspicacity concerning the danger to which the "industrial frenzy," in contrast to the "ascetic frenzy" of the Middle Ages, exposes our civilization.

The only real distinctions acknowledged by neo-Platonic metaphysics were degrees of unity, varying in perfection from the One in which all reality interpenetrates to matter which is complete dispersion. Bergson returns to the same vision of reality but in a manner that is completely original because his point of departure is intuitive awareness of duration. To him unification becomes tension, since degrees of tension are like a concentration of duration; for instance, what is dispersed in matter in the form of 510 trillion vibrations per second is in the human mind the sensation of the yellow light of sodium. At the summit of reality is God, the eternal being and creator with his duration fully concentrated. Relaxation or tension—relaxation in the direction of materiality, tension in the direction of spirituality—are the fundamental realities.

Some indications of Bergson's profound influence will be found in the following chapters. His philosophy rendered impossible the pseudoscientific conception of the universe which, under the influence of Spencer, Darwin, and Taine, had gained ascendancy around 1880. Works such as J. Segond's *Prayer* (1911), *Bergsonian Intuition* (1913), and *Imagination* (1922) shows his direct influence. But Bergsonism manifests itself above all as a kind of intellectual liberation, for he made possible or gave point to the movements that we are about to deal with: the philosophy of action, pragmatism, criticism of the sciences. Furthermore, intellectualism after Bergson was of necessity quite different from what it had been before him.[4]

[4] Cf., in addition to the works already cited, *Laughter: An Essay on the Meaning of the Comic* (*Le Rire*, 10th edition, 1910); *Durée et simultanéité*, 1922; *Mind-energy* (*L'Énergie spirituelle*, 1919) and papers on "L'Idée de Gause" (Paris, 1900), and "Parallélisme psychophysique" (Geneva, 1906). Bergson's articles on "Philosophical Intuition" (Bologna, 1911), "The Possible and the Real," "The Perception of Change," and "Introduction to Metaphysics" are collected in *The Creative Mind* (*La Pensée et le Mouvant*, 1934); of which the Introduction is a kind of intellectual biography. Concerning his philosophy, see H. W. Carr, *Henri Bergson: The Philosophy of Change;* A. D. Lindsay, *The Philosophy of Bergson* (London, 1911); H. Höffding, *La philosophie de Bergson* (Paris, 1916); Jacques Chevalier, *Henri Bergson* (1925); V. Jankélévitch, *Bergson* (Paris, 1931); B. Scharfstein, *Roots of Bergson's Philosophy;* I. W. Alexander, *Bergson, Philosopher of Reflection* (New York, 1957).

Bibliography

Texts

Bergson, Henri. *Quid Aristoteles de Loco Senserit*. Paris, 1889.
———. *Essai sur les données immédiates de la conscience*. Paris, 1889.
———. *Time and Free Will: An Essay on the Immediate Data of Consciousness*, trans. F. L. Pogson. New York, 1910.
———. *Matter and Memory*, trans. Nancy Margaret Paul and W. Scott Palmer. New York, 1911.
———. *Laughter. An Essay on the Meaning of the Comic*, trans. Cloudesley Brereton and Fred Rothwell. New York, 1910.
———. *Introduction to Metaphysics*, trans. T. E. Hulme. New York, 1913 and 1949.
———. *Creative Evolution*, trans. Arthur Mitchell. New York, 1911.
———. *Mind-Energy*, trans. H. Wildon Carr. New York, 1920.
———. *Durée et simultanéité*. Paris, 1922. 2d ed. with 3 appendices, 1923.
———. *The Two Sources of Morality and Religion*, trans. R. A. Audra and Cloudesley Brereton. London, 1935.
———. *The Creative Mind*, trans. Mabelle L. Andison. New York, 1946.
———, *Écrits et paroles*, ed. R. M. Mosse-Bastide. Preface by Édouard LeRoy. 3 vols. Paris, 1957–59.
———. *Œuvres. Édition du centenaire*. Annotated by André Robinet, introduction by Henri Gouhier. Paris, 1959.

Studies

Carr, H. W. *The Philosophy of Change*. New York, 1912.
Chevalier, Jacques. *Henri Bergson*. Translated by L. A. Clare. London, 1928.
Delhomme, Jeanne. *Vie et conscience de la vie: Essai sur Bergson*. Paris, 1954.
Les Études bergsoniennes. Vols. 1–5. Paris, 1948–59.
Hanna, Thomas, ed. *The Bergsonian Heritage*. New York and London, 1962.
Husson, Leon. *L'Intellectualisme de Bergson*. Paris, 1947.
Jankélévitch, Vladimir. *Henri Bergson*. Paris, 1959.
LeRoy, Édouard. *Une Philosophie nouvelle: Henri Bergson*. Paris, 1912.
———. *The New Philosophy of Henri Bergson*, trans. Vincent Benson. New York, 1913.
Marietti, Angele. *Les Formes du mouvement chez Bergson*. Paris, 1957.
Maritain, Jacques. *La Philosophie bergsonienne*. Paris, 1930.
Russell, Bertrand. *The Philosophy of Bergson*. London, 1914.
———. *Our Knowledge of the External World*. London, 1914.

Santayana, George. *Winds of Doctrine*. New York, 1913.
Scharfstein, Ben-Ami. *Roots of Bergson's Philosophy*. London, 1912.
Stephen, Karin. *The Misuse of Mind*. London, 1922.
Stewart, J. McK. *A Critical Exposition of Bergson's Philosophy*. London, 1912.

PHILOSOPHIES OF LIFE AND ACTION; PRAGMATISM

I *Léon Ollé-Laprune and Maurice Blondel*

In *Moral Certitude* (1880; 2d edition, 1888), written under the influence of Newman and also of Renouvier, Ollé Laprune, professor at the École Normale, had shown that certainty is never attained in a purely intellectual way and without the participation of the will. Applying this idea to religious life, he added that fallen man could not attain supernatural life unless grace aided his will.

Maurice Blondel, who studied under Ollé-Laprune, thought that these ideas were a first step toward a new solution to the relations between speculation and action. Philosophy, he wrote in an article published in *Annales de philosophie chrétienne* (1906, p. 337), has always fed on the uneasiness of souls inclined toward the mysteries of their future; furthermore, it is instinctively reflective and has always turned toward causes and conditions; it leaves an equivocal impression, for it is neither science nor life but a little of both; finally, the relation between speculation and practice is not clearly defined because action has usually been identified with the idea of action and practical knowledge with consciousness of practical knowledge. These observations show clearly the aim of Blondel's book, *Action, Outline of a Critique of Life and a Practical Appli-*

cation of Science (1893).[1] Action in its effective reality is the subject of this book. Action issues from a disequilibrium and would cease only if this end were attained. Here we have the basis for a dialectic of action: having posited an end and found it inadequate, action seeks in vain to discover a more satisfactory end in some of the concrete activities around us. This explains human uneasiness, fed constantly by an unsatisfied will. Science, individual action, social action, moral action all leave us face to face with an incomplete, unfulfilled destiny. In skeptical dilettantism, aestheticism, and immoralism Blondel sees vain attempts to shun the problem posed by the gaping void that separates what we wish to do from what we can do.

The will must make a choice. It must either accept the data of experience and remain powerless or cut himself off from objects that do not satisfy it. By cutting itself off from these objects, it renounces itself in the sense that it "somehow surrenders blindly to the great current of ideas, feelings, and moral rules which have gradually emerged from human actions by virtue of tradition and the accumulation of experiences." In other words, it surrenders to the authority of Catholicism and accepts the supernatural life in which God appears to be both transcendent and immanent, the source of whatever is infinite in our will and the ideal that satisfies this will.[2]

It would be a mistake for us to liken this philosophy of action to pragmatism. Here action is a means of gaining access to truth, but there is no question, as in pragmatism, of identifying truth with a practical attitude. G. Tyrrel focuses attention on this difference in an article on pragmatism.[3] He accepts the pragmatic view that the Absolute is not something external which the mind copies or which has no relation to our experience, but this does not in any sense

[1] *L'Action, Essai d'une critique de la vie et d'une science de la pratique;* 2d edition, 1937. *La Pensée* was published in 1934, *L'Être et les Êtres* in 1935.
[2] Cf. concerning M. Blondel: Boutroux, *Science et religion,* pp. 274 ff.; R. P. Lecanuet, *La vie de l'Église sous Léon XIII,* 1931, chap. xi; H. Urtin, *Vers une science du réel,* 1931, chap. ii.
[3] "Notre attitude en face du Pragmatisme," *Annales de philosophie chrétienne,* 1905, p. 223. Cf. also his *Christianity at the Cross-Roads,* 1909.

make the Absolute a relative term. "To deduce metaphysics from life and action instead of notions and concepts is to place it on a stable basis for the first time."

A. Chide's book, *Modern Mobilism* (1908) is a kind of history of this philosophy of immanence, whose principal moments are traced through the evolution of theology and philosophy.

Father Laberthonnière, founder of the *Annales de philosophie chrétienne* (1905), concerned himself particularly with the nature of faith. Is faith submission to an external authority employing coercion or justifying itself on intellectual grounds? Is it not rather "a vital experience," a manifestation of goodness, an effusion of grace through which God communicates his secret, letting man participate in his intimate life? Extrinsicality and intrinsicality—the choice goes back to the deep-seated opposition between the abstract idealism of Greek philosophy, which sees reality as fixed, inalterable essences that are in no way modified by human evolution, and Christian realism, which sees God not simply as a nature but as a person capable of entering through charity and love into a relation with other persons.[4] Agnosticism and intellectualism are equally opposed to intrinsicality. The first is the way chosen by Descartes, who, seeing God as an insuperable boundary on an obstacle to thought and action, relegated him to the domain of the unknowable;[5] the second, recognizing a dualism between nature and the supernatural, included intelligence in nature and reached the conclusion that dogma cannot be known but only intimated.[6]

Édouard le Roy's words suggest the significance of the new tendencies which were coming to light. "If old doctrines tried to find support in an impossible primacy of external being," he wrote, "if the universal criticism of this nineteenth century led logically to the solitary cultivation of thought for its own sake, in my judgment the mighty originality and solid truth of the new philosophy

[4] Cf. *Le Réalisme chrétien et l'Idéalisme grec*, 1904; *Dogme et théologie*, 1908; *Théorie de l'Éducation*, 7th edition, 1923; *Pages choisies* (Paris: Vrin), 1931.

[5] Cf. the trenchant criticism of Cartesianism in *Études sur Descartes*, a posthumous work published by L. Canet in 1935.

[6] *Annales*, 1909, p. 92 and p. 279.

springs from the recognition that ideas are subordinate to reality and reality to action," provided that action is interpreted to mean "the life of the spirit as well as the life of the body, and practical action is wholly dependent upon moral and religious life and subordinated to it." [7] His doctrine identifies the double opposition which appeared in the theories just outlined: intelligence and intuition in Bergson, speculation and action in Maurice Blondel. Then action is identical to experienced thought. In this anti-intellectualism, which he traces back to Duns Scotus and Pascal, he seeks to discover neither a philosophy of sentiment nor a philosophy of will but a philosophy of action; for action implies not only feeling and will, but also reason. In fact, he sees it even in the sciences, for scientific invention assumes the breaking of tyrannical intellectual habits and even acceptance of contradictories (for example, the invention of the infinitesimal calculus).[8]

In *Idealistic Exigency and the Fact of Evolution* (1927) and later in *Human Origins and the Evolution of Intelligence* (1928), taking into account facts now known in paleontology and anthropology, he tried to rediscover beneath these facts the vital surge which alone explains living beings and the evolution of humanity. His tentative explanation gave to the word "evolution" the meaning it had before Spencer and acquired once again with Bergson—that is, a creative process. "The history of life," he concludes (p. 267), "appeared to us to be the history of a concentration of thought. But the latter preexisted in the state of a diffuse tendency seeking to acquire substance and become precise. . . . Everything comes from it, no matter how remote its emanation from matter." [9]

Collectively, the philosophical tendencies mentioned here were defined as "modernistic philosophy" by Pius X, who condemned them in the encyclical *Pascendi* (1907). According to this encyclical, modernistic philosophy is rooted in agnosticism, which keeps human

[7] *Revue de Métaphysique*, 1899, pp. 424–25.
[8] *Ibid.*, 1905, pp. 197–99.
[9] Cf. besides the works cited: *La Pensée intuitive*, 2 vols., 1929–30; *Le problème de Dieu*, 1929; *Dogme et critique*, 1906; and L. Weber, "Une philosophie de l'invention," *Revue de Métaphysique*, 1932.

intelligence from ascending to God, and in immanentism, which relates religion to a vital need and identifies the truth of a dogma not with what it expresses concerning divine reality but with its vital capacity for producing religious feelings. But the essential traits of a philosophy of action can be divorced completely from any religious doctrine whatsoever. If action is conceived as adaptation, or tendency toward adaption, to reality (as in evolutionism), one can try to demonstrate that it subtends knowledge, and that is what Théodore Ruyssen maintained in his *Essay on the Psychological Evolution of Judgment* (1904); judgment, accompanied by belief, always facilitates an act adapted to the physical or social environment. The relation between knowledge and action is also the basis for pragmatism.

II *Pragmatism*

The theory of pragmatism was defined for the first time in the celebrated article, "How to Make Our Ideas Clear," [10] in which Charles Peirce (1839-1914) gave the following rule for getting a clear idea of the significance of the ideas we employ: "Consider what effects, which might conceivably have practical bearings, we conceive the object of our conception to have. Then, our conception of these effects is the whole of our conception of the object." Here "practical bearings" refers to the possibility of experimental controls.[11]

From this theory of signification William James (1842-1910), a Harvard professor, constructed a definition of truth. A distinction is ordinarily made between the truth of a proposition, defined by the equivalency of an affirmation and the thing affirmed, and the whole series of operations that must be carried out in order to gain possession of this truth. Pragmatism refuses to make this distinction and holds instead that truth depends on this series of operations.

[10] Originally written in French for the *Revue Philosophique,* the article was also published in a slightly different version in *Popular Science Monthly* (January 1878), pp. 286-302.

[11] Cf. Emmanuel Leroux, *Le pragmatisme américain et anglais,* 1922, pp. 90-96.

What is a *true* theory? It is a theory that leads us to expect the consequences of which we ascertain the actual production. In a much more general way, I know an object truly when I actually carry out or am capable of carrying out the series of operations which, by continuous transitions, will lead from my actual experience to an experience which places me in the presence of the object. A true idea is not the copy of an object; it is the idea which leads to the perception of the object.

But James offers yet another definition of truth: a proposition is true if adhesion to it produces satisfactory consequences, taking into consideration also the satisfaction of every possible need—whether simple or complex—of the human individual.

The first definition refers to direct perception of an object as the last phase of the operation called truth. The second, unrelated in principle to perception, refers to the idea of a proof or a successful plan of action. Error is failure. From the second point of view "truth" closely approximates Newman's conception of vital belief. But it was from his own father, Henry James, a theologian in the tradition of Emerson, that William James was able to learn that truth is truth only insofar as it is in the service of good, that a vital truth can never be transferred purely and simply from one mind to another mind, for life alone is the judge of the value of truths.[12]

These two notions of truth are quite "pragmatic" in the sense that they both define truth as a course of action. But whereas one of them gives truth an objective value, since the immediate perception envisioned is in the last resort the judge of the whole course, the other gives it the vital value of a belief that inspires actions. Neither of these two notions can be reduced to the other; further-more, the first seems not wholly in keeping with James's intentions, since it supposes at the very least a truth independent of any active operation—that of immediate perception. Of the two, which is properly, profoundly pragmatic? It is difficult for us to say, for there are in James two men: the disciple of Louis Agassiz, the Harvard

---

[12] Cf. J. Wahl, *Les philosophies pluralistes,* p. 26, and Maurice le Breton, *La personnalité de W. James,* 1928.

zoologist who taught him to go directly to nature, to take the facts in his own hands, to look and see for himself—the man for whom notions do not matter unless translated into concrete facts—and the son of Henry James, the mystical Swedenborgian transcendentalist who identified truth less with a theoretical vision than with participation in the divine life that animates things.[13] The student of Agassiz would not have tried to fathom the enigmas of the universe, mysterious and profound, investigated by James as theologian. An empiricist like Mill, he tried like a confirmed Hegelian to discover the great whole; the barrenness of English empiricism ran counter to his profoundly religious nature, however, and Hegelian absolutism, which absorbs individuals in the Whole, opposed his respect for experience. He respected experience not only as a scientist but also and perhaps even more as an artist who delights in the individual, the concrete, the irreducible.

Empirical verification of particulars—cold, objective, and capable of guiding external action—and vital, emotional belief serving as the inner source of action are the two poles of James's pragmatism. His philosophy is related to the preaching of Emerson as well as to the visions of Carlyle and Walt Whitman; its only fault is that it purports to be philosophy. That it is not is demonstrated by the application of the second pragmatic criterion of truth. What is a universe? It is the universe that corresponds to our tendencies, the universe in which we can act and assert our temperament. But that is not all. If this universe proves to be a modifying force, it follows that our belief transforms the universe and realizes it exactly as it is conceived. A universe that can be transformed by our action is one in which we can live; consequently we must reject both scientific determinism, which sees the world as a mechanism in which we are a cog, and idealistic absolutism, which denies even time and change. Time is the precondition of a serious action: "I accept time absolutely," Walt Whitman had said. "It alone is without flaw, it alone rounds and completes all." [14] To believe that our universe

[13] Leroux, *Le pragmatisme américain et anglais*, pp. 36–46.
[14] "Song of Myself," lines 480–81.

can be modified by our attitude is to believe that it contains forces and initiatives that are not indifferent to our action. But are they favorable or unfavorable? Here the "hard soul" and the "tender soul" have different visions of the universe. The "hard soul" is Whitman clamoring for enemies and opportunities for struggle: "O something pernicious and dread! Something far away, far away, far away from a puny and pious life!" "O to struggle against great odds; to meet enemies undaunted!"[15] It has been observed that his vision may reflect Calvinistic pessimism, which recognizes in the universe only the evil with which it is infected and the arbitrary will of an incomprehensible God, but it reflects this pessimism as it is interpreted by a strong, indomitable will. Rather than being hostile, perhaps, things are strange. The universe is wild—"a quarry which has the scent of a falcon's wing. Sameness returns only to introduce something different."[16] Those are the views of Benjamin Paul Blood, who had a strong influence on James. By contrast, the "tender soul" finds these forces favorable and helpful in his struggle; he feels that he is sustained not only by the comradeship of his fellows but by a providential God or, as in polytheism, by a multitude of helpers. James's personal vision oscillates, without becoming fixed, between the vision of the hard soul and that of the tender soul: there is one God, but he is a finite God whom we help in his work as much, perhaps, as he helps us; there is before all else an element of risk—a very real risk whose outcome is totally unpredictable; the history of the universe is not unfolded in accordance with a prearranged plan but is full of hazards, sudden shifts, circuits, returns. James believes in tychism or, in the language of Peirce, fortuitism—not only chance but the possibility of a wilful choice which can contribute to the final destiny of the universe. Success is but a hope, and James's meliorism defines not a spontaneous tendency of the universe but a law that man bestows on himself; the salvation of the world is not an end defined in advance but it is what each of us wants it to be.

---

[15] "A Song of Joys," lines 57–58, 158.
[16] Quoted by J. Wahl, *Les philosophies pluralistes*, p. 111.

This vision of the world seems to issue from the second pragmatic criterion, which apparently is less suited to judging truth than to creating it. The first criterion, which consists in minting a notion from facts, seems on the contrary to be intended for verification. Its application produces James's radical empiricism, his pluralism, his religious experience—factual proofs derived from the image of the world in which he lived. What is meant by "radical" empiricism? According to a tradition that had endured in English empiricism for more than a hundred years, the tissue of experience is composed of a mass of states of consciousness (feelings) which have no predetermined relations; gradually certain relations (causality, substance, etc.) are constructed in the mind through the interplay of associations. But James rejects associationism. As a psychologist he advocates instead the unity and continuity of the flow of consciousness; in contrast to the beliefs of both empiricists and apriorists, he holds that relations are in no way invested with an existence superior to immediate experience and, by the same token, that simultaneity, resemblance, and activity are experience. For example, Maine de Biran wrongly believed that effort was an experience of a special, irreducible kind, whereas it is merely the afferent sensation of muscular contraction. Emotions also must be ascribed to a common experience, that of changes in an organic state. It follows that relations are not principles introduced from above to unify the world; nor are they grounded, as Bradley thought, on their unifying terms, for experience shows that they remain outside these terms, which may be either joined or disjoined without affecting them. Empirical radicalism, which sees even relations as experiential facts, therefore leads to pluralism, which sees the universe as a chaos formed of separate blocks that are forever joining and disjoining, ready to enter into new combinations, like atoms or molecules. This pluralistic world of experience—this "multiverse"—obviously corresponds to the demands for action, the possibility of change, the free initiative replete with risks which the reality of time causes us to accept.

Radical empiricism accepts the religious experience just as it is, untouched by either the material interpretation which makes it a psychopathic state or theology and institutions based on theology.[17] The religious experience, taken in its concrete diversity as it is manifested in the lives of saints, mystics, and ascetics, brings joy and security, in the source of every moral initiative, and serves as a counterpoise to science, which, through a kind of animism that discovers individual consciousness everywhere, depersonalizes man.

James supports even the gross supernaturalism of spiritualism, which puts us in communication with the consciousness of invisible spirits and, like mysticism, helps us to erase the boundaries which ordinarily separate consciousness and to immerse our finite consciousness in a greater whole. The "fringes" which in James's psychology designate the obscure zone surrounding phenomena that appear distinctly on the plane of consciousness assure this possible continuity between consciousness. Here again the facts correspond to our requirements.

James's definition of truth would hardly make sense, of course, if detached from any vision of the universe that it introduces and by which it is itself introduced. Nor is it easy for us to understand how it can be applied in a strict sense to scientific, impersonal truths that passionately eliminate all passions. His philosophy is a deliberate, sincere return to a state in which nature seems to be inflated with all our emotions. It is a predication that claims to draw its support from the nature of reality but in fact ascribes to itself an image of the universe that conforms to its needs.[18]

F. C. S. Schiller, a professor at the University of Oxford, formulated a doctrine closely related to James's, which he called absolutism. Schiller seems to have been concerned primarily with the dangers inherent in any attempt to put idealistic absolutism into

---

[17] Cf. on this point H. Reverdin, *La notion d'expérience d'après W. James* (Geneva, 1913), especially chap. iv.

[18] Cf. Emmanuel Leroux, *Le pragmatisme*, pp. 90–109. The principal works of James are *The Principles of Psychology* (1892), *The Will to Believe* (1897), *The Varieties of Religious Experience* (1902), *Pragmatism* (1907), *A Pluralistic Universe* (1909), and his *Letters*, edited by his son, Henry James (1920). See also H. V. Knox, *The Philosophy of William James* (London, 1914); and R. B. Perry, *In the Spirit of William James* (New Haven, 1939).

practice: belief in the illusory character of action, change, or evolution leads to quietism. Absolutism is based on an error—the presumed necessity of conceiving a reality only as a part of a whole under the pretext that any truth is inwardly coherent and coherent with other truths. In contrast, pragmatism, which properly designates the human method of attaining truth, sees truth as something concrete and individual; generalities are coherent, and this coherence is lost in proportion as details become more precise on the level of experience. Moreover, there are in our experience several worlds lacking coherence one with another: the world of immediate, daily experience is not identical with the world of the scientist, and the physicist knows nothing of the biologist's concept of the world. Is there one true world, like Plato's ideal world, among all these worlds? By no means (and here pragmatism leans toward idealism), for each of these worlds is a construction relative to our human interests. Protagoras was closer to the truth than Plato. For knowledge implies no dualism, no reference to a determinate reality. It seems at times that Schiller borders on solipsism, but his doctrine is actually a kind of metaphysics of evolution. Here, however, evolution is not used in the Spencerian sense of a real, irreversible process of a perpetually incomplete world which is perfected by individual, unforeseeable initiatives. Schiller's evolutionism (and this sometimes explains the tendency toward solipsism) is monadological and stresses the interaction of free, active minds; but it is a monadology without continuisms, and new interactions can involve unknown worlds. Furthermore, Schiller accepts a kind of final salvation, a total harmony, and a unique, personal God.[19]

Along with Schiller, seven other members of the Oxford faculty published *Personal Idealism* (1902), outlining a common program of which the two principal tenets were that every idea should be tested by contact with reality and that every action is the action of a person.

Pragmatism apparently contradicts absolutism by accepting discontinuity as the sign of reality and incoherence as the necessary

[19] Cf. E. Leroux, *Le pragmatisme,* I, vi.

precondition of liberty and individuality. But there is perhaps another unity, wholly different from absolute totality, which the pragmatist ought to investigate. This seems to be the sense of the teachings of John Dewey.[20] According to him, philosophers vainly waste their energies in trying to rediscover a unity among the fragments of a universe which they themselves have torn apart, and their search for unity may embrace either the physical universe of science, wholly mechanical and devoid of morality, or the qualitative universe of common perception. In idealism physics is viewed as a mental construction, and the material world is reabsorbed in the spiritual world; in the spiritual world, however, there remains the duality of the sensible and the rational, or finite consciousness and total consciousness, and idealists cannot explain how and why absolute Thought was fragmented. In materialism, on the other hand, consciousness is absorbed in nature, but there is no explanation of the appearance, along with the strange epiphenomenon of consciousness, of a world of values distinct from the world of existences.

These false problems, according to Dewey, arise because knowledge is seen as contemplation. He proposes instead "instrumentalism" or "functionalism," which goes back to the most common conception of knowledge: that knowledge is a directed activity, a functional part of experience. Thought does not have its end in itself but is a phase of life, an event that occurs in a living being under certain definite conditions. It occurs (Spencer had already noticed this) in the event of a conflict between active impulses and consists in an attempt to reconstruct our interrupted activity by adapting it to the new situation. An idea, which is a hypothetical basis for action, refers only to the future and is true if it guides us truly. The rationality of nature, asserted by the physicist, is not a theoretical postulate but a belief that ascribes to intelligent activity the possibility of a rational intervention leading to a change. It means that man's intellectual activity is not something introduced into him from without; it is nature realizing its own potentialities

[20] Cf. E. Leroux, *Le pragmatisme*, pp. 140–160; *Revue de Métaphysique*, 1931, p. 107.

with a view to a fuller, richer production of events. By the same token, our moral activity is not directed by a stock, predetermined idea of moral goodness; it has at least three principles, each with a distinct origin—good conceived as an end, the rule of duty, and the estimation of others—and therefore gives rise to moral problems relating to the necessity of reconciling these three principles.[21]

These ideas betray Dewey's early indebtedness to Hegelianism. He claims to have realized spiritual unity but in a more perfect manner than Hegel. The uneasiness of contemporary thought, in his view and Hegel's, issues from the opposition between the ideal and the real, spirit and nature, which is expressed for example in the irreducible provinces of the historian and the mathematician, the moralist and the engineer. Ordinary pedagogy provides for this opposition by training men of action whose thought has been sacrificed or by cultivating abstract thought. Dewey falls short of reducing thought to action or even subordinating thought to action, but he does show that thought is an indispensable phase of action when the latter is complex and progressive; consequently his pragmatism, far from sacrificing thought, rehabilitates it. But his conception of thought persuades him to reverse the degrees of intelligibility. Most intelligible to him are the data, not of mathematics and physics, but of history and the sciences of humanity, which can be understood and realized intellectually better than the other sciences, for history is nothing less than the mind at work in nature and society.[22]

III *Georges Sorel*

Drawing his inspiration from Bergson, Georges Sorel (1847–1892) identifies *homo sapiens* with *homo faber*. The scientist who constructs hypotheses fabricates ideally a mechanism which should function like real mechanisms. Science is directed not toward specu-

---

[21] *Bulletin de la société française de philosophie,* October, 1930.

[22] Dewey's writings include *Studies in Logical Theory* (Chicago, 1903), *Creative Intelligence* (New York, 1917), *Human Nature and Conduct* (New York, 1922), and "Développement du pragmatisme américain," *Revue de Métaphysique,* 1922, No. 4.

lative knowledge, as men of letters insist that it should be, but toward the creation of an ideal workshop supplied with mechanisms that function with precision.[23] A hypothesis therefore is fully validated by its function as an instrument for dealing with things and is not required also to represent reality. Positivism excluded hypotheses in physics and at the same time admitted in history a necessary law determining the succession of events. Sorel holds that the important role of hypotheses must be restored and that in the determinism of the social future a place must be found for the obscure, the unconscious, and the unforeseeable. Just as hypotheses guide our actions in working with nature, beliefs should determine our actions with respect to this obscure social future. The social agitator makes use of the general strike just as the physicist makes use of his hypotheses; he knows that this strike is a myth just as the physicist knows that the future will consider his hypotheses obsolete—but his myth generates action. Between anti-intellectualistic philosophy and social revolution aimed at destroying the state and replacing it by syndicalistic organizations, Sorel sees a close relationship. It seems to him that this philosophy is the worker's philosophy, since it makes intelligence consist not in an ideology destined to curb appetites (such as the middle-class philosophy of progress at the end of the eighteenth century), but in a program of action centered on nature.[24]

[23] *Illusions du progrès,* p. 283.
[24] Cf. *Réflexions sur la violence,* 1900.

Bibliography

I

Texts

Blondel, Maurice. *L'Action: Essai d'une critique de la vie et d'une science de la pratique.* Paris, 1893. Rev. ed., 1950.
———. *La Pensée.* 2 vols. Paris, 1934.
———. *L'Être et les êtres.* Paris, 1935.
———. *L'Action.* 2 vols. Paris, 1937.
———. *La Philosophie et l'esprit chrétien.* 2 vols. Paris, 1944–46.
———. *Exigences philosophiques du christianisme.* Paris, 1950.

Studies

Duméry, H. *Blondel et la religion.* Paris, 1954.
———. *La Philosophie de l'action.* Paris, 1948.
Lefèvre, F. *L'Itinéraire philosophique de Maurice Blondel.* Paris, 1928.
Taymans d'Eypernon, F. *Le Blondélisme.* Louvain, 1935.
Trèsmontant, Claude. *Introduction à la métaphysique de Maurice Blondel.* Paris, 1963.

II

Texts

Sorel, Georges. *Contribution à l'étude profane de la Bible.* Paris, 1889.
———. *Le Procès de Socrate.* Paris, 1889.
———. *La Ruine du monde antique.* Paris, 1901.
———. *Essai sur l'église et l'état.* Paris, 1902.
———. *Saggi di critica del marxismo.* Palermo, 1902.
———. *Introduction à l'économie moderne.* Paris, 1903.
———. *Le Système historique de Renan.* 4 vols. Paris, 1905–06.
———. *Insegnamenti sociali della economia contemporanea.* Palermo, 1907.
———. *Reflections on Violence,* trans. T. E. Hulme and J. Roth. New York, 1914.
———. *Les Illusions du progrès.* Paris, 1908.
———. *La Décomposition du marxisme.* Paris, 1908.
———. *La Révolution dreyfusienne.* Paris, 1909.

———. *Matériaux d'une théorie du prolétariat.* Paris, 1919.

———. *Les Préoccupations métaphysiques des physiciens modernes.* Paris, 1921.

———. *De l'Utilité du pragmatisme.* Paris, 1921.

———. *D'Aristote à Marx.* Paris, 1935.

———. Variot, Jean. *Propos de Georges Sorel.* 1935.

IDEALISM

THE REVIVAL of interest in Hegelianism—particularly the idealism of Bradley and Bosanquet in England, Croce in Italy, and Hamelin in France—influenced the negative philosophies of the second half of the nineteenth century, but not in the same way as the doctrines of action discussed in the previous chapter.

1 *English Idealism: Bradley, Bosanquet, Royce*

With Green, Kant's synthetic unity of apperception became a metaphysical principle, and the law of knowledge, a law of being. The doctrine of F. H. Bradley (1846–1924), an Oxford professor, is more complex.[1] Two themes dominate his philosophy, which he himself refuses to call a philosophy of idealism: first, the insufficiency of all relations, categories, or concepts such as substance or cause in defining absolute reality; second, the attainment of the Absolute by direct contact with things in sensation, one indivisible and diversified experience characterized by concrete richness beyond measure, even though it cannot be said to be as diverse as if it were composed of fragments. But at times these two themes fuse and interpenetrate in a complicated manner.

[1] Bradley's works include *The Principles of Logic* (1883; 2d edition, 1922, corrected 1928) and *Appearance and Reality* (1893; 2d edition, 1897). Concerning Bradley, see A. K. Rogers, *English and American Philosophy Since 1800* (1922), pp. 250–63; Duprat, "La métaphysique de Bradley," *Revue philosophique*, 1926; and R. W. Church, *Bradley's Dialectic*, 1942.

The first is demonstrated by the illusory character of a notion which since the criticism of Hume and Kant had seemed to enjoy almost universal acceptance—the notion of external relations. A spatial, temporal relation such as causality, or any other relation, exists in itself as a kind of mold, outside the terms that it connects. For Bradley, only inner relations exist. In other words, he returns to Leibniz' point of view and maintains that all relations between two terms have their rationality and their foundation of existence in the terms themselves. If the notion of geometric space—a simple juxtaposition which does not involve these terms—is raised as an objection, he answers that space so conceived is a pure abstraction which does not bring us directly to the tissue of internal relations constituting reality.

Does the negation of external relations leave any room for the idea of a relation? We might entertain doubts at the outset when we see the first of these themes transformed into the second: no relations, said Hume, with the result that reality is resolved into a cloud of isolated states; no external relations, said Bradley, with the result that reality is a coherent whole, one and individual, which coincides with the given, with sensed and sentient experience—experience that is not a "relation" between subject and object but a particular presence of an object, which is an indescribable and inexplicable fact.

That the immediacy of this datum or experience is the reason for the exclusion of external relations seems clear at the outset but becomes less clear when this immediate experience is seen, first as the end of a dialectic which tends toward it as the Hegelian dialectic tended toward spirit, and second as a point of departure, in a certain sense, toward a new dialectic. Let us begin by taking up the first point. The conceptual determination or category which is in one sense a false determination of reality is in another sense an incomplete determination. Any judgment, according to Bradley, is the determination of reality by a concept, of *that* by *what,* but this determination always proves inadequate to reality and must be completed. A judgment can be true only if it embraces all the conditions on which its truth depends; moreover, little by little we see that these conditions are integral experiences, for only in an integral experience do we note the disappearance of the otherness which consciousness always finds before it but does not absorb. In an integral experience false determinations will acquire their truth as if by transmutation; it follows that the difference between appearance and reality corresponds to the difference between fragmentation and totality, provided that we do not conceive totality as a collection of fragments but fragmentation as the result of a discursive and superficial reason.

But this theory of judgment is visibly imbued with Hegelianism, for it directs philosophical speculation toward a *Geist,* a concrete universal reality. Does it not for this reason collide with the thesis that defines reality in terms of concrete individual experience? Such experience is finite and cannot appear to be real. Proof of this is change, in which we see it assume, successively, diverse forms. Phenomenal change, according to Bradley, is the symptom of incompleteness, by the same token as the dialectic of concepts. Is not this total reality beyond the finite centers constituted by each individual experience? But if this is true, what is Bradley's doctrine? Is it a philosophy of experience which defines the real as an authentic datum or a Hegelian dialectic which places it above any datum?

It is as a Hegelian that Bradley feels the need for a kind of theodicy—and one of the most traditional—to justify evil, error, and the particular by considering them to be parts of a whole, which they enrich, provided that they are not isolated from it and considered abstractly. It is as a Hegelian also that he makes the Absolute a total reality more than an individual and moral one. But can we be certain that it is as a philosopher of experience that he sees the self and the system of individual selves as our highest possession,[2] as something that inclines us toward the idea of a sense of time peculiar to each individual and not associated with one unique time, or even toward the idea of a multiplicity of spaces?

[2] See J. Wahl, *Les philosophies pluralistes,* 1920, p. 13.

Or should we say rather that he, in keeping with a certain idealistic tradition—that of Plotinus, Spinoza, and Hegel—accepts the absolute only as being richly endowed with individual determinations, which he transmutes into eternal modes? A Scottish Hegelian of the same generation, Simon Laurie (*Synthetica*, 1906), sees divine reality in the act of self-revelation in finite human selves, nature being the medium of this revelation.

The particular contribution of Bernard Bosanquet (1848–1923), professor at St. Andrews (*Logic*, 1888; *The Value and Destiny of the Individual*, 1913; *What Religion Is*, 1920) was to demonstrate all that experience can bring to the verification of a system of idealism as Bradley's: experience of common life in society and politics, experience of unity and permanence of the physical environment, experience of another world such as the world of art whose values complement ours. The element common to all these great experiences, especially our aesthetic and religious experiences, is that they satisfy the spirit, enabling it to escape from contradiction not by an ideal construction but by an experienced reality in which everything is coherent. For Bosanquet there is no pure thought, no pure logic, no universal that is not a general predicate. Logic, which makes things conceivable, is knowledge of the structure of reality; a universal is a plastic unit in a system that includes particulars.

The origin of absolutism is traceable to a reaction against individualism. In his reaction Bradley goes so far as to deny the individual, with his temporal life and daily exertion, any true reality; here he follows the example of Plotinus, who saw the true reality of the individual only in an eternal intelligence which the individual, through practical exertion, tried in vain to imitate. Is absolutism incompatible, then, with any view of the universe giving serious consideration to the sufferings, struggles, and actions of the individual? Do the demands of speculative thought condemn the certainties of practical life? In America, Josiah Royce (1855–1916) tried to unite both in his system of idealism (*The Spirit of Modern Philosophy*, 1892; *The World and the Individual*, 1900–1901). The fundamental theme of Royce is an idea quite characteristic of the American religious mentality: the world in which free man holds himself upright and advances is the world of God even as it is his own. An idea has practical worth only if it is wholly individualized and is not similar to any other idea; generality is the sign of a defect. The absolute Self would have this deficiency if it were not expressed by a great variety of individuals each of whom freely shapes his own destiny. Royce remains a monist, for any thought implies monism: to think of an object is generally to have an image of it, with the result that the object remains external to thought; thought, however, is not in the image but in the judgment that signifies the object or subjects it to doubt. This judgment is valid only if we posit a consciousness more perfect than ours, which possesses the object, and for which there is no longer any question or doubt; there is truth only if a single self includes every thought and every object. The life of this absolute self is the knowledge of the diverse individuals in which it is realized, and in consequence this absolute self is forever incomplete.

Did Royce succeed in his undertaking? He was perhaps closer than he seemed to the thought of his predecessors and Hegel, their common instigator. They all wanted to conceive a rich universe, which far from being withered and abstracted by thought, would be justified in its concrete reality by thought. We find in an idealist like Lord Haldane (also famous as an English statesman) the deep-seated notion that knowledge is not the relation of one substance to another but the fundamental reality (*The Pathway to Reality*, 1903); here knowledge denotes not logical generality but everything that confers meaning on what we sense. John Muirhead, professor at Birmingham (*Contemporary British Philosophy*, 1924, p. 316), accepts the principle of Bradley's philosophy; he thinks, however, that it invites criticism by denying the separate reality of the finite, and that progress in philosophy depends on an attempt to demonstrate the positive value of the finite. J. B. Baillie (*The Idealistic Construction of Experience*, 1906) has something quite similar in mind when he acknowledges several kinds of mutually irreducible experiences; some of them seem almost complete, like sensible experience; others, like scientific experience, are growing even as the individual grows by means of them; the individual confers on them a very different value, depending on the degree of perfection that they enable him to attain; consequently the struggle for unity involves great variety.

This interpretation of the concrete individual finally conflicts with the theory of the concrete universal. Joachim (*The Nature of Truth*, 1906) acknowledges the impossibility of our understanding how the Absolute, total and coherent, requires for its preservation finite knowledge such as ours, an incomplete logical systematization, a precarious determination of *that* by the migratory adjective *what*. J. M. M'Taggart (*The Nature of Existence*, 2 vols., 1921–27) even went so far as to give Hegelianism an individualistic interpretation. The only substances he recognizes are selves, parts of selves, or groups of selves; as with Mill and James, God himself is a finite being with limited power. The method of idealism rather than the doctrine seems to persist in M'Taggart, who claims to be able to deduce all categories of reality from two empirical principles—something exists, and this something is differentiated. George Howison, who sees the Absolute as a community of selves rather than as a singular self (*The Limits of Evolution*, 1901), plainly tends toward pluralism even though he remains an idealist and a Kantian. That every existence is reduced to that of spirits, that nature exists only as their common representation and is objective only because it is common to the community of spirits, that this community is motivated by a rational ideal under the leadership of a God who acts not as an efficient cause but as a final cause—all these ideas decisively separate idealism from absolutism. The idea of this community of spirits appears again in G. T. Ladd's *Theory of Reality* (1899), and Galloway also sees in the world a series of monads constituting a hierarchy (*Philosophy of Religion*, 1914). A similar trait reappears in America in the writings of W. E. Hocking (*The Meaning of God in Human Experience*, 1912; *Human Nature and Its Remaking*, 1918), who bases his "social realism" on the necessity, to give a validity to knowledge, of a relation between my spirit and another spirit which is independent of nature, which knows all things, and through which alone I can share a relation with kindred spirits. Independence of individuals, dualism in knowledge, reality of the temporal process, God himself evolving in time—all of these notions led Andrew Seth Pringle-Pattison, the Scottish philosopher (*Hegelianism and Personality*, 1887; *The Idea of God*, 1917), to criticize Hegelianism, but without abandoning Bradley's idea of an all-embracing experience which resolves the contradictions of our own experience.

Thus, in England and America, especially after 1900, we see the inner dissolution of this idealistic absolutism which had gone too far in its protest against individualism. But we should note in addition that this destruction was carried out under the pressure of other doctrines centered less on the problem of reality than on that of certain human values which philosophy was supposed to justify.

These doctrines of belief opposed both naturalism and absolutism, equivalent in the sense that they destroy the values of finite beings. The poetry of Tennyson (1809–92) probably did much to cultivate a state of mind unfavorable to these scientific doctrines, which substituted impersonal laws for the God of religion. A. J. Balfour (*The Foundations of Belief*, 1895), a distinguished statesman, showed that naturalistic philosophy was incapable of explaining not only the value that man attributes to art, morality, and religion, but even the value of truth; for if our belief in truth is traceable to the causes adduced by naturalism (natural selection, association, etc.), these causes suppress the objective value linked to the word "truth." And W. R. Sorley (*On the Ethics of Naturalism*, 1885; *Moral Values and the Idea of God*, 1918) insists that nature, far from being an absolute, is part of the same rational universe as our values; that it is, indeed, merely an instrument for the discovery of the values that bring the self to perfection.

Naturalism called into existence the consciousness and spirit of nature. One of the most common refutations of naturalism, beginning with the Stoics and Plotinus, had been to start from the other extreme and to attribute spirits or souls to natural forces. Quite different from critical idealism, this doctrine has often had its supporters, during the modern period, in England and America. Hinton (*The Life in Nature,* 1862) maintained, like Plotinus, that our belief in the inertia of matter issued solely from a defect in our perception; to apprehend life everywhere we need only rely on the organs of spiritual knowledge instead of the intellect; our vision of inert matter issues from sin; wherever there is an absence of love, there is matter. The principle of continuity is for Read (*The Metaphysics of Nature,* 1905; *The Origin of Man,* 1920) the true argument of panpsychism. Consciousness could never emerge if it were not originally in every being. James Ward, whose celebrated article on "Psychology" in the *Encyclopedia Britannica* was instrumental in substituting voluntaristic psychology for associationism, draws support from the critical movment in the sciences, especially the work of Stanley Jevons, in his attempt to combat naturalism by showing the purely hypothetical and methodological character of the concepts of mechanism (*Naturalism and Agnosticism,* 1899; *The Realm of Ends,* 1911). He argues that the question of relations between soul and body is insoluble unless panpsychism is accepted, and that the monads of the body are subordinate to the central monad and utilized by it, in somewhat the same manner as the services of the state are utilized by the citizen. This monadology leads to a theism, for only in God do we find a foundation to insure the correspondence of monads and the final triumph of Good.

II *Italian Idealism*

The development of the Hegelian influence in Italy dates from the middle of the nineteenth century and is linked to the political movement aimed at the liberation and unification of Italy. The notion of the state as a totality and final end to which individuals submit then appeared as the central notion of the system. Translations of Hegel's works and commentaries multiplied; Spaventa (1871–83), of Naples, was one of those who contributed most to spreading his ideas. Today Hegelianism is firmly supported by Benedetto Croce and Giovanni Gentile.

"Partial philosophy is a contradictory concept; the act of thinking encompasses everything or nothing, and any limit it might have would be a reflective limit and consequently one transcended by it" (*The Philosophy of the Practical,* 1909). This is the Hegelian dictum used by Croce to defend absolute idealism against Kantian criticism. Having translated the *Encyclopedia* into Italian, Croce was aware of the "scabrous part" of Hegel's teachings in the false sciences—the philosophy of nature and of history—but he kept Hegel's discovery, his "Columbus' egg," which is the synthesis of opposites. "Opposites are not an illusion, and unity is not an illusion. Opposites resist each other but not unity, for true, concrete unity is simply the unity or synthesis of opposites." [3] Thus Croce's philosophy is immediately a philosophy of spirit. It has in its structure four moments or degrees, corresponding to the four parts of his *Filosofia dello Spirito*: the spirit is the first intuition or representation of the individual and constitutes the subjcet matter of aesthetics (*Aesthetic as Science of Expression and General Linguistic,* 1902); then it is consciousness of the universal and its unity with the individual (*Logic as the Science of Pure Concept,* 1909). These two degrees constitute the theoretical sphere, which has as its counterpart the practical sphere or the sphere of will. Willing relates at first to the particular; it is an economic activity, which seeks and realizes only what relates to the actual conditions in which man finds himself. Willing relates next to the universal; it is an ethical activity, which seeks and realizes what relates not only to man's actual conditions but also to something that transcends them (*Philosophy of the Practical*).

The periodical *La Critica*, founded by Croce in 1903, did much

[3] *What Is Living and What Is Dead of the Philosophy of Hegel,* 1907 (English translation, 1915).

to spread Hegel's political realism throughout Italy. In his *Philosophy of the Practical* (Part 3, Chap. 3) Croce shows that laws are merely abstract generalities, incapable of predicting the concrete; they should be treated as simple aids to real volitions, like scientific theories, which, taken independently and apart from their role in interpreting the concrete, are merely pseudo-concepts. In much the same vein, in a recent monograph he condemns antihistorical views, abstract rationalism "which extols the construction of human life by separating it from life itself, which is history . . . , materializes spiritual values and renders them inert by making them transcendent." [4] This tendency toward the concrete (the universal concrete, in the Hegelian sense of the word) inspired Croce's numerous works on aesthetics, literary criticism, and historiography.

In *The Theory of Mind as Pure Act* (1916) Giovanni Gentile, Croce's contemporary, relates his own philosophy to the Italian tradition and identifies the absolute with a creative act of the spirit which is immanent in all reality. A historian of the philosophy of the Middle Ages and the Renaissance and editor of the writings of the Italian philosopher Giordano Bruno, he states his own doctrine in terms of history, from which he considers his doctrine to have developed. "Our theory," he writes, "frees the spirit from all limits of space or time as well as from all external conditions . . . ; it sees history not as something presupposed but as the real, concrete form of the spiritual reality, and in this way it establishes absolute liberty. It is summed up in two principles: the sole concept of reality is a concept of self . . . ; there is no matter in the spiritual act except from itself as activity." It follows that philosophy is not contemplation but participation, through moral and political life, in this creative activity.

III *Octave Hamelin*

The doctrine of Octave Hamelin (1856–1907), set forth in *The Principal Elements of Representation* (1907; 2d edition, 1925), has

[4] *Revue de Métaphysique*, 1931, p. 7.

Renouvier's neocriticism as its point of departure and is actually the construction of a table of categories, the first of which is relation. His list of categories—number, time, space, movement, quality, alteration, specification, causality, personality—obviously owes its origin to reflection on Renouvier's list. He reverses the order of time and space as well as the order of movement (that of becoming in Renouvier's writings) and quality, adding specification to quality and alteration to movement; but this does not change in any way the spirit of the table, which goes from abstract relations that determine objects to concrete relations that determine subjects. Furthermore, each category is presented as the synthesis of a thesis and an antithesis; for example, with Hamelin as with Renouvier, number is a synthesis of unity and plurality, and Hamelin generally followed Renouvier in these determinations. Finally, as with Renouvier, categories are elements of representation and not, like the Hegelian Idea, definitions of the absolute.

In addition, however, Hamelin sought to resolve a problem which had simply been stated by Renouvier in these terms: "To construct the system of general relations among phenomena, to raise an edifice of which these relations determine the principal lines, so that facts known or to be known will all have their places marked off or implied, is the problem of science" (2d edition, p. 323). Renouvier, who considered categories to be experiential data, had not completed this construction. Hamelin tried to complete it by a synthetic method which was supposed to leave no notion isolated—that is, by a method analogous to that of Plato and Hegel.

But there is a serious discrepancy between the Heglian system and the Renouvierian spirit that inspired Hamelin. Hegelian dialectic leads to Spirit, to a concrete universal, which, according to Hamelin, is simply the absolute One of Alexandrian philosophy, in which any trace of individuality is lost. In the personalism of Renouvier, on the other hand, as in Hamelin's system, the supreme category is the person. It follows that the synthetic method must be divorced from these conclusions, and Hamelin claims to accomplish this very goal. In contract to Hegel, he interprets the relation between thesis and antithesis, not as a relation between contradictory terms which are mutually exclusive, but as a relation between opposing or correlative terms which evoke each other and therefore lead to complementary affirmations instead of tending toward the nothingness of negative theology.

From this angle, the most fragile part of Hamelin's system is that discussed in the previous chapter. Here he shows how personality, born of the synthesis of causality and finality, completes the dialectical movement. We can readily understand how different causal series governed by a particular end can form what Hamelin calls an active system containing all the conditions of its activity and consequently its independence. But that this active system is precisely what we call the conscious, free person (rather than the world or cosmos, for example, or simply a living organism) seems less clearly demonstrated. Having acknowledged this point, Hamelin offers us a vision of the universe similar to that of personalism.

But it is not by a new dialectical step that he passes from the human person to the divine, free, creative, and providential person; it is by an urgent longing for perfection. Necessity no longer has a part. "Indeed, thought is actualized and can be actualized only in and through will. The first moment is the moment when mind accomplishes its first act; the first cause is that which mind makes the first." Necessity, which was seen to reign supreme in the lower, abstract regions of representation, no longer has a place here, and at the same time this necessity is revealed to be only the most superficial aspect of reality.[5]

iv German Idealism

The idealism of R. C. Eucken's *Intellectual Currents of the Present* (1904) is that of a reformer who holds that the moral predication of a spiritual world is revealed in action and contemplation. But

[5] On Hamelin, see Darbon, "La méthode synthétique dans l'Essai d'Hamelin," *Revue de Métaphysique*, January 1929; and H.-Ch. Puech, "Notes sur O. Hamelin," *L'Esprit*, 1927.

there was also a great revival of Hegelianism after 1918, and this was attested in 1928 by the creation of an international Hegelian society, whose first congress was held in Holland in 1930. In a recent work, *The Dialectic in Contemporary Philosophy* (1929–31), Siegfried Marck studies this movement, particularly the neo-Hegelian dialectic in R. Kroner's *From Kant to Hegel* (1921–24) and *Prolegomena to the Philosophy of Culture* (1928).[6]

v *The Idealism of Jules de Gaultier*

The nature of Jules de Gaultier's idealism is clearly indicated by the title of his book: *From Kant to Nietzsche* (1900). Far from trying to restore values destroyed by naturalism, as proponents of other doctrines of idealism had done, Gaultier seeks to prove that the problem of values does not fall within the province of philosophy. Moral sensibility and metaphysical sensibility are two points of departure for two distinct visions of the world. If we start from the former, we fashion for ourselves a world which has some influence on our conduct, our destiny, our happiness; it is ruled by a finality which affords room for knowledge and action; furthermore, these requirements are at the heart of almost all philosophies, which are generally linked to the Messianic hope of a final state of bliss. If we start from the latter, we have a vision of the world as a "spectacle" which confers true reality on no subject, which makes thought the only activity spread throughout the universe; all objects and all subjects are merely the means of representing this infinite reality. "Bovarysm" is the doctrine that exposes the illusions hidden in the first of these two visions. "Existence is necessarily conceived as being different from what it actually is—such is its principle.[7]

[6] Cf. Heinrich Levy, *Die Hegel-Renaissance in der deutschen Philosophie*, 1927.
[7] See *Le Bovarysme*, 1902; *La fiction universelle*, 1903; *La dépendance de la morale et l'indépendance des mœurs*, 1907; *La sensibilité métaphysique*, new edition, 1928.

Bibliography

I

Texts

Bosanquet, Bernard. *A Companion to Plato's Republic*. London and New York, 1895.
————. *The Psychology of the Moral Self*. London and New York, 1897.
————. *Three Lectures on Aesthetics*. London, 1915.
————. *Some Suggestions in Ethics*. London, 1918.
————. *Implication and Linear Inference*. London, 1920.
————. *What Religion Is*. London, 1920.
————. *The Meeting of Extremes in Contemporary Philosophy*. London, 1921.
————. *Essays and Addresses*. London, 1889.
————. *The Civilisation of Christendom*. London, 1893.
————. *Social and International Ideals*. London, 1917.
————. *Science and Philosophy and Other Essays*. London, 1927.

Studies

Cotton, J. H. *Royce on the Human Self*. Cambridge, Mass., 1954.
Cunningham, G. Watts. *The Idealistic Argument in Recent British and American Philosophy*. London and New York, 1933.
Fuss, Peter. *The Moral Philosophy of Josiah Royce*. Cambridge, Mass., 1965.
Loewenberg, Jacob. *The Philosophical Review* 26 (1917): 578–82.
Marcel, Gabriel. *Royce's Metaphysics,* trans. V. Ringer and G. Ringer. Chicago, 1956.
Muirhead, John H. *The Platonic Tradition in Anglo-Saxon Philosophy*. London, 1931.
Rand, Benjamin. *The Philosophical Review* 25 (1916): 515–22.
Smith, John E. *Royce's Social Infinite*. New York, 1950.

III

Texts

Hamelin, Octave. *Essai sur les éléments principaux de la représentation*. Paris, 1907.
————. *Le Système de Descartes*. Paris, 1910.
————. *Le Système d'Aristote*. Paris, 1920.
————. *Le Système de Renouvier*. Paris, 1927.

THE CRITIQUE OF THE SCIENCES

TOWARD THE BEGINNING of the period under study many thinkers, working independently, realized that the positive sciences simply do not have the meaning and metaphysical significance attributed to them by Spencer and Taine. As early as 1870 Lachelier, drawing support from Kant's *Critique of Judgment,* had shown that investigation of the laws of nature assumes the principle of finality as well as that of causality. Émile Boutroux in his *Concerning the Contingency of the Laws of Nature* (1874) had shown through an internal analysis of scientific knowledge that determinism becomes less rigorous as one moves to higher levels of reality—from matter to life and from life to consciousness.

Then began the critical trend which was the characteristic expression of the years around the turn of the century: the investigation of the meaning and value of the fundamental concepts used in the sciences. This trend had two distinctive traits. In the first place, it was technical in nature; investigations concerning the principles of geometry derived from the purely technical investigations of non-Euclidean geometers; at the head of the movement were mathematicians like Henri Poincaré and later Cantor, Whitehead, and Russell, and physicists like Duhem. In the second place, it was wholly positive in nature, since it examined the principles of the sciences, not in themselves and in the absolute or by referring to very general principles such as the principles of contradiction or sufficient reason, but in their actual and indispensable role in scientific knowledge, for it was assumed that principles could be examined only in the context of which they were a part. Thus the deductive ideal of a perfect science was sacrificed not to empiricism but to a much more complex ideal.

1 Henri Poincaré, Pierre Duhem, and Gaston Milhaud

Henri Poincaré (1854–1912), inventor of a new method of solving differential equations and author of notable works on celestial mechanics, investigated as a philosopher the conditions under which he carried out his studies as a scientist. Generally speaking, Poincaré believed that in the sciences an insufficienct distinction was made between experimental truth, definition, and theory. When we say, for example, that the stars follow Newton's law, we are mingling in this proposition, which has the appearance of a factual truth, two other propositions: one of these—that gravitation follows Newton's law—is a definition and consequently remains immutable and unverifiable; the other—that gravitation is the only force which acts on stars—can be verified. Poincaré's critique is grounded largely on this distinction. He holds that the properties which we confer on mathematical space—homogeneity, isotropy, three dimensions—are not given facts, and that the properties of mechanical force (equality of action and reaction, etc.) are simple definitions. But what is the source of these affirmations and definitions? They are simple conventions, which, in theory, are completely free. In practice, however, we choose the most convenient ones—that is, those which enable us to arrange phenomena according to the simplest constructions. Poincaré accepts Mach's principle of economy of thought or simplicity. But it is clear that experimental data remain independent of this convention. The mechanical explanation of a fact is entirely conventional, and it can even be demonstrated that a fact has an infinite number of possible mechanical explanations. Yet the fact is the boundary at which our liberty stops.

Thus Poincaré indicated the role of the scientist's initiative even though his conventionalism sheds little light on the degree to which the scientist who remains in the sphere of the relative can gain direct access to reality. The opposite is true of the physicist Pierre Duhem (1861–1916). According to his *Physical Theory, Its Object and Structure* (1906), one may try to make physical theory a real explanation of laws and boast of reaching reality just as in Cartesian mechanics; then the theory will merge with a certain metaphysical conception of reality and lead to discussions concerning the Absolute; or one may make physical theory nothing more than a summary, schematic representation of experimental knowledge, which does not in any way penetrate reality. Henri Bouasse also maintains in his *Theory of Mechanics* that equations derived from a physical theory are of utmost importance and that there is no basis for choosing between theories that lead to the same equations. It must also be noted that physical experience (and here Duhem anticipates, in an article written in 1894 for the *Revue des Questions scientifiques,* ideas taken up a little later by Milhaud and Edouard le Roy) already contains a theoretical interpretation that adds to the immediate data: the physicist does not ascertain that a gas occupies a certain volume but that a column of mercury reaches a certain mark, and he can reach his conclusion only by resorting to all kinds of abstract notions and hypotheses. In his *System of the World,*[1] Duhem traced the history of this double conception of physical theory in astronomy: one of these—the one which seeks to penetrate reality—establishes for science a routine more and more remote from facts; the other yields without resistance to new experiences.

Gaston Milhaud (1858–1918), who taught mathematics before becoming a philosopher and a historian of science, shows with utmost clarity how Taine's and Spencer's conceptions of the world derived from an illegitimate transformation of science into metaphysics. "Everything which, according to the laws of modern science, seemed to contradict the fact of liberty is contained, in reality, not in these laws but in an a priori opinion which holds that nothing escapes determinism. . . . The progress of science has not changed in any

---

[1] *Système du Monde, Histoire des doctrines cosmologiques de Platon à Copernic,* 5 vols., 1913–17.

way the form of determinism as it might have been conceived by the first thinker who had the notion of linking by a relation of quantity the two simplest phenomena imaginable."[2] Science, far from being a simple, passive account of external relations, as Bacon and Comte assumed it to be, is a work of the spirit, and as such implies, in its very creativity, a certain contingency.[3]

It was in the same spirit that J. Wilbois, in his articles in the *Revue de Métaphysique* (1899–1901), presented a critique of the famous methods of Mill. Their application seems to imply only a simple recording of facts, but these presumed facts (for example the position of Neptune in Le Verrier's discovery) are the result of theories and calculations which are wholly independent of methods.

II *The Critique of the Sciences and Citicism*

If science is the work of the mind, one can undertake to go back to the Kantian method, enlarge it, and show that it is guided by the necessities of the mind. That is what Arthur Hannequin (1856–1905) tried to accomplish in his *Critical Essay on the Hypothesis of Atoms*. When regressive analysis has been carried to the limit, the physicist is persuaded to identify motion as the final principle of reality, yet motion itself contains a wholly unintelligible element—continuity—which supposes both the continuity of time and the continuity of place. It follows that mechanics is not a purely intelligible science. There is but one science which attains the perfect intelligibility required by the understanding—the science of numbers or discrete quantities. There is but one means of attaining perfect intelligibility in the science of motion—by introducing the science of numbers. That is what atomism does. Hannequin shows that atomism is necessary in mechanics and chemistry; in chemistry, notably, it cannot be treated as a raw datum of experience, since the

[2] *Essai sur les conditions et les limites de la certitude logique,* 1894, p. 143.
[3] *Le Rationnel,* 1898; *Le positivisme et le progrès de l'esprit; Études critiques sur Auguste Comte,* 1902.

laws from which it is tentatively deduced—Gay Lussac's law of combining volumes and the law of specific heat formulated by Dulong and Petit—are only approximate. It was in a similar spirit that A. Darbon wrote *The Mechanical Theory and Nominalism* (1910). The Cartesian view that mechanism expresses the profound reality of things is no longer tenable. Does it follow that one must treat this view as a pure fiction and fall back upon the nominalism of Mach or Duhem? The study of probability and the different forms of induction suggests "that the mind has the power to draw from its own resources ideas that illuminate experience—not preconceived ideas but ideas that are constantly being formulated and sharpened to provide better explanations as facts become better known. Darbon maintains that the agreement between an idea and all available facts provides him with the most reliable demonstration permitted by the form of our intelligence.

Spiritual necessities, says Hannequin with reference to scientific theories. Vital necessity, says Hans Vaihinger in his *The Philosophy of As If* (1911).[4] Vaihinger's doctrine, moreover, is simply a brilliant elaboration of theories which were then commanding attention, such as the Darwin-inspired theory of biological determination of intellectual functions in Nietzsche and Bergson, and Poincaré's conventionalism. He tries to prove that there is no such thing as a theoretical thought that contains its own end and has inherent value. This doctrine contains two distinct theories. The first is that the role of thought is not to apprehend reality but to adapt us to our environment; thought is an instrument which enables us to move safely from one part of reality to another, thanks to prevision. We should note that by itself this theory does not in any way contradict the view that thought also represents reality; for example, Bergson shows that intellectual categories, though biological by origin, penetrate to the heart of reality when we limit them to knowledge of inert matter and fail only when we try to apply them to life. Vaihinger

[4] *Die philosophie des Als Ob,* 1911; 8th edition, 1922; English translation by C. K. Ogden, 1924.

has the unique distinction, however, of forging a permanent link between the theory of thought as a biological function and his second theory—that thought is composed of fictions which make adaptation possible but do not in any way represent reality. The only reality is the aggregate of our sensations, whereas things endowed with properties and causality are merely fictions. When they are not acknowledged as fictions, Vaihinger tries to find proof of their fictive character in their inner contradictions. For example, the fundamental concepts of physics and mathematics are contradictory; attenuated atoms and infinitesimal quantities which can be eliminated as zeros are fictions because they are incoherent notions. But some fictions—such as negative, irrational, or imaginary quantities in mathematics—are acknowledged outright. Political economy works with the fiction of the *homo oeconomicus* who is insensitive to anything other than his own interests, and Condillac's statue as well as Fichte's closed commercial state are fictions. This notion of fictions is quite different from the notion of hypotheses, which are suppositions subject to verification independently or in terms of their consequences; fictions, by contrast, do not have to be verified—in fact, such a requirement would make no sense. Still to be demonstrated is the success of fictions in our adaptation to our environment, not in spite of the fact that they are fictions but because they are fictions. On this point Vaihinger's thinking seems much less clear. Paper money seems to provide a convenient analogy: by serving as a substitute for heavy commodities, it greatly facilitates exchanges.[5] By the same token, if I consider experience *as if* it were composed of things, matter *as if* it were composed of atoms, and a curve *as if* it consisted of infinitely small straight lines, I find it easier to govern myself within the realm of experience. In no case is our aim to mitigate an unyielding reality; we must rather yield to it.

Vaihinger insists that this doctrine should not be confused with pragmatism, and rightly so. Pragmatism is a doctrine of truth, and it assumes that our action transforms things; Vaihinger envisions, not the impossible mitigation of things, but the growing flexibility

[5] *Ibid.*, pp. 288 ff.

of thought by virtue of the invention of fictions. Furthermore, James seeks a true religion which is actually experienced; Vaihinger thinks it "plebeian" to search for the truth of a religious myth and, in the words of Lange, his teacher, maintains that one can no more refute a religion than a mass by Palestrina. To his doctrine he gave the names of positivistic idealism and idealistic irrationalism.

III *The Critique of the Sciences and Modern Scientific Developments*

The period that began around 1910 differs in many respects from the preceding one. The general tendency of philosophy at the beginning of the twentieth century was to return to the immediate reality beneath the rather fragile constructions created by human intelligence. Poincaré's conventionalism joined with Bergson's intuitionism and James's pragmatism to show that intelligence either fails to penetrate true reality or disfigures it. In the profound revolutions that have occurred in physics since 1910, in new views concerning the evolution of living beings, in transformations in psychology, and in juridical theories—everywhere we find manifestations of a spirit which we unquestionably have difficulty in isolating and defining but which seems to carry our whole intellectual civilization in the same direction. Generally speaking, it seems to be marked by the abandonment of the old oppositions which for a long time were the lifeblood of philosophy—discontinuity and continuity, specific stability and transformism, introspection and objective observation, right and deed. The tendency was to attribute the point of view of human intelligence and the conditions under which this intelligence is capable of approaching reality to the first term in each of these pairs; the second was treated as an irreducible, irrational term. But discontinuity is perhaps a profound characteristic of reality, and continuity the aspect of things revealed by a superficial acquaintance, for the Leibnizian adage is reversed by contemporary physics—nature proceeds only by leaps. Putting discontinuity at the very heart of reality does not mean fitting the objects of experience into preconceived molds; instead, it means renouncing the critical idealism of Kant, which, with greater or lesser obviousness, inspired practically every philosophical theory of the nineteenth century. One would scarcely have dared, only a few years ago, to speak of the discontinuous realities familiar to physicists and biologists today without adding that they were intellectual constructions or forms to be imposed on things. At the moment when the nuclear theory of matter and energy was about to score a prodigious success, it was generally thought that atomism was a way of looking at reality, imposed by the nature of mind, or even that it was simply a convenient fiction.

The critical problem could be stated as that of determining the point of view that the mind must adopt in each instance when considering things. But are we not rather to eliminate the point of view in the mind in each instance and, in general, everything that is merely a point of view? The theory of relativity, in physics, offers an illustration of this trend of thought, for here the problem is to express physical laws by eliminating any point of view peculiar to a particular observer.

It seems, in fact, that in its general development Einstein's theory of relativity tends toward a realistic epistemology. It has been shown time and again since Kant that homogeneous, uniform time, in which the physicist sees events unfold, and Euclidean space, in which he accommodates these events, is the characteristic elaboration of a mind desirous of apprehending relations between phenomena. Our representation of the universe is a mixture, then, of something that comes from us and something that comes from things; it depends on the point of view of the observer. Is it possible for us to discover notions of space and time that will enable us to describe the events of the universe as they are in themselves, independently of any particular point of view? That is the question posed by Einstein. His theory generalized what the Greek geometers had done for proximity and remoteness. In the geometric space invented by the Greeks, the properties of a figure are completely independent of the accident of its being near or distant from the observer. As

Bergson said, however, "the reduction of gravitation to inertia was properly an elimination of ready-made concepts which, by coming between the physicist and his data or between the mind and the constitutive relations of a thing, were preventing physics from being geometry." [6] The course of events is expressed in a manner independent of their practice of entering *our* duration at a certain moment of our *time*.

Theoreticians of science are accustomed to considering determinism either as a characteristic of reality itself or as a convenient fiction or convention, which, though successful, does not express the essence of reality. According to Arthur S. Eddington, however, one consequence of the appearance of the quantum theory has been that physics is no longer bound to a framework of laws that implies determinism. Immediately after recent theories of theoretical physics were formulated, determinism collapsed, and it may well be asked whether it will ever regain its former place.[7] Thus philosophy was persuaded to return to the so-called necessity of subjective conditions in science, which became frameworks—but only frameworks—under critical examination; and positive developments in science show that they are biases which, if we cease to consider things indiscriminately and in terms of mediate results, cannot be justified by observation.

IV *Epistemology and Positivism*

The central idea of positivism was to withhold from philosophy any content but the data of science. This idea appears in the works of Abel Rey, who identifies philosophy with reflection on the positive sciences, and who assumes the point of view of the conditions governing scientific progress in order to defend mechanism against the energetics of Ostwald and Duhem (*Theory of Physics Among Contemporary Physicists,* 1908; *Mechanism and Energetics from the Point of View of the Conditions of Knowledge,* 1908). The superiority of mechanism is proven by its traditional characteristics, its

[6] *Durée et simultanéité,* 1922, p. 241.
[7] *The Nature of the Physical World,* 1928.

intelligibility and clearness, its tendency to suggest new experiences. In the second edition of his *Theory* (1923) and in his recent works, Abel Rey, reflecting the tendency manifested by science itself since 1900, stresses the realistic nature of his views: "Nothing authorizes us to make the atom a metaphysical entity. But everything compels us to consider it a coherent bundle of experimentally given physicochemical relations."

Henri Berr, who began as the theoretician of *Synthesis in History* (1911), for which he founded his *Revue de synthèse historique,* was now attempting, in a much larger work, an unqualified synthesis which, through the effective collaboration of all scholars, was to realize the synthesis of scientific knowledge on which Auguste Comte grounded philosophy. The same tendency toward synthesis is found in Rignano, the Italian philosopher who, in 1906, founded the international journal *Scientia.*

Distinct from such endeavors is epistemology, which analyzes the conditions governing scientific knowledge and therefore fits into a general philosophy of the spirit.

Émile Meyerson begins his epistemology by refuting positivism (*Identity and Reality,* 1908; *On Explanation in the Sciences,* 1921; *Relativistic Deduction,* 1925; *The Progress and Processes of Thought,* 1931). Before all else, however, he sees positivism as legalism—that is, the doctrine of philosophy of the sciences which confines scientific knowledge to the statement of relations. That was the view not only of Comte but also of Mach and the energeticists, who were opposed to any theory concerning the structure of reality and were closely linked to the critique of the sciences prevalent at the beginning of the century. Meyerson held that scientific knowledge as it actually existed did not in any way justify their view. The scientist constructs theories to provide an explanation of phenomena and to lead him to real causes. To discover the cause of an effect is ultimately to identify both by showing that the effect is not different from the cause. That is why physics is governed wholly by principles of inertia and conservation which, in so far as they are able to do so, eliminate diversity and heterogeneity in favor of unity and homogeneity. Physics seeks to eliminate time because its irreversibility implies a direction in the course of causal series and therefore interferes with the identification of causes and effects; it seeks to eliminate the quality of matter and gain direct access to its unity which, in extreme theories, is identical with homogeneous space. Is this procedure of identification peculiar to science? Certainly not, for it is the very same procedure associated with common sense, which Meyerson studies in his last work, *The Progress and Processes of Thought*, in which he compares spontaneous thought and scientific thought. The aim of *Relativistic Deduction*, on the other hand, is to show that the recent theory of relativity exhibits the same tendency, since it is truly a comprehensive system of deduction.

But the mind discovers instances of resistance. Carnot's principle states that the transformation of energy is not arbitrarily reversible. Furthermore, there are "irrationals": sensible qualities that cannot be reduced to motion; collision and remote action, equally incomprehensible; finality, which seems to govern everything irrational in science.

It would seem that these very instances of resistance should suggest certain metaphysical problems: Where is the real? Is it associated with identity, to which everything is reduced, or with differences? Or are there, as in Bergson, two kinds of reality—a slack, homogeneous reality like space and matter, and a qualitative reality? (It should be noted that one part of the Bergsonian doctrine is Meyerson's epistemology, for Bergson discovers the natural course of physical speculation in a reduction of diversity to homogeneity.) Limiting himself to pure epistemology, Meyerson refuses to deal with these questions. It is nevertheless true that the agreement— partial at any rate—between our principles of conservation and reality suggests the idea of a certain realism which is far removed from theories of expedients, fictions, and conventions. This realism was already accepted by Bergson, who is identified with pragmatism only through erroneous interpretations; for according to him, it is the absolute characteristics of material reality that the mind accedes to in the principles of conservation.

Bibliography

Texts

Duhem, Pierre. *Le Potentiel thermodynamique et ses applications à la mécanique chimique et à la théorie des phénomènes électriques.* Paris, 1886.
———. *Le Mixte et la combinaison chimique. Essai sur l'évolution d'une idée.* Paris, 1902.
———. *Les Théories électriques de J. Clerk Maxwell: Étude historique et critique.* Paris, 1902.
———. *L'Évolution de la mécanique.* Paris, 1903.
———. *Les Origines de la statique.* Paris, 1905–06.
———. *The Aim and Structure of Physical Theory,* trans. P. P. Wiener. Princeton, N.J., 1954.
———. *Études sur Léonard de Vinci, ceux qu'il a lus et ceux qui l'ont lu.* Paris, 1906–13.
———. "Physics—History of." In *Catholic Encyclopedia,* vol. 12. New York, 1911.
———. *Le Système du monde: Histoire des doctrines cosmologiques de Platon à Copernic.* 8 vols. Paris, 1913–58.
Poincaré, Jules Henri. *Œuvres de Jules Henri Poincaré.* 11 vols. Paris, 1928–56.
———. *Science and Hypothesis,* trans. W. J. Greenstreet. London, 1905.
———. *The Value of Science,* trans. G. B. Halsted. London, 1907.
———. *Science and Method,* trans. Francis Maitland, with a preface by Bertrand Russell. London, 1914.
———. *Mathematics and Science: Last Essays,* trans. John W. Bolduc. New York, 1963.
———. "Analyse des travaux scientifiques de Henri Poincaré, faite par lui-même." *Acta Mathematica* 38 (1921).

Studies

Nadal, A. "Gaston Milhaud," in *Revue d'histoire des sciences* 12.
Poirier, R. *Philosophes et savants français.* Vol. 2. *La Philosophie de la science.* Paris, 1926.

PHILOSOPHICAL CRITICISM

IN PHILOSOPHIES of action and in idealism we have
seen the reaction that was taking place in favor of spiritual values,
which had no place in the representation of the universe fashioned
by preceding generations. In these doctrines, particularly Édouard
le Roy's, the criticism of science was already playing a significant
role. Also to be discussed in this chapter are doctrines intimately
linked to the scientific movement, particularly in Germany and
France. In Germany we witness the revival of Kantian criticism and
the birth of the philosophy of values; in France, the movement was
strongly reinforced by Xavier Léon's foundation of the *Revue de
Métaphysique et de morale* (1893), which encouraged the collaboration of scientists and philosophers. International congresses of
philosophers convened through Xavier Léon's efforts (the first was
held in Paris in 1900 and the last, also in Paris, in 1937) and sessions
of the Société Française de Philosophie (since 1900)—sessions often
devoted to the discussion of theories proposed by men like Langevin,
Perrin, Le Dantec, and Einstein—helped to forge close ties between
science and philosophy, which had been separated for a long time.

1 Neo-Kantianism of the Marburg School

At the crux of pure Kantianism, as we have already seen, was
the distinction between the transcendental aesthetic and the tran-

scendental analytic. The intellectual functions cannot be exercised unless sensibility provides them with materials and this need for sensible data leads to idealistic phenomenalism and to the thing in itself as the unknowable foundation of phenomena. The negation of this duality constitutes the essential characteristic of the Marburg school of neo-Kantianism. For Hermann Cohen the activity of pure thought is at the same time its content, and the act of producing is itself the product (*System of Philosophy: Logic of Pure Knowledge,* 1902; *Ethics of Pure Will,* 1904; *Aesthetics of Pure Feeling,* 1912). Thus Cohen contradicts Fichte, for whom any product is a suspension of production and for whom the ideal of making the activity of thought its own object is unrealizable. Nor does Cohen accept the "absurd concept of formal logic," which issues, in Aristotle, from the unhappy union of logic and universal grammar; as Pythagoras and Plato had seen, thought which constitutes the object peculiar to logic belongs to the "dominant science" in which thought and reality merge—the mathematical science of nature. Such thought is not a synthesis, for this would assume, as its necessary precondition, a prior datum; it is wholly original, and its principle is the principle of the "origin" or generation of objects by thought—for example, in the infinitesimal calculus, the essential tool of the science of nature, which shows clearly that thought is not the simple organization of a preliminary datum but the production of an object. An infinitesimal quantity allows us, in fact, to apprehend the intellectual reality of the motion, acceleration, and laws of nature; far from being an arithmetic expedient, it is the true unit, prior to extension and number. Thus we come to the true signification of logical "concepts," which when confused with ideas—that is, with representative elements—gave birth to everything associated with "Romantic decadence." A concept, as Kant saw, is one of the threads in the tissue that constitutes an object, and the object itself is nothing but a tissue of concepts. The problem of philosophy is to apprehend it as such and to reintroduce not only geometric and mechanical determinations but also the objects of chemistry and biology; at the antipodes of the philosophy of nature, the aim of Cohen's philosophy, then, is to expel immediate intuition everywhere in favor of concepts.

He introduced this rigorous intellectualism into ethics, aesthetics, and religion. It is wrong to set ethics against science, making the first the study of moral obligation and the second the study of being; for the object of ethics, without being an actual existence, is a being—the being of pure will, determined by moral obligation. His aesthetics reveals a "pure" sentiment, independent of any desire. In *The Concept of Religion* (1915), he shows that religion, freed from the mystical theology of the history of religions—*Religionsphiloso-phie*—is intended to bring the inner life of the individual to perfection and in this way to complement ethics, which absorbed the individual in mankind. The concept to these three disciples is that of Man: ethics requires humanity, art makes humanity the object of its love, and religion frees the individual.

Cohen's intellectualism was a revelation, in 1885, to Paul Natorp, who saw in it a means of combating naturalism and empiricism, prevalent at that time, and especially impressionism, which irremediably divides reason and experience, nature and humanity, the universal and the individual. In *Plato's Doctrine of Ideas, An Introduction to Idealism* (1903) Natorp attempts to demonstrate through history that Cohen's doctrine is related to Plato's philosophy. His main thesis is the unity of thought and being, which reappears in the Logos of Heraclitus, the One of Parmenides, and especially the Idea of Plato. Here he is not concerned in any way with a synthesis between thought and being; existence is proved by reflection itself, for existence is "the vital act of positing oneself"; what he has in mind is not a creation but a construction. In keeping with these principles, Natorp tries in *The Logical Foundations of the Exact Sciences* (1910) to lay a purely logical foundation for mathematics without resorting to intuitive knowledge of space and time. Still, he understands, perhaps more clearly and decisively than Cohen, the necessity of assuming facts, data, nonconstructions. Sometimes, however, he considers the notion of a fact as meaning only that a construction is incomplete and that knowledge has not yet reached its end; sometimes also, and more especially in psychology, he accepts, under the influence of Bergson, the thesis that knowledge can develop in a direction contrary to intellectual constructions and return from an object to a pure subject. Thus our knowledge would go in two directions but without ever reaching the goal: toward objectivation culminating in absolute knowledge of the laws of nature, or toward a subject which, though pure, is only "the power of every determination accomplished or to be accomplished in it by knowledge, which objectivizes." It was natural, under these conditions, for him to take into consideration the objections of anti-intellectualistic philosophers who thought that the logical schematism was superficial and did not reach being. His answer is that true logic assumes an inherent opposition, since it is production or passage from nonbeing to being. It seems that the common element in the philosophical speculation of Cohen and Natorp is the direction given to an integrative procedure, illustrated by mathematical analysis but infinitely more general. Thus Natorp sees it further illustrated in the abstractive procedure through which Plotinus arrived at his supreme principle, "a victory of action over everything which is simply done" ("Sieg der Tat über alles bloss getan").

Natorp's intellectualism culminates, in practice, in a situation not without similarity to that of the philosophy of enlightenment at the end of the eighteenth century: that the diffusion of the intellectual heritage is more important than purely economic and material methods of resolving the social question. His *Socialidealismus* (1920) was written to support the thesis of the unique school.

Ernst Cassirer, in *The Problem of Knowledge* (1906–20), argued that the evolution of philosophy since the Renaissance has tended always in the direction of a clearer statement of the critical problem. In *Substance and Function* (1910) he also advanced a theory of mathematics which throws much light on the spiritual directions of the Marburg school—the theory that mathematics is not a science of quantity but a universal combinative science that discovers the relations between all possible modes. Finally, he tried to apply Cohen's suggestion to chemistry; the energetistic conception of chemical phenomena seemed to him to lay the basis for transforming chemistry into a mathematical science of nature. Cassirer claimed that Einstein's theory of relativity confirmed his own idealism, proving that physics does not seek to provide an image of reality but resolves the events studied by it into certain numerical combinations. For the Marburg school the notion of pure data is illegitimate. As Liebert indicates in *The Problem of Value* (1906), philosophy investigates not being but its value, and this value consists in admitting no affirmation of being except within a systematic order, as a member of a series. According to the juridical sociology of Stammler (*Economy and Right*, 1896; *Theory of Jurisprudence*, 1911), the concept of law should have a role in society analogous to that of concepts which, in physics, integrate all facts into a system; law is the pattern or norm governing social relations of every kind, and it tends to bring about an ideal state in which each individual adopts the goals of others when they are objectively justified.

II Neo-Kantianism and the Baden School

Kantian criticism defined objective knowledge not as the image of an external reality but in terms of its universality and necessity, introducing into our knowledge of reality an element of value which seemed to be peculiar to moral or social standards. This is the tendency of Kantianism stressed by Wilhelm Windelband (*Preludes*, 1884; *Introduction to Philosophy*, 1914). A true representation is one that ought to be thought, just as a good action is one that ought to be done and a good thing one that ought to please. This notion of moral obligation enables him to unite all the philosophical disciplines: philosophy does not create values; it simply separates from the chaos of experience the values which, as a system, constitute the normal conscience and represent human "culture." Windelband therefore rejects relativism in favor of absolute values; he offers no systematic means of discerning them, however, and he makes the very existence of this normal conscience a matter of personal belief or a postulate of thought.

Heinrich Rickert is faithful to the spirit of Windelband. His idealism should be called transcendental, to set it apart from subjective idealism, since he gives logical priority to values and "oughts" (*Sollen*) in the determination of truth. A value is independent of reality (for example, the value of a painting is independent of the chemical substances used by the painter); it is independent of the act of evaluation which posits it, independent even of the ought which posits a relation between it and a subject who takes it as a standard; consequently value constitutes a separate realm, which transcends both subject and object. Philosophy seeks to define not only this realm of values but also the relations between the realm of reality and the realm of values, that is, the signification or sense (*Sinn*) of objects or events in relation to determinate values. Like Windelband, Rickert fails to indicate a single principle for defining these values, with the result that their determination seems to be completely arbitrary (*The Object of Knowledge*, 1892; 6th edition, 1928).

The danger inherent in this procedure comes to light particularly in Rickert's treatment of the philosophy of history. Developing ideas already advanced by Windelband, he makes a radical distinction between history and the sciences of nature: history deals with individual things as such, events that occur only once; the sciences of nature investigate the universal laws of beings. This difference relates less to realities themselves than to the different aspects under which a particular reality can be apprehended; for example, the difference between natural science and history is reflected in Newtonian astronomy as opposed to Kant's cosmogony. But to say that history deals with events that "occur but once" is not enough; the historian chooses only events that have value, or more precisely, events that have value for "culture"; this choice therefore owes its value to the concept of culture. The degree to which this procedure is susceptible to arbitrariness is obvious (*Science of History and Natural Science*, 1899).

The philosophical speculation of Ernst Troeltsch (1865–1923) might also be related to Windelband, at least in its initial stages. In his philosophy of religion he seeks support for religion in a rational a priori, an immanent necessity which points to the necessary place of religion in the economy of the human conscience. The life of God is marked by a separation manifested in two contexts: first, in the natural, spontaneous life of the soul; second, in the world of reason, in which personalities take shape and the conflicts of history arise. In *Christian Thought, Its History and Application* (*Der Historismus und seine Überwindung*, 1921; English translation, 1924) he sees the general problem of the philosophy of history in the context of historical relativism and cultural values. History comprises "individual totalities"—Hellenism, Germanism—which are completely autonomous and cannot be explained through simple composition of antecedent elements. The historical sense consists in apprehending, not a series of events bound by a causal tie, but the unity of the evolutionary process that animates them.

It is obvious that the Baden school of neo-Kantianism abandoned any hope of categorical deduction. Bruno Bauch maintains in *Concerning the Concept of Natural Law* (1914) that the system of categories itself cannot be considered closed since natural laws continue to increase in number and are veritable categories for coordinating experiences. But the notion of value and the absence of any transcendental deduction place "theoretical reason" and practical reason on the same level, resulting in a profound modification of both these concepts. B. Bauch seeks in his *Ethics* (1921) to complete the categorical imperative by introducing a system of "cultural values" of which Kant failed to apprehend the importance; moreover, the consequence of these "obligations" is immediate; and since culture can be realized in history only through force, the final consequence of what amounts to absolutism in values is that politics, if it is to serve the ends of culture, can and should in good conscience be a politics of force. This absolutism is manifested especially in *The Philosophy of Values* (1908) in which Münsterberg seeks a principle in Bauch's system of values but finds it only in "a primitive action which confers meaning on our existence, in our act of willing the existence of a world and impressions which not only matter to us as impressions but also assert their independence."

III *The Relativism of Simmel and Volkelt*

Quite different from the uniform doctrines of the Baden school is the vital, receptive relativism of Georg Simmel (1858–1918). His most characteristic works are perhaps his monographs on Kant (1903), Schopenhauer and Nietzsche (1906), Goethe (1913), and Rembrandt (1916). For Simmel a philosophy is the expression of a *type of mind;* unlike the sciences, it arrives at an intuitive apprehension of the world, which is the expression of the being of the philosopher himself and of the human type inherent in him. In Kant, for example, the intellectual type predominates; each thing seems to him to be destined to be known; his problem is not things but what we know of things. Goethe, on the contrary, searches for the unity of mind and nature; he collects every fact in nature which seems to have an affinity with mind and, in mind, every fact which seems to have a kinship with nature.

Mental type appears here as an active agent of selection. It is the true, psychological a priori. Our psychophysical organization admits only representations useful to its own preservation. Knowledge is not to be construed in terms of the deductive type, as originating in a principle, itself not proved, which proves everything, but as a wholly free process involving interdependent elements which draw support from each other and owe their position to each other.

Introduction to Moral Science (1892–93) shows the emptiness of purely formal principles. From the pure form of moral obligation one can deduce nothing—any more than from the pure form of being, in metaphysics—for moral obligation is consciousness of a certain ideal of conduct which is contrary to reality. But what is this ideal? Experience alone can provide us with an answer. By observing the variety of answers provided by the history of morals, we find that determination of the ideal embraces not only a general form but also different mental dispositions, which together shape our sense of moral obligation. A persistent feeling of compulsion may give rise to a ceremonial or rite which, after its purpose has been forgotten, becomes obligatory in itself. Some minds assume the obligation of struggling against the existing state of affairs, others that of preserving it. It is the determination of these moral types, even more than of the details associated with them, that interests Simmel.

Simmel's thought moves always in a region halfway between the empty a priori and the indefinite fragmenting of facts. Just as his *Introduction to Moral Science* can be considered as a critique of a certain apriorism, his *Problems of the Philosophy of History* (1892; 4th edition, 1921) proves that it is futile to search for pure facts in history and, consequently, for causes and laws. The only historical realities are ideas and feelings; physical causes—climate or soil—and economic causes can produce results only by modifying psychological states. These feelings are too varied and complex to be accessible to us. How can we represent to ourselves in detail the psychic forces which converged to produce the victory of Marathon? Let us add that these causes are accessible only through the intermediary of the feelings and ideas of the historian, for the thought patterns of the historian are a veritable a priori, and the picture he paints for us is less an image of reality than a creation of his mind. Factual materials are transformed into history only by virtue of a formative principle to which they are subjected.

Similarly, in his *Sociology* (1908) Simmel does not investigate social structures themselves or become hopelessly involved with countless varieties of societies. Instead, he seeks to isolate the general forms of social interaction, each of which is like the organizing nucleus of societies which may differ strikingly. What constitutes social superiority? What is competition? What are the essential traits of a secret society? It is problems of this type that he thinks sociology capable of solving.

Simmel was always careful not to allow skeptical subjectivism to confuse his forms or types with an individual temperament. In his support for this belief and maintained that it introduced into experience a connection or cohesion (*Zusammenhang*) different from simple logical coherence.

With Simmel, philosophy is essentially meditation on culture. Especially in Germany after the World War, doubt concerning the soundness of the values associated with European culture inspired a pessimistic movement which found its clearest expression in Oswald Spengler's *The Decline of the West* (2 vols., 1920–22). Hermann Keyserling was concerned particularly with the limitations of our culture: "The West is obsessed with exactness. It pays almost no attention at all to meaning. If it ever does grasp the meaning of things, this will help it find its perfect expression and will establish complete harmony between the essence of things and phenomena" (*Travel Diary of a Philosopher,* 1919). Such statements have rightly been interpreted as an indication of a resurgence of romanticism, which transforms all things into symbols.[2] The works of Ludwig Klages (*The Being of Consciousness,* 1921; *Principles of Characterology*) exhibit the same tendency, particularly when the author separates soul and spirit (*Geist*). The *Geist,* outside the world and consciousness, is an alien absolute, a bad demon that introduces itself into the life of the soul; it tries to contain the course of evolution through the unity of the ego and to impose its law on the world by resorting to logic. This "parasitic intellectual life" breaks the bond that originally existed between the human soul and the world of images, which was expressed in myths whose meaning we have lost. These reflections on Western culture are connected with belief in a deep-rooted dualism which is expressed, from the point of view of culture, in the opposition between West and East, but which also finds its psychological expression in the psychoanalysis of Freud. With Freud the subconscious becomes an independent life based on a fundamental desire that is repressed and can no longer appear in consciousness except in the form of images in dreams or myths—always symbols of this deep-rooted vitality of which we are unconscious.

[2] Ernest Seillière, *Le néoromantisme en Allemagne,* 3 vols., 1928–31.

last works he insisted on the objective character of ideal contents or values, such as logical norms or natural laws. Besides these values, which govern our interpretation of data, however, there are "ideal requirements," which not only are those of a temperament but also constitute an impersonal order. They are not simply a priori forms that guide our actions; what they require of us is not simply obedience but the intimate transformation of our being. For Simmel, goodness refers not to an action but to being itself. *Philosophy of Life* (1918) is the elaboration of this tendency toward mysticism. Drawn to negative theology, he seeks to understand the immortality of the soul without accepting its substantiality, and he reasons that the soul is perhaps only a functional law, which will remain the same under wholly different conditions of reality, which are its variables.[1]

Johannes Volkelt has nevertheless shown that this relativism was not a type of subjectivism (*Experience and Thinking*, 1886; *The Sources of Human Certainty*, 1900; *Certainty and Truth*, 1918). Any truth is seen only as a form of certainty, and that is the basis of criticism. But there are several orders of certainty: the certainty of pure experience, the data of consciousness, which form only a tangled skein; the certainty of the necessities of thought which are not data in the realm of experience, such as causality or legality; finally, the intuitive certainty of a transsubjective reality, grounded on the certainty of the existence of consciousnesses alien to our own, the existence of continuous, permanent things bound by laws and constituting an identical world for the same persons. There was nothing to prevent his introducing into the "subjectivistic subjectivism" still other orders of certainty; and Volkelt does in fact accept an intuitive type of certainty, under the name "philosophy of life," in metaphysical and religious matters. But is he not escaping from subjectivism at the price of arbitrariness? Immediate data do not go beyond subjectivity; as soon as we try to think, however, a transsubjective minimum is introduced—by means of a belief, to be sure—into the act of knowing. Later Volkelt tried to find more definite

---

[1] Cf. Vl. Jankélévitch, "Simmel philosophe de la vie," *Revue de Métaphysique*, IV (1922).

IV *Italian Neo-Kantianism*

In Italy, beginning around 1880, Kantianism developed as a reaction against determinism. Cantoni (1840–1906), who devoted a long work to Kant (*E. Kant,* 3 vols., 1879–84), sees Kantianism as the answer to the reduction of spiritual reality to the physical world undertaken by the evolutionists. As early as 1878, Barzelloti (1844–1917) in *The New School of Kant* had acquainted his compatriots with the significance of the neo-Kantian movement. A. Chiappelli held that Kantian criticism should be the point of departure of a new idealism and a spiritualistic monism. Thanks to philosophy, "the totality of reality becomes an ideal whole, that is, a conception subordinate to the knowing subject and to the mind." A vigorous resurgence of antinaturalism, he reasoned, would restore the classical heritage, preserve art and religion as ideal ends, and save the ethics of pure opportunism.[3]

V *The Relativism of Höffding*

Harald Höffding (1843–1931), professor at Copenhagen, defended a positivistic and critical doctrine in all his works. In his *Outline of a Psychology* (1882) he maintained that methodical presuppositions necessary for science are to be found in "soulless psychology" and in the theory of psychophysical parallelism. His *Ethics* (1887) is closely related to Hume's, but he distinguishes between a "motive principle of judgment," which is sympathy, and the objective content or value contained in the moral judgment. In *The Philosophy of Religion* (1906) he makes a clear-cut distinction between religion as an attempt to provide a complete explanation of the world and religion as an affirmation of the existence of a system of values; in the first sense, religion can only arrive at a negative result; in the second, it must be submitted to the test of criticism, which accepts only affirmations that do not conflict

[3] *Revue philosophique,* I (1909), 233.

with the modern conscience. "A philosopher must always guard against using theological expressions," he wrote. "Theological dogmas correspond to problems in philosophy"—for example, the problem of value. It is obvious, then, that Höffding is extremely reluctant to approach reality without taking critical precautions; he does not believe in intuition in metaphysics, and is one of those who believe that Bergsonism blazes the trail to a kind of artistic perception (without real value) rather than to a superior science. He finally developed a theory of relativity which he expounds in *Philosophical Relativity*. Here metaphysical oppositions are reduced to distinctions of value and perspective. For instance, in a mass of elements one can study either the elements themselves or the inner relationship which causes the whole to offer properties possessed by none of the elements when these are taken separately; this is the opposition between the two tendencies that can be designated, respectively, by the names of mechanism and vitalism, associationism and spiritualism, individualism and socialism.

VI *Spiritualism in France*

The notion of force, together with the law of the conservation of force, was the central idea from which Spencer deduced his evolutionistic determinism. But whereas Spencer held that action was the very essence of reality, Alfred Fouillée notes that force, defined as the tendency toward action, is apprehended directly as a universal characteristic of the data of consciousness. There cannot be a mind distinct from a will—an idea that is simply known and a spontaneous or reflective activity that is governed by this idea. Any idea is already a force or a tendency toward movement which is realized independently by acts unless this idea is counteracted by another idea.

Thus the notion of force makes possible an interpretation of both mind and matter. At the same time (here the aim of Fouillée's vast enterprise becomes clear), without violating the conditions imposed by positivism, it opens up the possibility of preserving the reality of spiritual values, which seemed to be hopelessly compromised by the unlawful application that Spencer had made of them. Take the problem of free will, discussed in *Liberty and Determinism* (1872). As soon as we admit that any idea is a force, we must also admit that the idea of liberty is a force. The conduct of a being who believes he is free is not the same as that of one who believes he is unfree, for the former modifies himself through the alternatives he thinks he can posit. Consequently, everything that participates in the spiritual life has the distinctive trait of reacting on itself indefinitely. *The Psychology of Ideas as Effective Causes* (1893) shows how the complete life of the spirit, particularly intellectual life, develops from consciousness as action. It is consciousness in action which, by itself, posits itself as existing, along with the other beings on which it acts or with which it interacts, and at the same time the intellectual categories (like causality) which are deduced from conditions determining the exercise of will. *The Ethics of Ideas as Effective Causes* (1908) shows the practical applications of his doctrine, the inner force of an ideal which is attractive and persuasive. Thus nature and spirit coincide in the notion of force, making it the sign of an absolute reality which is not an absolute unknowable, as Spencer insisted, but a relative unknowable, and this is enough to prove that consciousness is not an epiphenomenon.

Spiritualistic positivism, which originated with Ravaisson, is essentially an attempt to apprehend the production of spiritual activity. Many philosophical works published in France since 1880 are attempts to guide reflection toward this spiritual productivity.

In *Genius in Art* (1883), Gabriel Séailles sees the very essence of spirit in the inventive genius of the artist. Spirit is greater than consciousness, which knows only the results produced by spirit. The obscure, spontaneous operation of inspiration—manifested not only in the invention of works of art or scientific hypotheses but also in the most common acts of perception (since our perception of the world is its operation)—is spirit or life; not a confused and disordered life, however, but one tending toward harmony, intelligence, and order. The freedom of the genius is the vital law that he follows. Spirit, like the Good of the *Republic,* includes both the full warmth of love and the clearness of reason.

The union of life and spirit also has a central place in Charles Dunan's *Essays in General Philosophy* (1898) and his *Two Idealisms* (1911). "All our preferences," he wrote, "are for an experimental idealism. . . . The object of metaphysics is to conceive ourselves and the other beings of nature in their concrete reality. . . . Metaphysics is a concrete experience because it is a vital, personal experience. . . . To feel in oneself, in thought and action, the thrill of universal nature, alive and palpitating in each of the beings it creates, . . . to see without the eyes of the body or even the spirit but only through the identity of our being and the being of things, is this not as good as saying to oneself: I know everything that can be known about this point, and I know it with certainty?" Spiritual life is "unanalyzable knowledge, divine intoxication."

Paul Souriau maintains in *Rational Beauty* (1904) that beauty consists in the spiritualization of being, in expression, and in life (nothing is more opposed to spirit than inert matter); consequently this expressionistic aesthetic, which is in the tradition of Plotinus and Ravaisson, interprets art as a means of tempting us to pursue spirit.

Jules Lagneau (1851–94), who models his reflective analysis on that of his teacher, Lachelier, is also deeply indebted to the meditation of Spinoza.[4] For the other writers under discussion here, spiritualism, even if it never reaches its goal, tended toward a vitalism which discovered the reality of spirit in the obscure, spontaneous forms of life. With Lagneau we return to the idea of a spiritual method or system of analysis that rediscovers in stable products the spiritual activity that has engendered them; in this way philosophy will identify the activity of the mind in external perception. Lagneau's analysis does not stop with the finite self, the spirit-self, but moves on to the universal spirit; to investigate the individual self is futile, for "the thinking subject is not a being but

---

[4] See "Fragments," *Revue de Métaphysique,* 1898; *Écrits réunis par les soins de ses disciples,* 1924; *L'existence de Dieu,* 1923.

the totality of principles—that is, the connections that link empirical thoughts to spirit, to absolute unity." Reflection, according to Lagneau, is not an egotistical withdrawal into oneself. The reason it discovers is not simply a principle of independence but, even more important, a principle of order, unity, and sacrifice; it is the power to emerge from self. Reflection recognizes "its own insufficiency and the necessity of an absolute action originating from within." It is in this action that one reaches God immediately, for God is not an external power but an immanent power, the principle of moral goodness within us. Thus Lagneau did not limit himself to pure speculation and was, with Paul Desjardins, the founder of a union for moral action (*Union pour l'action morale*). Émile Chartier (Alain) wrote a book on his recollections of Lagneau (*Souvenirs concernant Lagneau,* 1925) and drew his inspiration from Lagneau in writing *Words of Alain (Propos d'Alain,* 1920) and numerous essays. I can only call attention to this intellectualism which asserts the rationality of truth, which sees in beauty the light of intelligence, which thinks that thought can be apprehended in a production as it is being produced—in artistic technique, for example, better than in any speculation.

VII *Léon Brunschvicg*

The spiritualistic theories of the philosophers discussed above were more or less alien to the scientific ferment of the period. Léon Brunschvicg, beginning with his first work on *The Modality of Judgment* (1894), subscribed to the reflective method of Lagneau and Lachelier. "The mind no longer gives itself an object that is stable, which stands motionless before it," he wrote (p. 4). "It seeks to apprehend itself in its own movement or activity, to seize the vital act of production, not the product, which only an ulterior process of abstraction can posit separately," But it is mainly in the sciences as they have developed since the Greeks that he seeks, in a positive manner, to discover this spiritual activity. In *Stages in Mathematical Philosophy* (1913), he shows that the reflections of mathematicians and philosophers concerning mathematical study contain two distinct conceptions of intelligence. "According to one of them, an idea is a concept in the Aristotelian and Scholastic sense; the essential role of the mind is to seize the most general terms of discourse, even at the risk of exhausting itself in the effort to fit them into an initial definition. The second is the intellectualistic doctrine of the Platonists and Cartesians, in which an idea is an action of the mind as it becomes a relation and expresses the very fact of perceiving—τὸ *intelligere*" (p. 37). On one hand an ideal of logical deduction in which the intellectual operation could be replaced by a material mechanism on the order of the calculating machine; on the other, an activity which does not originate in ready-made ideas but which constitutes "the idea itself by virtue of an inherent truth," exemplified in the development of the idea of number, produced in the very operations made possible by it. In *Human Experience and Physical Causality* (1921) Brunschvicg shows the sterility, in the discovery of laws, of the mechanism of induction as it was understood by Mill, with its ready-made frames and passive registry of facts; by contrast, the transformation of pure physics into geometry in the theory of relativity shows the action of the mind as it invents, through its own resources, concepts for the interpretation of nature. But in a much more general way Brunschvicg shows the functioning of this spiritual activity in *The Progress of Consciousness in Western Philosophy* (1927). This is the history of the struggle, beginning with Socrates and continuing through the centuries, between spiritual activity and a philosophy which considers concepts as fixed things, or between spiritual activity and a vitalism which confuses spirit with vital activity. Moral consciousness and aesthetic consciousness are identical with the intellectual consciousness that has produced science; they are linked to a humanism that considers spirit not as a transcendent reality in which all science is eternally realized but as a productive activity in man. Reflective analysis, interpreted in this way, is far removed from what we generally associate with inner experience. At the beginning of *Human Experience* Brunschvicg calls attention to the illusion of Maine de Biran, who thought that he could apprehend causality by simply retiring into himself. In reality, knowledge of self is knowledge of the spirit in the vast multiplicity of its acts, from the inventive activity of *homo faber* to science and morality. That is the theme of the book entitled *Knowledge of Self* (1931). In short, Brunschvicg's spiritualism, which identifies spirit with intellect, marks a decisive break with the vitalistic theories of Ravaisson and Lachelier.

VIII   *André Lalande and Rationalism*

Spencer's evolutionism, widely prevalent around 1890, was one of the doctrines most opposed to the intention of spiritualism, since it was presented, as a necessary result of the law of evolution, a mechanization of society of which the very perfection made all spiritual activity useless or impossible. André Lalande began by examining the validity of this law of evolution in *The Idea of Dissolution Contrasted with That of Evolution in the Method of the Physical and Moral Sciences* (*L'idée de dissolution opposée à celle de l'évolution dans la méthode des sciences physiques et morales,* 1899; 2d edition, under the title *Les illusions évolutionnistes,* 1930). Evolution is passage from homogeneity to heterogeneity, from the undifferentiated to the differentiated. "The Carnot-Clausius law shows that transformations of energy tend always toward the realization of a more complete homogeneity. Even more important, spiritual activity in all its forms—in sciences, ethics, and art— accounts for progress in assimilation, which is opposed to the disordered variations of life. Positive science assimilates minds (this is its objectivity) and things (this is what Émile Meyerson interpreted as an explanation); it assimilates things to the mind, making them intelligible. As civilization advances, the diversity of morals and legislation disappears. Art itself, which would seem to favor the theory of divergence between individualities, exists only by virtue of a spiritual communion which gradually embraces humanity as a whole. That assimilation is particularly useful in indicating the true direction of social development is proved by many facts: egalitarian tendencies, dissolution of castes and classes, regression of the family as an independent social unit, increasing equality, both legal and moral, of men and women, and finally progress in international relations. Nor should assimilation be treated as a kind of Spencerian fatum of evolution in reverse; instead, it is the principle of voluntary activity and the unit of measure of rational values. Far from diminishing and utterly destroying the individual, it fortifies the essential elements of individuality, countering the individualistic anarchism of Stirner, perhaps, but adhering to individualism, which defends the rights common to all rational beings against the encroachments of groups. *Theories of Induction and Experimentation* (1929) also shows that the fundamental tendency of spirit toward universality is the true guarantee of induction. These books conclude with an invitation to act in the direction of a spiritual assimilation. *Technical and Critical Vocabulary of Philosophy* (1926), a collection of articles drafted by André Lalande and submitted to the members of the Philosophical Society, is another attempt to achieve unity in intellectual matters.

It was possible, at the time of Mill, to imagine a conflict between the positive sciences and rationalism, between a well-founded empiricism and an arbitrary a priori. All of Edmond Goblot's works (*Essay on the Classification of the Sciences,* 1898; *Treatise on Logic,* 1918; *The System of the Sciences,* 1922; *The Logic of Value Judgments,* 1927) are intended to show that progress in science has caused the positive reality of experience to be suffused with rationality. Sciences which now are intelligible and deductive—the mathematical sciences, for example—reached this state only after accumulating empirical rules and inductive truths; moreover, that empirical science tends to become intelligible science is a general law. The assimilation of reality by intelligence is the essence of science, and it is also the essence of logic. That is why the syllogism, which simply marks time, does not illustrate true reasoning; deduction is rather a constructive operation which enables us to pass from the simple to the complex, as in any mathematical demonstration. As defined by Sigwart, logic is a part of psychology that studies spirit in so far as it acts only through intelligence, and without recourse to feeling, which if introduced, causes the spirit to interpret things as good or bad—that is, as being consistent or inconsistent with its ends—and to place value judgments on them. These value judgments in turn can be investigated by logic, and to them Goblot has devoted his most recent work, *Barrier and Level* (1925). Censurable, in this book, are paralogisms such as the one which tries to make the value of spiritual activity depend on the metaphysical affirmation of a substantial soul distinct from the body (*Logic of Value Judgments,* sec. 71).

The practical and moral side of rationalism is illuminated in Paul Lapie's *The Logic of the Will* (1902). According to him, voluntary acts are determined by judgments concerning ends and means. Every action implies a "volitional argument," which states the end in the major premise, the middle term in the minor premise, and the act in the conclusion. Defects of will are explained by the doubts of a mind not sufficiently enlightened concerning ends and means, or by positive mistakes. It follows that ethics is a science which ultimately must allow us to measure the moral worth of men and classify them accordingly.

In *The Moral Problem and Contemporary Thought* (1909; 2d edition, 1921) D. Parodi defends rationalism in ethics, showing that characteristics universally identified with moral activity are characteristics of rational activity. To begin with, an action is moral only if the impulse that produces it is accepted and approved "by something that belongs to a different order and can be called either conscience or reason." It is moral only if we are sure, while accomplishing it, that an impartial spectator would not judge it differently, and this impersonality is a characteristic of reason. A heroic sacrifice, which might seem to transcend reason, nevertheless is moral only if it tends toward an end found by reason to be universal and obligatory. Finally, moral conduct necessitates a sincere examination of our motives, and this examination is not possible in the absence of the eminently rational act of abstraction (pp. 288 ff.). *In Search of a Philosophy* (1935) defines a spiritualistic rationalism which makes aspiration after ideas the very heart of nature and humanity, and which posits as the ideal reason for this aspiration a God who is above all else the locus of ideas. *Human Conduct and Ideal Values* (1939) shows the role of this aspiration in the pursuit of the True, the Beautiful, and the Good.

Inspired by his reflections on Hamelin's theories, René Le Senne —who is also the author of an *Introduction to Philosophy* (1925; 2d edition, 1939)—developed a moral rationalism in which the main role is assigned to the Hamelinian notion of reason, considered as a synthetic function. In *Duty* and *Falsehood and Character* he shows that contradiction is at the root of moral life. The ego can answer with skepticism, but moral activity consists in answering with courage, which "implies that any eventual future should not contain an irreducible nucleus, before which the spirit could only feel ashamed." Active thought begins by accepting as an axiom the necessity of reducing contradictions to identity, and this reduction is the goal or ideal on which moral consciousness should confer a concrete content.[5]

IX *Frédéric Rauh*

The doctrine of Frédéric Rauh (1861–1909) provides a completely different kind of solution to the antithesis of science and conscience. In his works *On Method in the Psychology of Feelings* (1889) and *Moral Experience* (1903) he shows that there is no difference between the way in which moral truths and scientific truths are established and obtain our assent; in their nature and in the attitude that they require, moral certainty and scientific certainty are not different. In the sciences, in fact, there is no proof other than contact between ideas and experience, and this proof is wholly relative, since experience itself can always increase. In ethics, the situation seems to be different, for our moral conscience provides us with general principles endowed with an absolute, definite character, and

[5] Cf. also his *Traité de morale générale* (1942), particularly pp. 706–07.

their application to particular cases is a simple question of logic. But appearances are deceptive, and moral realities are something else entirely. We are forever finding ourselves in new, unexpected situations created by all the changes, individual and social, that make each moment different from all others. Generalities are of little use to us; we must free ourselves from all theories, assume the impersonal attitude of the scientist in each situation, and put relevant ideas to the critical test by comparing them with reality and with other ideas. "To search for certainty in an immediate adaptation to reality instead of deducing it from abstract ideologies, to utilize everything that passes for the principle of a belief as a means of testing this belief, to make eternal or objective truths serve the living ideal instead of trying to find rules for action in these truths—this would be a revolution, a renaissance for men stunted or misled by academic doctrines" (p. 235).[6]

[6] Cf. Léon Brunschvicg, "L'expérience morale chez Rauh," *Revue Philosophique,* I (1928).

BIBLIOGRAPHY

V

Høffding, Harald. *Harald Høffding in Memoriam,* ed. Kalle Sandelin. Copenhagen, 1932. Excellent bibliography.

VII

Texts

Brunschvicg, Léon. *Les Âges de l'intelligence.* Paris, 1934.
―――. *Écrits philosophiques.* 3 vols. Paris, 1951, 1954, 1958.
―――. *Introduction à la vie de l'esprit.* Paris, 1920.
―――. *La Raison et la religion.* Paris, 1939.
―――. *Spinoza et ses contemporains.* Paris, 1923.

Studies

Cochet, M. A. *Commentaire sur la conversion spirituelle dans la philosophie de Léon Brunschvicg.* Brussels, 1937.
Deschoux, Marcel. *La Philosophie de Léon Brunschvicg.* Paris, 1949.
Messaut, J. *La Philosophie de Léon Brunschvicg.* Paris, 1938.

VIII

Texts

Lelande, André. *L'idée directrice de la dissolution opposée à celle de l'évolution.* Paris, 1899.
―――. *Les Illusions évolutionnistes.* Paris, 1930.
―――. *Quid de Mathematica vel Rationali vel Naturali Senserit Baconus Verulamius.* Paris, 1899.
―――. *Lectures sur la philosophie des sciences.* Paris, 1893 and 1907.
―――. *Précis raisonné de morale pratique.* Paris, 1907.
―――. *Les Théories de l'induction et de l'expérimentation.* Paris, 1929.
―――. *La Raison et les normes.* Paris, 1948.
―――. *Vocabulaire technique et critique de la philosophie.* 8th ed. Paris, 1962.

Studies

Lavelle, L. *La Philosophie française entre les deux guerres.* Paris, 1942.
Smith, Colin, *Contemporary French Philosophy.* London, 1964.

196

REALISM

1 English Realism

Seeking to define idealism in the most general terms, Wildon Carr (1857–1931) states that it is grounded on the principle that knowledge is not an external relation (*A Theory of Monads: Outlines of the Philosophy of the Principle of Relativity*, London, 1922). This is a form of the general principle of relativity. It is futile to try to apprehend physical realities independently of the conditions of experience. With respect to this principle, critical idealism, also represented in England by M. G. F. Stout (cf. *Mind and Matter*, 1931, p. 308–9) agrees with Hegelian idealism and pragmatism.

The differences between pragmatism and Anglo-American Hegelianism, moreover, amount to nothing more than a friendly quarrel which does not rule out a deep-seated community of ideas. An obvious preference for the concrete, the non-truth of the abstract, the tendency toward self-realization in things—here is something Hegelian as well as pragmatic, which refers not merely to scientific experience in its true sense but to a kind of immediate apprehension of a vital inner development. Man, according to Dickinson, is an unfinished creature, full of possibilities, in the process of creating himself. He favors anything real that is divine; he resists anything real that is diabolical.[1] We shall see, however, that real things are inimical to both the divine and the diabolical.

The strictly philosophical debate between Hegelian idealists and

[1] See Wahl, *Les philosophies pluralistes*, p. 171.

197

pragmatists could be reduced to this question: "Are relations internal or external?" If they are internal—that is, if a term cannot be apprehended in itself, independently of its relations with others —the universe forms a unique, immutable, eternal whole; that is the view supported by the absolutists. If they are external, the universe is no more than the summation of independent parts; that is the theory of pragmatistic pluralism. A relation is external when the entrance of a term into this relation does not alter the nature of this term—for example, the relation *near, separated from,* or *similar to.* Among the pragmatists, one relation is treated (implicitly) as an exception to this rule—the cognitive relation or the relation between subject and object—since the very essence of their doctrine is that knowledge is a modifying action of the object. Neorealism can be defined as the doctrine which rigorously accepts the doctrine of external relations and extends it to the cognitive relation, returning in this way to a doctrine of common sense according to which the fact of being known in no way alters the object known. According to this theory, the object of knowledge can have a non-mental nature; it is not a state of consciousness; and we must not suppose that the knowing subject and the object have a common nature, or that they are linked by anything like an idea or an intermediate mental state, for this takes us back to the doctrine of immediate perception.

But from the exclusive existence of external relations, several neorealists draw other consequences, which are closely linked to pragmatic views. The first is that an assertion about an object can be true in itself apart from every assertion having to do with relations between this object and other objects; this is in a sense a restoration, against Hegelianism, of an atomistic philosophy grounded on the principle that the existence of the complex depends on the existence of the simple. The second is a kind of Platonism, based on the principle that relations are independent of terms and, by virtue of the exteriority of the cognitive relation, exist in themselves, independently of the fact of being known, as essences.[2]

---

[2] Concerning the connection between this realism and logistic, cf. Brunschvicg, *Les Étapes de la philosophie mathématique,* pp. 370–411; Couturat, in *L'Infini mathématique* (1896), supported a realism of the same kind.

On the whole, these are the ideas developed by Moore in *Principia ethica* (1903) and "The Nature of Judgment" (*Mind,* 1901), and by Russell in *Principles of Mathematics* (1903). In ethics, Moore's intention is to show that goodness is a final entity, existing objectively and capable of being perceived but not analyzed. The same is true of truth, which is an undefinable property of certain judgments. The impossibility of defining truth is the main distinction between neorealism and pragmatism, because realism treats knowledge as an immediate presence of objects to intuition. Consequently the truth of a judgment does not depend on its correspondence to reality; to say that a judgment is true is to say that a certain connection between concepts appears among existents, and this connection cannot be defined but must be recognized immediately. But that also implies that reality is composed of concepts related to each other. The world of realism is therefore a world of entities which are logical but do not constitute a systematic unity.

"Logic," says Russell, "has become the great liberator," * and this statement might well serve as an epigraph to his work. He rejects, not without distaste, the idea of making philosophy serve human interests. Philosophy requires a detached mind which is satisfied only by logical demonstration. Logic "liberates" us in the sense that it studies the relations that pertain to all possible worlds: free logical constructions between which experience is to decide. A characteristic example of Russell's approach is his theory of the perception of external objects. Beginning with the self-evident data of experience, which are not things but forever changing *qualia,* he proposes to construct, using the laws of logic, the notion of permanent objects. It is commonly believed that objects exist in a common space and that the *qualia* are the appearances or aspects which the objects present from my point of view and which must change with my point of view. For Russell, however, these appearances themselves constitute reality; they are not in a common space but

---

* Translator's note.—Asked to identify this quotation, Lord Russell replied that he had no recollection of making the statement attributed to him.

constitute my private world in my private space. An object is a purely logical construction which involves no other entities but *qualia* and no inference concerning any reality whatsoever. It is the complete system of all possible appearances, and Russell attempts to demonstrate that the system has precisely the properties that common sense attributes to objects. Common space is constructed logically, beginning with the private spaces of individual observers. Thus we see how Russell manages to substitute logical constructions for spontaneous beliefs, and this may well explain his attraction to communism, a logical reconstruction of society beginning with pure private interests and without recourse to a common instinct (cf. also *Principia mathematica* [with Whitehead], 1910–13; *Scientific Method in Philosophy*, 1914; *An Analysis of Mind*, 1921; *The Problems of Philosophy*, 1912).

If realism is interpreted in its strict sense, everything pertaining to objects must be eliminated from the mind; an object is always a non-mental reality. Samuel Alexander (*Space, Time, and Deity*, 1920), a professor at Manchester University, pursued this thought to the limit and reduced mental life to pure acts of will, everything knowable being on the side of objects. Yet Alexander acknowledges, alongside contemplative knowledge which is "awareness" of objects, a kind of direct possession of reality in which the duality of subject and object disappears, which he calls "enjoying." It follows that memory cannot be the contemplation of an event in the past, which would mean introducing an object into the mind; it consists in reliving an experience in the past. Alexander assumes that the essential datum of this inner experience is the direction of mental activity—a direction which changes with the content of the object, like a beam of light aimed at the thing to be known.

Alexander's realism, in direct contrast to Russell's, tends like pragmatism and absolutism toward a vision of the universe which nevertheless, in somewhat the same way as neorealism, is divested of emotion and, in a manner of speaking, without interiority. He sees the composite reality of Space-Time as the matrix of all things and deduces every possible category from its determinations: existence, the occupation of a portion of space-time; substance, space limited by a contour where events succeed each other; things, constituted by a combination of movements; relations the spatio-temporal connections of things; causality, the transition from one continuous event to another. All of these categories, which to a Kantian idealist seem to imply the act of a mind that unifies the diversity of space and time, are for him objective determinations. Furthermore, in describing the mind, he also goes as far as possible in identifying it with the nervous system which is but a determination of space-time; to him the direction of mental activity referred to above is perhaps merely the direction of the nervous process, which is arrested only by the radically new quality of awareness. In a general way, the order of qualities seems irreducible to space-time, since they introduce the idea of levels of reality and, consequently, of progress. The universe has, not a God, but a divinity that is merely the tendency to produce progressively higher forms, each supported by a lower form just as the mind is supported by the body.[3]

Also different from Alexander's realism is the realism of Shadworth H. Hodgson (*The Metaphysics of Experience*, 4 vols., 1898) and R. Adamson (*The Development of Modern Philosophy*, 2 vols., 1903). According to Hodgson, consciousness is not an activity and therefore is incapable, by itself, of producing representations of the external world; these representations find the necessary conditions of their existence only in matter. Adamson shows, against Kant, that self-consciousness is a product of spiritual evolution and therefore can provide no support whatsoever for the reality of objects. Also worth noting is F. E. Moore's article, "The Refutation of Idealism" (*Mind*, 1903); like Alexander, he assumes a distinction between the act of representing, which alone belongs to consciousness, and the thing represented. If the knowable is wholly on the side of objects, it follows that consciousness is not knowable. We have just seen how Alexander avoided the difficulty. The American neorealists chose a wholly different solution. They adopted the

[3] Cf. Philippe Devaux, *Le système d'Alexander*, 1929.

position of J. B. Watson ("Psychology as the Behaviorist Views It," *Psychological Review*, 1912), the psychologist who began by studying animals and assumed that if there is a psychological science, it can only be a science of corporal attitudes, comportment or behavior. Such was the origin of *behaviorism,* a psychology not only without a soul but also without consciousness, just as their metaphysics is without an epistemology.[4] The neorealistic movement gained strength with the publication of *The New Realism* (1912), a collaborative work by six different writers. One of them, R. B. Perry (*Present Philosophical Tendencies,* 1912; *The Present Conflict of Ideals,* 1918), once a disciple of James, demonstrates the uselessness of consciousness in this way: only the human organism and its environment exist; the same objects that are physical facts can become conscious facts, subject only to the condition that they have a particular connection with the body which reacts; a psychic fact is simply a particular aspect of a physical fact.

Thus neorealism in general, particularly with Russell and his American disciples, stands in direct contrast to romanticism, the philosophy of life and continuity. Even in Russell, however, we find a dualism between the laws of logic and the data of experience. This dualism becomes more pronounced with Marvin (*A First Book in Metaphysics,* 1912) and leads to a kind of irrationalism which treats a singular experience as a datum which thwarts all attempts to place it under any assignable number of laws whatsoever, with the result that any particular event is a final logical term. Is not this unanalyzable kind of reality opposed in many respects, as Jean Wahl has observed, to the intellectualistic analysis of neorealism?[5]

America witnessed the birth of doctrines related to neorealism because of their realistic elements, but different because of the role assigned to mind. George Santayana (see *Three Proofs of Realism,* 1920; *The Life of Reason,* 1905–06) holds that mechanism is the

[4] Concerning this movement in psychology, see A. Tilquin, *Le Behaviorisme, Origine et développement de la psychologie de réaction en Amérique,* 1942; concerning its relations with neorealism, pp. 98 ff.

[5] *Les philosophies pluralistes,* p. 231.

only rational explanation of things, matter the sole causal agent, and consciousness a simple relation of everything occurring in an organism, an echo of whatever concerns the body. By contrast, he treats consciousness as the sole source of values, and insists that reason has the task not only of providing a mechanistic explanation of things but also of establishing a set of ideal values, in which the demands of life are adjusted to the ideal, and the ideal to natural conditions. The same sense of spiritual values is found in the wholly different doctrine of Alfred North Whitehead (*The Concept of Nature*, 1920; *Science and the Modern World*, 1925, *Process and Reality*, 1929). In his view, any satisfactory cosmology is excluded by the separation between perception and emotion, between these psychological facts and efficient causality, and finally between efficient causality and intelligent design. Still, this separation had been felt in almost every aspect of European philosophy since Descartes, who first separated thinking substance from extended substance; and since each substance requires only itself in order to exist, incoherence becomes a virtue. This method made it possible for certain principles to be used as points of departure for deduction, wrongly considered to be the method of philosophy; a God was posited as the eminent reality from which all things proceed. Whitehead, influenced by the wisdom of India and China, always disagrees with this view. He tries to grasp a reality in the making instead of using a ready-made reality as a point of departure for deduction. He adopts the principle that consciousness presupposes experience and not the reverse; an actual entity, in so far as it is subjective, is nothing except what the universe is for it, including its own reactions. Whitehead, not unlike Bergson is this respect, holds that an organism is wholly oriented toward the constitution of this subject, choosing from the universe the elements to be integrated in it. Whitehead starts from the ideas expounded by William James, in 1904, in his article "Does Consciousness Exist?" Physical things are not substantially different from mental things; between them there is only the distinction between the public and the private. There is in the creative process a kind of rhythm: from a "public" universe composed of a multiplicity of things, the process jumps to private individuality, which is the main point, the ideal center, the goal toward which things move; then, from the private individual, it jumps to the "publicity of the objectified individual" who plays his role in the universe as an efficient cause. According to White-head, universal progress is like an idealized description of the reaction of an organism to its environment; the organism is enriched through interaction with the environment and returns what it has received. This doctrine is indeed a form of realism, though certainly not in the sense attributed to the word by Whitehead, who identifies realism with materialism, but in the sense that it seeks to reach the things beneath the conceptual constructions interposed between them and the mind.[6]

In short, like every preceding English doctrine since Bradley, it is a description of the universe. These doctrines are all solutions to the "riddle of the sphinx" which rely, not on a critical standard which seeks in the knowable universe the expression of the very conditions of our knowledge and in this way leads to phenomenalism, but on the boldness of a vision which scorns epistemology and goes directly to things.

II Realism in Germany: Husserl and Rehmke

Is logic independent of psychology? The dispute over this question continues even today to have a profound influence on the development of German philosophy. "Psychologists" are generally opposed to Kantianism, and the outflanking movement executed by antipsychologists shows that their opposition to it is even more implacable.

We have already seen the role ascribed to psychology by the school of Fries. Similarly, in *Psychology and the Theory of Knowledge* (1891) Carl Stumpf attributes the defects of Kantianism to separation of the theory of knowledge and the theory of psychology.

[6] Cf. J. Wahl, "La doctrine spéculative de Whitehead," *Revue philosophique,* V (1931).

If the theory of knowledge has the special task of determining the most universal knowledge, the question of discovering how these universal truths are possible, according to Stumpf, is the province of psychology.

Noteworthy among psychologically oriented logicians is Sigwart. In *Logic* (1873–78) Sigwart insists that logic is restricted to the study of certain acts of thought but that it differs from psychology, first by intention since it tries to discover the conditions of true thought and universal judgments, then by content since it considers only the sphere of thought in which there can be truth or error of judgment. But his discussion concerning the nature of negative judgments clearly indicates the place which he assigns in logic to mental attitudes. A negative judgment, according to him, is neither original nor independent like a positive judgment. It has meaning only in relation to an unsuccessful attempt at a positive affirmation, and its subjective character is indicated particularly by the fact that what is to be denied concerning a subject cannot be stated exhaustively. If Aristotle was able to oppose affirmation to negation as the union of predicate and subject to their separation, the reason is that he implicitly accepted the thesis of Platonic ideas, considering the predicate as an independent being. Similarly, in *The Function of Judgment* (1893) and *Critical Idealism and Pure Logic* (1905) Wilhelm Jerusalem also sees logic as nothing but a theory of true thought, and it is an act of thought that he studies judgment when he shows that its traditional forms do not correspond to the act actually effected. This act consists essentially in separating, in a single representation, a "center of force," which is the subject from an event that expresses it (for instance: the rose smells). In *Logic* (1892) Benno Erdmann, dealing with the relations between logic and psychology, considers thought expressed by language to be the object of logic and concludes that logic is part of the subject matter of psychology. Logic is not a part of psychology, however, for it is a formal, normative science. Antipsychologists interpreted the independence of logic in a totally different sense.

The antipsychologists are indebted to Franz Brentano (1838–

1917), a Catholic theologian who became professor at Würzburg. He makes a rigid distinction between the logical validity of a thought and its psychological genesis. He separates from logic a psychognosis, which seeks to discover the ultimate psychic elements of which all psychic phenomena are composed, making possible a universal characteristic, such as that envisioned by Leibniz, instructing us in the laws governing the birth and disappearance of phenomena.[7] The ideas of Alexius Meinong (1853–1920) are developed along the same lines. In *Concerning Objects of Higher Classification* (1899) he insists that any object (for example a round square) can be the object of scientific knowledge even if it does not exist and even if it is not possible. Thus his object theory (*Gegenstandtheorie*) conceives the object free of existence (*daseinsfrei*) in its greatest generality, independently of the fact that it is or is not apprehended by us, or that it has or does not have a value for us. The object itself contains objects of a higher order (such as relations), which imply objects of a lower order (*relata*).

Edmund Husserl, professor at Göttingen, then Freiburg, and a pupil of Franz Brentano, began by writing a *Philosophy of Arithmetic* (1891), of which only the first volume appeared. Here he shows that the invention of numerical symbols and their manipulation are destined to compensate for a defect in the intuition of the human mind. There was nothing in this work to cause us to anticipate his *Logical Investigations* (1900).[8] The first volume (*Prolegomena to Pure Logic*) contains, in addition to a lengthy critique of psychologism, the delimitation of the sphere of logic; the second (*Investigations of Phenomenology and Theory of Knowledge*) contains only preliminary works for constructing a system of pure logic.

The critique of psychologism rests on the opposition between psychological laws, which are empirical, vague, limited to prob-

---

[7] Cf. O. Kraus's Introduction to Brentano's edition of *Psychologie vom empirischen Standpunkt* (Philosoph. Bibliothek), 1924, pp. xvii–xciii.

[8] *Logische Untersuchungen*, 1900 (2d edition, 1913–21). Vol. I: *Prolegomena zur reinen Logik;* Vol. II: *Untersuchungen zur Phänomenologie und Theorie der Erkenntnis.*

ability and verifications of fact, and logical laws, which are precise, certain, and normative. Husserl never ceased to reflect on this opposition, which remained the center of his work. *Formal and Transcendental Logic* (1929) indicates the final state of his thinking on this point. It is not easy, he reasons, for us to separate logical forms from the psychological events with which they are intimately fused (p. 137). Concept, judgment, and reasoning are said to be psychological events, and logic is a branch of psychology. But the roots of psychologism are in sensualistic naturalism, in the "anti-Platonism" that originated in Locke and Hume. The only immediate data are ascribed to sensible impressions, and the only thing left to explain logical forms is a causal connection governed by psychological laws—for example, habitual association. The implication is that sensible reality is the only datum and that the ideal or unreal cannot be given. But what constitutes an independent object (*Gegenstand*)? Here the criterion of truth is numerical identity with respect to the multiple appearances of the object to consciousness (p. 138), and this numerical identity can be attributed, for example, to the whole set of logical relations which demonstrate the Pythagorean theory as well as to a sensible thing. Husserl's thought, directed against Kant as much as against the empiricists, is that the notion of an object, reduced in this way to its distinctive characteristic, covers a much larger field than mere sensible objectivity.

Here Husserl makes use of the notion of intentionality, developed earlier by Brentano. What is the subjective and distinctively physical characteristic in knowledge? It is its direction toward or application to an object. It is what Brentano, returning to the vocabulary of the Scholastics, calls *intention*: everything toward which intention is directed is an object (*Gegenstand*). What leads to error in this matter is the false, narrow idea formulated concerning evidence; it is accepted as a criterion of truth which provides us with absolute assurance against error; in fact, it designates "the general form of intentionality or awareness of something, in which the conscious object is conscious, in such a way that it is apprehended by itself and seen by itself." There are as many kinds of evidence—which is another way of saying experience—as there are kinds of objects; for example, an external experience is one specific kind of evidence because it is the only way in which the objects of nature are possessed by themselves; and there is also the experience or evidence of ideal or unreal objects, each of which remains numerically identical no matter how often it is experienced. The transcendence of an object is merely this identity. The philosophy of Mach or Vaihinger, for whom this identity is only a fiction, is simply a form of psychologism, all the more absurd in so far as it fails to see that these "fictions" have their own evidence.

This antipsychologism obviously represents an extreme attempt to bring philosophical thought well within the range of Hume and criticism. Though related to naïve realism, it differs radically by virtue of its theory of the objectivity of the unreal.

Pure logic, as delimited and defined by Husserl, differs significantly from formal logic in the traditional sense. Husserl also calls it a doctrine of science (*Wissenschaftslehre*), a theory of theories, finally *Mathesis universalis*. Its aim is to determine the essence that is found in every theoretical science. Its necessity, according to an observation which he had already recorded in *Philosophy of Arithmetic* and which might have been the moving force behind all of Husserl's philosophical speculation, is traceable to a deficiency in the mind, capable only in rare instances of arriving at immediate knowledge of facts and obliged therefore to resort to the circuit of proof. Pure logic studies every element that enters into a proof: the disjunctive, conjunctive, or hypothetical linking of certain propositions to produce new propositions; categories that describe an object—objectivity, unity, plurality, number, relations; investigation of laws based on these categories, such as syllogistic reasoning; theory of numbers. Finally it arrives at theories, such as the mathematical theory of groups. Roughly, then, Husserl's doctrine embraces, along with traditional logic, the field of mathematical principles, interpreted in the spirit of Leibnizianism.

But before approaching the construction of this logic, Husserl considers it vital to define what he calls phenomenology. This word, in the traditional vocabulary, designates the preliminary part of philosophy, which, before studying reality itself, investigates the way in which reality is manifested in consciousness. Hegel's "phenomenology of the spirit" contains the steps through which man passes in becoming aware of the spirits. In Husserl's *Logical Investigations* phenomenology is the pure psychological description (without any attempt to explain or account for their origin) of the acts of consciousness through which we reach logical objects, expressed by significative words. What is expression? What is signification? These are phenomenological questions. Genetic psychology resolves these questions by resorting to associations; for Husserl, expression is an irreducible quality of a word, and this explains how one thinks something by means of words. Signification or meaning, far from depending on arbitrary, variable associations, is absolutely fixed—for example, the meaning of the number one; consequently it is a true object. It is in fact the object of pure logic, whose species and relations it studies. For it, a "universal signification" (*animal, red*) exists by the same token as an individual signification (*Caesar*).

Another question of phenomenology as defined by Husserl is this: what is the act of thinking (*Denken*)? We have seen that thought is an intentional act, a direction to a meaningful object, but if this object is the same, "intention" can be different. It can be conceived by pure thought, represented, predicated—these are different "qualities" of intention. Furthermore, if only pure thought is involved, an identical object can be a whole composed of different thoughts; for example, the same object can be interpreted as equiangular or equilateral. A distinction must be made between thought and knowledge, which Husserl describes as accomplishment (*Erfüllung*) of intention. Knowledge can be perfect when the object to which thought tends—for instance, number—is itself in the consciousness; it is imperfect in external perception, in which an object is apprehended only from a certain perspective.

Phenomenology, interpreted in this way, presents one of the

characteristic traits of mathematicians who are also philosophers—
among them Descartes—a kind of delineation resulting in the accumulation of principles, treated as ideal data. The mathematician
never tries to unite principles but has as his prime concern the
tabulation of all the principles which are necessary and sufficient
for deduction. But Husserl never wrote the logic for which these
investigations were supposed to be the preliminary. In *Ideas:
General Introduction to Pure Phenomenology* (1913), for instance,
he interprets phenomenology as the fundamental philosophical
science which should place philosophy on an equal footing with
exact sciences like mathematics.[9] This does not mean that it should
take the form of deduction starting from a unique principle, as
it might have done during the seventeenth or eighteenth centuries,
but that it should investigate its principles mathematically—as ideal
terms which are constant, juxtaposed, and independent of the flow
of experience—without concerning itself with their genesis. Phenomenology, also called *science of essence* or *eidetic science,* is intended to provide the means of discovering these terms. Its principle
is simply to take the things that present themselves originally to
intuition just as they are given. The most naïve and habitual
intuition of the world, however, provides us with a flow of events
intermingled with constant terms which alternately appear and disappear but remain immutable: blue, red, sounds, the act of judging,
etc. This involves nothing like general or abstract ideas, formed
by combination and union, but immutable essences similar to Platonic ideas, which are known through a particular intuition, the
intuition of essences (*Wesensschau*). This intuition is a priori
and independent of experience, but it can be separated from experience only by a phenomenological analysis, which in Husserl's
thought almost takes the place of the Platonic dialectic. Its essential
procedure is *expulsion* (*Ausschaltung*) and *putting in brackets.* A

---

[9] Book I of Husserl's *Ideen zu einer reinen Phänomenologie und phänomenologi-
schen Philosophie* was published in the first volume of the *Jahrbuch für Philosophie
und phänomenologische Forschung* (Halle, 1913); English translation by W. R. Boyce
Gibson, 1952. Books II and III were published posthumously in *Husserliana,* edited
by H. L. van Breda, 1950–52.

typical example is given by the essence of thought or intentionality that is obtained by excluding objects from knowledge and preserving only the direction to objects, but what is excluded and "put in brackets" can in turn be analyzed phenomenologically by an exclusion in the opposite direction. It is clear that the data serving as the starting point for this analysis are concrete but not necessarily real data; the concrete fiction allows us to identify the same essences that reality identifies. Philosophy (and it is in this way that Husserl claims to relate his thought to Descartes' in *Cartesian Meditations*) should "put in brackets" temporarily everything given—not only physical realities but also mathematical essences—in order to arrive at the intuition of the essence of consciousness (proceeding by signs, images, or pure thought, etc.).[10]

Thus *Ideas* is a preface to a philosophy which has not yet been written. In his last book, *Formal and Transcendental Logic* (1929), Husserl returns to the problem of the delimitation of logic, investigated earlier in *Logical Investigations*. But here he has a wholly new preoccupation: reaffirming the rights of formal ontology proscribed by Kantianism. This is the substance of his demonstration: both traditional mathematical analysis and modern mathematics, which introduces the notions of set, permutation, and combination, relate to an object in general or to an entity in general; they teach us every imaginable form of deduction (groups, combinations, series, whole and part), which allows us to discover ever new properties; consequently mathematics is a formal ontology. In contrast, Aristotle's logic seems to be a science of demonstration which has as its sole theme judgments involving subjects and predicates; it is not a theory of objects but a simple theory of propositions. To be sure, we can treat formal logic as an algebraic calculation and, like Boole, make arithmetical calculation a particular case of logical calculation; that does not prevent logic from remaining the theory of propositions or predications concerning things. In Husserl's opinion, this opposition should vanish, for the forms of every

---

[10] Cf. E. Lévinas, "Sur les Ideen de Husserl," *Revue philosophique*, III (1929); G. Berger, *Le Cogito dans la pensée de Husserl*, 1941.

object, connection, relation, or set appear in the forms of a judgment. For example, the operation through which a "plural judgment" (one which has a plural subject) is transformed into a judgment in which the predicate is affirmed of a collection, introduces the same notions of objects as mathematics. It follows that formal logic, like mathematics, is a theory of objects; against Kant, Husserl maintains that formal logic is already transcendental and therefore, like transcendental logic, requires a critique based on phenomenological analysis of subjective conditions relating to knowledge of logical essences.

Husserl is first of all a mathematician and a logician, but the spirit of his doctrine can penetrate and has in fact penetrated every domain of philosophical thought. Psychology, ethics, philosophy of religion—every discipline in which the ideas of genesis, slow formation, and reduction of the complex to the simple predominated throughout most of the nineteenth century—seemed to be exceptionally unfavorable to the doctrine. Still, it was in this domain that Max Scheler (1874–1928), professor at Cologne, drawing his inspiration from phenomenology, made original contributions. Moral and religious values in particular seem to depend more especially on feelings or the course of history. They depend at best on ways of judging which can be humanly necessary but are unrelated to being. Scheler nevertheless finds in values the characteristic of numerical identity across diversity of manifestations which is for Husserl the sign of an object and an essence. Pleasingness and holiness are qualities which, like sound and color, remain the same no matter how different the subjects to which they are attached may be. It follows that value, independent of a psychic subject and desires, is in no way susceptible of genesis; only the capacity of sensing values is susceptible of development. Scheler's notion of value is closer to the neo-Kantianism of Windelband than to naturalism, and under these conditions his proposed classification of values exhibits the kind of delineation characteristic of Husserl's *Wesensschau*. No bond or common principle unites the four kinds of values that he identifies: pleasingness and displeasingness, vital values (such as nobility and vulgarity), spiritual values (knowledge, art, law), religious values or holiness (*Formalism in Ethics and Ethics of Material Values,* 1913–16; *Revolution of Values,* 1919).

Apriorism in ethics, according to Kant, necessitated formalism, since freedom of will is not guaranteed if morality depends on knowledge of a good. Scheler, with his theory of values which are known a priori, claims that he can establish a material moral apriorism. Kant's formalism made religion depend on morality as a postulate. Scheler's material apriorism frees religion from this dependence. In general, phenomenology is favorable to religion. Since the Renaissance the main philosophical argument against religion had been that it destroyed mental and intellectual unity. It might have found a place in the intellectual system by retaining a rational or natural character, but as a positive system of faith grounded on tradition or on mystical intuition, it remained on the margin of the intellectual current. It seems certain, in so far as one can judge the present, that the twentieth century is witnessing an abatement of the intellectual passion expressed in Descartes' idea of the unity of science. The effect of this abatement is to initiate a disclocation that eliminates the rational need for unity, which is condemned as a superficial monism. One example of this is the delineation of essences in phenomenology, which actually originated in one of the requirements of the mathematical method (independence of the points of departure indispensable to any demonstration), but quickly left its birthplace and became the basis of a doctrine that puts ethics, aesthetics, and religion on an equal footing by making each discipline depend on an intuition of distinct, irreducible essences.

For Max Scheler, who personally reached the decision to embrace Catholicism, the philosophy of religion is not a psychology which analyzes and reduces but an intuition of certain essences which are manifested in an original, irreducible religious experience. There is no truly religious evolution, according to Scheler, because the fundamental essence apprehended intuitively by religion is the essence of holiness, which remains identical whether applied to a finite or an infinite being. The only faith is the one based on intuition; for example, the Christian faith has its origin in the intuition of God through Christ. The essences that are discovered by analyzing religion as it is given to us are the following: the essence of the divine, that is, of the being who possesses absolute holiness; the forms of revelation of the divine; the religious act, which is man's subjective preparation for apprehending absolute value by revelation. These values cannot be reduced to other values, particularly to moral values, even though Scheler does acknowledge the impossibility of separating moral attitudes and religious attitudes. His image of the world is dominated by his religious faith. According to *The Eternal in Man* (1921), since the original Fall the world has moved naturally in the direction of gradual decay; in this universe, which the physical theory of relativity has proved to be finite, the law of degradation of energy shows us the qualitative diminution of energy; the evolution of history is in the direction of gradual enslavement of society to economic needs alone and reveals a satanical power engaged in a struggle against God.

Like the postimpressionistic painters, Scheler tends to single out or emphasize certain distinctive traits. This tendency is also manifested in his psychology, in which he acknowledges, as immediate and intuitive data, five completely distinct spheres: outer world, inner world, body, consciousness of others, divinity. In addition, we perceive these realities only through the intermediary of "senses" which let only what is actually useful to life pass into consciousness. From this point of view the inner sense is in the same situation as the outer sense and also has illusions, for it apprehends only a part of the inner states.

Martin Heidegger, professor at Freiburg, devoted his early works to Scholasticism, publishing them until 1929 in the journal which Husserl had edited since 1919 (*Jahrbuch für Philosophie und phänomenologische Forschung*). He bases his reflection in *Being and Time* (1927) and *The Ground of Being* (1929) on certain fundamental feelings which relate not to this or that particular object but to existence in general and its modalities: uneasiness, anxiety, anguish, familiarity, boredom, loneliness, astonishment, embarrassment. Such feelings reveal the essence of the world. What we might call his anti-Cartesianism will serve as a starting point for a brief exposition of his views.[11] Descartes determined the essence of the world, exclusive of the thinking thing, and the essence of the thinking thing by using methodical doubt to deny the existence of the world; this dualism of substance caused him completely to discard Scholastic ontology. His subject without a world is a fiction, however, for the given—existence—is being-in-the-world (*Sein-in-der-Welt*), and this refers not only to our involvement with external things around us but also to our feeling of being in the totality of the existent. "If it is true that we never apprehend the totality of the existent in itself and absolutely, at least there is no doubt about our being placed in the middle of this existent, the totality of which is hidden from us in one way or another. . . . To be sure, it seems that in our usual proceedings we attach ourselves to this or that being; that is why daily existence may seem fragmentary even though it maintains the cohesion of the existent in its totality, hidden in darkness, of course. It is when we are not especially absorbed in things or ourselves that this totality appears to us, for example, in a state of general and profound boredom. . . . Reaching into the depths of existence like a silent mist, profound boredom strangely blends things, men, and ourselves, producing a general indifferentiation. This boredom is a revelation of the totality of the existent." [12] In the same way "Angst," a feeling quite different from fear, since it has no precise object and its object is experienced as a totality, reveals to us the nothingness that encompasses the existent. What oppresses us in anguish is the absence of a feeling of familiarity or strangeness and, with it, the disappearance of things.

We can state the essential philosophical problem—the problem of being as being or the being of the existent—only by using the liberating cultivation of these feelings of totality to escape from the idols

[11] An outline of *Sein und Zeit* is given in *Existence and Being,* edited by Werner Brock. See also *Mind,* new series, XXXVIII (1929), 355–70.

[12] *Was ist Metaphysik?* (Bonn, 1929). Cf. A. de Waelhens, *La Philosophie de M. Heidegger* (Louvain, 1941).

we have forged for ourselves for the purpose of avoiding them, "toward which each is accustomed to crawl in search of salvation"—for example, the divine absolute on which we ground the existent or, more simply, the feeling of familiarity linked to our involvement with things.[13]

The works of Nicolai Hartmann (*Main Features of a Metaphysic of Knowledge*, 1921; *On Laying the Foundation of Onthology*, 1935; *Possibility and Reality*, 1938; *The Structure of the Real World*, 1939) manifest the same basic tendencies as the preceding works. For Hartmann, the problem of knowledge envelops the problem of being and cannot be studied apart from it even though the two problems are distinct. The being of an object is not reduced to being an object for a subject; the relation called knowledge is a relation between beings that exist independently of this relation. The theory of knowledge of necessity originates in a theory of being, and, even when it is purely critical, implicitly affirms that being is relative to knowledge. The solutions cannot be indicated here, but in the position of the problem we see an affirmation of realism.

Johannes Rehmke's doctrine, set forth in *Philosophy as the Primary Science* (1910), is absolutely distinct from phenomenology. Still, it contains an element of realism even though it considers the idea of a reality other than consciousness to be devoid of any meaning. Rehmke claims to have demonstrated that pantheism on one hand, and psychologism as well as phenomenalism on the other, are mistakes. A thing is real when its action is linked to something else; no action is performed or suffered except between individuals, and nothing acts on itself; moreover, the action of one individual governs change in another individual; consequently a universal reality, such as the God of pantheism, is an unintelligible expression. By contrast, consciousness and body are absolutely different individualities, and the body-consciousness union never constitutes one individual; therefore man is not an individual but a union of two individual actions. In this way Rehmke avoids phenomenalism, which re-

---

[13] Cf. Gurvitch, *Les tendances actuelles de la philosophie allemande*, 1930; Lévinas, *La théorie de l'intuition dans la phénoménologie de Husserl*, 1931.

duces everything to consciousness. The whole doctrine seems to be the development of the ancient aporia introduced in Plato's *Charmides*: nothing acts upon itself. This is the negation of any immanent action.

III Neo-Thomistic Realism

Thomism had been the official philosophy of the Catholic Church since the encyclical *Aeterni patris* was issued in 1879. Because of its realism and reactionary tendency with respect to Descartes and Kant, it attracted the sympathy of phenomenologists, of whom many were also Catholics by origin. Father Erich Przywara of the Society of Jesus, outlining the history of the movement in Catholic Philosophy in *Kantstudien* (XXXIII, 73), singles out three tendencies: the pure Thomism of the Dominican schools; the study of the birth of Thomist philosophy in the Middle Ages as an independent philosophy (historical works of Ehrle, Grabmann, Bäumker, and Gilson); finally, a creative neo-Scholasticism which itself follows several different currents. The author identifies two of these currents: Christian metaphysics and neo-Thomism. Christian metaphysics deals with philosophical questions which theology attempts to answer—truth, existence of the outer world, nature of the soul—and is studied in the works of Gutberlet, Cardinal Mercier, Geyser, and Gemelli. According to the author, it is quite different from neo-Thomism. He calls it neo-Molinism because its two fundamental theses are that "the intellection of singular things is prior to the intellection of universal things"—a thesis that is the basis of a "critical realism," opposed to the "naïve realism" of Thomism, in which essences are supposedly apprehended in singular things—and that "individuals are grounded on forms," which leads to a metaphysics based on concrete things and not on first principles.

Father Przywara insists on making a distinction between this neo-Molinism, which is Aristotelian, and French neo-Thomism as formulated by Father Sertillange and Father Garrigou-Lagrange, in which he claims to see the influence of Bergsonism. On one hand he acknowledges that metaphysics, which apprehends being, takes precedence over the sciences, that the *intellectus universalium* and *quidditatum* is prior to the *intellectus singularium* and the *intellectus dividens et componens;* on the other hand nature is a dynamogenic being, a process of becoming, which never realizes essences. The real distinction between essence and existence contrasts with the rational distinction of Molinism. Neo-Thomism was completed by Father Maréchal's position with respect to Kant in *The Point of Departure of Metaphysics,* in which he seeks to revive Kantian criticism without falling into agnosticism.

Thus the neo-Thomist movement, which has an important place in contemporary thought, has manifested diverse tendencies but is linked by its realism to the doctrines analyzed in this chapter.

Its intellectualistic realism conflicts with Kantian idealism or phenomenalism as well as with vitalistic Bergsonian realism. The second of these conflicts has been stated explicitly by Jacques Maritain in particular, in *Bergsonian Philosophy* (1914): "By substituting intuition for intelligence and duration, becoming, or pure change for being, Bergson annihilates the being of things and destroys the principle of identity" (p. 149). An action, which is reality, and grows and creates itself as it advances, is following a law directly opposed to the principle of contradiction. If likeness engenders otherness, if a being can give more than it has, if movement requires no body in motion and body in motion no moving force, the reason is that the principles of sufficient reason and substance are not exact. In sum, these criticisms view Bergsonism as the reversal of the great Aristotelian principle, which had been revived by Thomism, and is the crux of its intellectualism: actual being is prior to potential being. By contrast, in *The Degrees of Knowledge* (1929) Maritain tries to show that "Thomistic realism, using a truly critical method to save the validity of knowledge of things, allows us to explore the universe of reflection intimately and to construct what might be termed a metaphysical topology." He also rejects "contemporary idealism," which "shows the whole mind on a single plane of intellection," and proposes instead different planes: knowledge of sensible nature, metaphysical knowledge, mystical experience.

The position of Thomist realism with respect to Kantian idealism has been clearly defined by Father Maréchal in *The Starting Point of Metaphysics* (5 books, Louvain, 1923–26). Maréchal's detailed historical study of doctrines of criticism of knowledge from antiquity to Kant leads him to conclude that Kantianism is grounded on the interdependence of these two theses: negation of intellectual intuition and negation of knowledge of noumena if such knowledge depends solely on intellectual intuition. He does not try to refute Kant by defending the existence of intellectual intuition, but he insists that its negation does not entail the negation of knowledge of noumena. Kant himself had shown in his *Critique of Practical Reason* that noumena, God, and free beings acquire an objective value as conditions governing the exercise of practical Reason. "Let us suppose that it can be shown that the postulates of practical Reason, . . . at the very least the divine absolute . . . are also conditions governing the possibility of exercising the most fundamental of the faculties of knowing. . . . Then the objective reality of these postulates would be founded on a necessity pertaining to the speculative domain," yet would not involve intellectual intuition (Book III, p. 237). This is possible as soon as we reject the break that Kant claimed to have established between phenomena and noumena, and we can reject it without having to embrace Platonism, which claims to apprehend the intelligible directly. Thomism teaches us a middle way. Our concepts do not go beyond sensible quiddities, but they have an "element of signification" of which the object, indirectly representable, envelops an ontological relation to the absolute. The conditioned reality which is given to us implies, through this element, a reference to the Absolute. "The Kantian critique proves only that *if* an immanent object is simply a formal, synthetic unity of phenomena, it would be futile for us to hope to deduce a metaphysics from it by way of analysis." In reality, however, a faint trace of divine knowledge subsists on the modest plane on which human intelligence is laid out; it appears in prescience of the products of our action and in the apriority of our agent intellect which actuates intelligibles; there is a dynamism which impels intelligence toward the Absolute, and this is the very being of intelligence. Every mistake of modern idealism originates in the "unfortunate disjunction" accomplished at the end of the Middle Ages between the vital or dynamic aspect and the conscious aspect of knowledge.

The relationship between neo-Thomism and modern philosophy is obviously one of "necessary intolerance" (Book IV, p. 462) based on the belief that neo-Thomism is in possession of the touchstone. Still, aware of the indefinite perfectibility of human expressions of truth, Scholasticism remains "generously receptive to the successive enrichments of human thought," precisely because it adopts only those alien elements which can assimilate.

Neo-Thomism contains a precise thesis concerning the sense of history and philosophy. Hence the considerable importance of neo-Thomist works devoted to the history of medieval philosophy, the most important of which have been mentioned above in chronological order

Bibliography

Texts

Brentano, Franz. *Von der mannigfachen Bedeutung des Seienden nach Aristoteles.* Freiburg, 1862. Republished Darmstadt, 1960.

———. *Die Psychologie des Aristoteles.* Mainz, 1867.

———. *Untersuchungen zur Sinnespsychologie.* Leipzig, 1907.

———. *Die Lehre Jesu und ihre bleibende Bedeutung,* ed. Alfred Kastil. Leipzig, 1922.

Hartmann, Nicolai. *Ethics,* trans. Stanton Coit. 3 vols. London, 1932.

———. *New Ways of Ontology,* trans. R. C. Kuhn. Chicago, 1953.

———. *Teleologisches Denken.* Berlin, 1951.

———. *Ästhetik.* Berlin, 1953.

———. *Kleinere Schriften.* 3 vols. Berlin, 1955–58.

Heidegger, Martin. *Die Kategorien und Bedeutungslehre des Duns Scotus* ("Duns Scotus' doctrine of categories and concepts"). Tübingen, 1916.

———. *Being and Time,* translation of *Sein und Zeit,* vol. 1, by J. Macquarrie and E. S. Robinson. New York, 1962.

———. *Kant and the Problem of Metaphysics,* trans. J. S. Churchill. Bloomington, Ind., 1962.

———. *Existence and Being,* ed. Werner Brock. Contains "Remembrance of the Poet," "Holderlin and the Essence of Poetry," (both trans. Douglass Scott), "On the Essence of Truth," "What is Metaphysics" (both trans. by R.F.C. Hull and Alan Crick). Chicago, 1939.

———. "The Way Back into the Ground of Metaphysics," trans. Walter Kaufmann in his *Existentialism from Dostoevsky to Sartre.* New York, 1956.

———. *An Introduction to Metaphysics,* trans. R. Manheim. New Haven, 1959. New York, 1961.

———. *Question of Being,* ed. W. Kluback and J. T. Wilde. New York, 1958.

———. *What is Philosophy?,* trans. W. Kluback and J. T. Wilde. London, 1958.

———. *Essays in Metaphysics: Identity and Difference.* New York, 1960.

Husserl, Edmund. *Husserliana, Edmund Husserl, Gesammelte Werke.* The Hague, 1950———. Nine volumes have been published thus far, and other volumes are in preparation. Vols. 1–10 primarily contain unpublished writings and relevant working notes.

———. *Philosophie der Arithmetik.* Halle, Germany, 1891.

———. *Logische Untersuchungen.* 2 vols. Halle, Germany, 1900–1901.

———. "Philosophy as Rigorous Science," trans. Quentin Lauer. In Husserl, *Phenomenonology and the Crisis of Philosophy.* New York, 1965.

———. *Ideas—General Introduction to Pure Phenomenonology,* trans. W. R.

Boyce Gibson. London, 1931. The second and third volumes were published posthumously in *Husserliana* (see above), vols. 4–5 (1952).

——. "Phenomenonology," trans, C. V. Salmon in *Encyclopaedia Britannica*, 14th ed., vol. 17. Chicago, 1929.

——. *Formale und transcendentale Logik*. Halle, 1929.

——. *Cartesian Meditations*, trans. Dorion Cairns. The Hague, 1960.

——. *Die Krisis der europäischen Wissenschaften und die transcendentale Phänomenologie*, in *Husserliana* (see above), vol. 6 (1954).

Rehmke, Johannes. *Unsere Gewissheit von der Aussenwelt* ("Our Certainty about the External World"). Heilbronn, 1892.

——. *Grundlegung der Ethik als Wissenschaft* ("Foundations of Ethics as a Science"). Leipzig, 1925.

——. *Die Willensfreiheit* ("The Freedom of the Will"). Leipzig, 1925.

——. *Gesammelte philosophische Aufsätze* ("Collected Philosophical Essays"), ed. K. Gassen. Erfurt, 1928.

——. "Selbstdarstellung." In *Die Philosophie der Gegenwart in Selbstdarstellung*, ed. Raymund Schmidt. 7 vols. Leipzig, 1921–29.

——. *Grundwissenschaft. Philosophische Zeitschrift der Johannes-Rehmke-Gesellschaft*. Vol. 1, 1919; vol. 10, 1931.

Studies

Bachelard, Suzanne. *La logique de Husserl*. Paris, 1957.

Diemer, Alwin. *Edmund Husserl, Versuch einer systematischen Zusammenstellung seiner Phänomenologie*. Meisenheim am Glan, 1956.

Fink, Eugen. "Die phenomenologische Philosophie Edmund Husserls in der gegenwärtigen Kritik." *Kantstudien* 38 (1933).

Kastil, Alfred. *Die Philosophie Franz Brentanos: Eine Einführung in seine Lehre*. Bern, 1951.

Kraus, Oskar. *Franz Brentano: Zur Kenntnis seines Lebens und seiner Lehre*. Munich, 1919.

Spiegelberg, Herbert. *The Phenomenological Movement*. 2 vols. The Hague, 1960.

Szilasi, Wilhelm. *Einführung in die Phänomenologie Edmund Husserls*. Tübingen, 1959.

SOCIOLOGY AND PHILOSOPHY IN FRANCE

IN HIS BOOK *Sociologists of Yesterday and Today* (1931, p. 34), Georges Davy calls attention to four directions taken by French sociology from 1850 until the present: the one "which goes from Saint-Simon and Auguste Comte to Durkheim; the one which, under the name of social reform and especially of social science, goes from Le Play to Paul Bureau by way of H. de Tourville and Demolin"; Espinas' organicism, derived from Spencer; finally, the direction represented by Gabriel Tarde. Here we can consider only a few cursory details relating to the importance of these diverse directions in the history of philosophical thought.

Frédéric Le Play's *Social Reform in France* (1864) was intended to put an end to social instability arising from revolution by introducing the method of observation. In contrast to ready-made principles, Le Play advocates experience in every sense of the word—the experience of the great industrialist, the experience acquired by observing alien nations, the experience associated with nations whose institutions (like those of the British) originate in immemorial customs. Thus (p. 89) against philosophical rationalism, which links civilization to the weakening of religious beliefs, he sets the experience of Russia, Britain, and the United States, nations in which progress is most evident and beliefs most constant. This same theme was taken up again by Paul Bureau in *Moral Crisis of the New Age* (10th edition, 1908), a book devoted to the social justification of our religious sense. "The intimate, penetrating, vivid awareness of the relation which unites us to a higher, infinite being, . . . alone can exercise on us the pressure necessary for the establishment of an inner, truly fertile discipline for the collective good." Experience is here the first and last word; consequently this school, which even supports the superiority of the English (indeed, that is the title of Demolin's work) has some of the features of pragmatism.

All the writings of Gabriel Tarde (*The Laws of Imitation,* 1890; *Social Logic,* 1895; *Universal Opposition,* 1897; *Social Laws,* 1898) aim to reduce all social facts to the phenomenon of imitation, in which an act, an idea, or a feeling tends to be transmitted from one person to another. The starting point of imitation is invention, an essentially individual and nonsocial fact. That invention is an individual act in social phenomena such as those associated with religion and language, often vaguely attributed to some ill-defined collective force, was at bottom a singularly new principle. This principle casts doubt on the generally accepted notion that the essential social fact is constituted by an interdependence, based on coordination without imitation. Are not animal colonies—in other words, inferior societies—founded on the most perfect form of interdependence? Judicial custom provides a superior social bond, for it is based on imitation in morals and laws. The sociologist's aim is to determine how imitation occurs and is modified under real circumstances of every kind. Social imitation is itself perhaps only one aspect of a characteristic essential to reality as a whole, for the phenomena associated with repetition are the elementary phenomena studied in physics and biology—for example, successive, repeated vibrations, and the facts of heredity. Cyclic recurrence becomes a universal category.

The organicism of Alfred Espinas (1844–1922) finds its clearest expression in the following passage: "For us and for all evolutionistic naturalists, organs and individuals belong to the same series. They are separated only by a purely accidental difference of degree. . . . Otherwise we could not understand how every organ tends toward unity and individualization even when the complexity and interdependence of the organism of which it is a part makes separation from the whole impossible." [1] It was the study of animal societies, particularly animal colonies, which had led Espinas to conclude, in *Animal Societies* (1877), that organs in an organism are equivalent to individuals in a society. Individuals, animal societies, and human societies are alike in that they are all organisms, and as an assemblage of cells an individual is a society. Espinas' aim is to identify different patterns of organization, beginning with colonies and animal societies designed to satisfy simple vital, elementary needs and extending to human societies based on understanding and sympathy.

The aim of Émile Durkheim (1858–1917) was above all to institute a positive sociology which would disregard Comte's dream of discovering the general law of evolution of humanity, abandon all philosophies of history or general theories of the essence of society, and seek instead to discover by ordinary methods of observation and induction the laws that connect certain social phenomena to certain others—for example, suicide or division of labor and population increase. Durkheim justifiably complained that his critics took the provisional definitions or maxims—which he, like any scientist, employed in his investigations—for general theories of society; for example, when he defined a moral act in terms of the sanctions that accompany the violation of a standard, he believed that he had provided a means of recognizing morality, not that he had explained it or identified its essence.

Durkheim's sociology nevertheless raises and resolves questions which are in the province of philosophy, and this transmutation of philosophical problems into sociological problems is of particular interest to us here. Durkheim was very sensitive to the "present disorder of moral ideas" and the "crisis that we are now undergoing." The search for a remedy to this situation may have been

---

[1] *Revue philosophique*, I (1882), 99. As quoted by G. Davy, *Sociologues d'hier et d'aujourd'hui*, p. 33.

the dominant force behind all his activity. One form of this crisis was the hostility that existed around 1880 between science and conscience—between empiricism and relativism, which seemed to lead to a utilitarian morality and to acceptance of every individual fancy, and, on the other hand, the rational and moral exigencies of an impersonal and absolute justice. Durkheim's doctrine seeks to satisfy entirely the exigencies of a scientific method without relinquishing any of the benefits of a rational aprioristic method. In practically every instance the "a priori" of rationalism is replaced by "society" in Durkheim's writings. In fact, in relation to the individual, society has attributes quite similar to those which philosophy ascribes to reason: it is relatively permanent, whereas the individual vanishes; it transcends individuals since social standards of opinions are imposed on them as something not created by them, yet is immanent since it alone makes us truly human, civilized beings and is the foundation of all higher mental functions. This being, which is to us as reason is to the individual, is at the same time the object of experience and science. Methodical experience enables us to identify the cause of certain social phenomena in other social phenomena and to arrive at positive laws. For the sociologist, a social rule, aprioristic and absolute for an individual in a society, is relative to a certain social structure of which it is the effect, and the respect it inspires does not prevent it from being an object of science. With respect to incest, for example, Durkheim tries to prove that its prohibition in primitive societies derives from the rule of exogamy— that is, the interdiction of marriage within the same clan; furthermore, he relates this interdiction to certain beliefs concerning blood, reducing the moral rule to its primitive source and at the same time explaining an emotional efflorescence associated with this rule— the contrast between the regularity and firmness of the sentiments that bind us to the family and the irregularity of passionate love, purely individual and personal. Our "moral conscience" reveals none of the motives behind the standard; the individual's feeling of aversion for incest is at once sacred and incomprehensible. This attitude is possible, of course, only if we assume that "once incorporated into our manners and morals, a rule persists, outliving its own cause." Our conduct originates in social prejudices that we find absurd today, which, before disappearing, nevertheless gave birth to patterns of behavior by which we are bound. But the objection raised against Hume and all others who sought to discover a naturalistic origin of intellectual or moral apriorisms—that to identify their motives is to destroy and desecrate them by robbing them of their holiness—must also apply to Durkheim. Does this not tilt the balance in favor of relativism? Durkheim's answer is hard to reconcile with the preceding statements. "It is an essential postulate of sociology," he says, "that a human institution cannot be based on error and deceit, for otherwise it would not have been able to endure. If it were not rooted in the nature of things, it could not have overcome the resistance encountered in things." It follows that the permanence of a rule is not the product of an individual or hereditary habit, as in Hume or Spencer, but a proof of its truth. Curiously, Durkheim concludes from this principle, formulated earlier by De Bonald, that there are no religions "which are true in contrast to others which might be false. All are true in their own way." Similarly, all religions were once viewed as forms of deformations of a single primitive religion.

Durkheim's answer obviously sets him apart from Comte, who grounded social unity on the gradual rescinding of explicit errors by intellectual progress. Limited by method to special questions, Durkheim recognizes no such progress; besides, he does not base his sociology on the system of the positive sciences. For him society is an immutable factor, at least formally, since at any point in time it is the source of juridical, moral, religious, and intellectual standards which, at any point in time, are true because they have society not only as their source but also as their object. The "collective representations" of the social conscience, never fully assimilated by each individual conscience, always refer only to the society from which they have originated. The gods of religions represent society itself in its sacred aspect; collective representations, encumbered with qualifications (left and right, lucky and unlucky days, etc.), are predicated on the beliefs or positive social activities which establish their truth.

In society facts and ideals blend; thanks to sociology, an ideal seems to be equivalent to a fact. Abnormal social facts—suicide, for instance—support the view that an aberrant moral conscience can appeal to a reformed moral conscience. The true collective representation is not necessarily the common representation; an inspired individual like Socrates may be the only one in possession of the true morality of his time. Society is separated from the individual conscience by a distance which can be increased to the point where the true collective representation vanishes from the individual conscience. Hence the practical and reformative import of sociology, which advocates a well-informed society instead of a badly formed society, and which has the ultimate goal of reinforcing the social conscience of the individual. That is why Durkheim proposes in a perfectly logical way to restore guilds, under conditions suitable to modern life. Communion between the individual and society cannot be established by the state, which is too big and too distant, or by the reduced monogamic family of our time, which is too narrow. A guild is a social body which conforms to the individual conscience, like the Society of the Divine Word.[2]

In 1896 Durkheim founded *L'Année sociologique* (1896–1913; new series, 1925) which groups works inspired by his method according to the areas of specialization of sociology. Religious sociology is studied in the works of Henri Hubert and Marcel Mauss: *Essay on the Nature and Function of Sacrifice* (1897–98); *Outline of a General Theory of Magic* (1902–03). Juridical sociology is studied by Paul Fauconnet in *Responsibility* (1920), and by Georges Davy in *Sworn Testimony* (1922), *Law, Idealism and Experience* (1923),

---

[2] Durkheim's principal works are *The Division of Labor in Society* (*De la division du travail social*, 1893; English translation by George Simpson, 1947); *The Rules of Sociological Method* (*Les règles de la méthode sociologique*, 1895; English translation by G. E. G. Catlin, 1950); *Suicide* (*Le suicide*, 1897; English translation by J. A. Spaulding and George Simpson, 1951); *The Elementary Forms of Religious Life* (*Les formes élémentaires de la vie religieuse*, 1912; English translation by J. W. Swain, 1947); *Sociology and Philosophy*, translated by D. F. Pocock, 1953; and *Education and Sociology*, translated by S. D. Fox, 1956.

and *Elements of Sociology I* (1924). Maurice Halbwachs—*The Working Class and Living Standards* (1912); *The Causes of Suicide* (1930); *Social Morphology* (1938)—deals with social facts of a general nature. All these works are inspired less by the same doctrine than by the same method.

It is on this method that Charles Lalo bases his studies of aesthetics: *Contemporary Experimental Aesthetics* (1908); *Aesthetic Feelings* (1910); *Art and Life in Society* (1920); *Art apart from Life* (1939). He would extend to art a sociological method of explanation which heretofore has been applied almost exclusively to primitive art, known through ethnological findings.

Gaston Richard, on the other hand, maintains a critical attitude toward the sociological method of Durkheim. In his works—*The Origin of the Idea of Law* (1892), *The Idea of Evolution in Nature and History* (1902), and *General Sociology and Sociological Laws* (1912)—he tries to found a general sociology distinct from a simple corpus of the social sciences to which Durkheim sought to reduce it; and he finds its unity in a theory of social forms derived from Fichte, who showed how social facts issued from natural relations between individuals should be subordinate to the community, which represents ideal ends, law, religion, etc. In *Egalitarian Ideas* (1899) and *Essays on the Caste System* (1908) C. Bouglé maintains that Durkheim's sociological explanation is but one step toward a total explanation. It is a sociological law that the development of egalitarian ideas is connected with an increase in population density; but one can also search for the reasons behind this connection and discover them in the psychological modifications produced by social concentration; thus simple concomitances lead to intelligible relations. In *Teachings of Sociology concerning the Evolution of Values* (1922) Bouglé examines the thesis that collective representations are the source of intellectual, moral, or aesthetic values, and he takes pains to show that the ideal, spiritual character of these values is imcompatible with such an origin.

In *Ethics and Moral Science* (1903; English translation, 1905) Lucien Lévy-Bruhl (1857-1939) adopts the sociological point of view and denies that there can be anything resembling what philosophers understand by theoretical ethics—that is, a science of rules of conduct based on a uniform human nature and constituting one harmonious whole. There is instead an existing code of ethics which science can study as a datum. To this science, if it is sufficiently advanced, might be added a rational art which would be to moral science what medicine is to biology. The works of Albert Bayet—*Suicide and Ethics* (1922) and *The Ethics of the Gauls* (1927-31)—are devoted to the study of this moral science.

If standards of conduct or moral rules are relative to a fixed state of society, cannot as much be said of mentality in general and in particular of the guiding principles of intelligence, which, according to both empirical and idealistic philosophers, are identical throughout time and constitute a universal human reason? This is the question investigated, within the limits of ethnology, in the works of Lévy-Bruhl: *How Natives Think* (1910; English translation, 1926); *Primitive Mentality* (1922; English translation, 1923); *The Primitive Soul* (1927); *Primitives and the Supernatural* (1931; English translation, 1935); *Primitive Mythology* (1935); *The Mystical Experience and Symbols among Primitives* (1938). Most ethnologists assumed that mental functions were identical among primitives and civilized men, and that the same functions produced science in our case and myths in theirs. Still, upon examination, these functions are found to imply well-defined concepts, precise, ordered, not susceptible of confusion. Far from thinking with the help of well-defined ideas that logically include or exclude one another, the savage thinks with the help of images that flow together in a way that seems most unusual to us, as if he were unaware of our principle of contradiction; experience often fails to reveal any similarity between beings declared by him to be identical; they are identical by virtue of a kind of participation—an ultimate fact, which defies any attempt at logical analysis. This prelogical thought is the only explanation of a belief in the supernatural, which attributes to objects mystical powers capable of producing happiness or unhappiness, and of the deep-rooted fear that the social order will be disturbed unless man respects the traditional rules of conduct with respect to these powers.

Durkheim's sociology ascribes the initiative of intellectual, juridical, and ethical norms to society as a whole. Thus it is connected, in spite of many differences, with the objective theory of law proposed by jurists like Léon Duguit. In *Transformations of Public Law* (2d edition, 1927) Duguit compares society to a vast cooperative workshop, in which each individual has a task to perform and derives the rule of law from the intimate constitution of this society.[3]

Gustave Belot, in Studies in *Positive Ethics* (2d edition, 1921), assumes that both rationality and reality must enter into positive ethics, and that the second of these conditions forges a close link between ethics and sociology. "Morality, viewed in the context of its reality, would be . . . a set of rules imposed by each collectively on its members." Belot therefore turns to sociology for all data associated with the problem, but he maintains that the rational need (reflective acceptance on the part of the subject) belongs to a wholly different order and cannot be satisfied by sociology.

The philosophical question posed by sociology remains, in effect, that of determining the degree to which mental functions are social functions or a set of collective representations. On this point Daniel Essertier's book on *Lower Forms of Explanation* (1927) provides a counterpart to the thesis of the social origin of reason by separating mental evolution from social evolution. The birth of reason seems to have occurred in spite of the collective consciousness and even in opposition to it; by itself the collective consciousness always remains at a lower stage.

[3] Cf. the exposition and critique of this conception and related conceptions from the Durkheimian point of view in Georges Davy's "L'Evolution de la pensée juridique contemporaine," *Revue de Métaphysique*, 1921; and *Le Droit, l'idéalisme et l'experience*, 1922.

Bibliography

Duguit, Léon. *Études de droit public,* 2 vols. Paris, 1901–2.
———. Preface. In vol. 1, Woodrow Wilson, *L'état: Éléments d'histoire et de pratique politique.* Paris, 1902.
———. *Traité de droit constitutionnel,* 2d ed., 5 vols. Paris, 1921–25.
———. *Law in the Modern State,* trans. Frida Laski and Harold J. Laski. New York, 1919.
Durkheim, Émile. *The Division of Labor in Society.* Glencoe, Ill., 1960.
———. *The Rules of Sociological Method,* 8th ed., ed. George E. G. Catlin. Glencoe, Ill., 1958.
———. *Suicide: A Study in Sociology.* Glencoe, Ill., 1951.
———. *Sociology and Philosophy.* Glencoe, Ill., 1953.
———. *Prefaces to L'année sociologique:* Preface to vol. 2. In *Émile Durkheim, 1858–1917: A Collection of Essays With Translations and a Bibliography,* ed. Kurt H. Wolff. Ohio, 1960.
———. *Moral Education: A Study in the Theory and Application of the Sociology of Education.* New York, 1961.
———. "The Determination of Moral Facts." In *Sociology and Philosophy.* Glencoe, Ill., 1953.
———. "Value Judgments and Judgments of Reality." 80–97 in *Sociology and Philosophy.* Glencoe, Ill., 1953.
———. *The Elementary Forms of the Religious Life.* London and New York, 1954.
Durkheim, Émile, and Mauss, Marcel. *Primitive Classification,* trans. and ed. Rodney Needham. Chicago, 1963.
Lévy-Bruhl, Lucien. *History of Modern Philosophy in France,* trans. G. Coblence. London and Chicago, 1899.
———. *The Philosophy of Auguste Comte,* trans. K. de Braumont-Klein. London, 1903.
———. *How Natives Think,* trans. L. A. Clare. London, 1926.
———. *Primitive Mentality,* trans. L. A. Clare. London and New York, 1923.
———. *The "Soul" of the Primitive,* trans L. A. Clare. London, 1928.
———. *Primitives and the Supernatural.* London, 1936.
———. *La Mythologie primitive: Le monde mythique des Australiens et des Papous.* Paris, 1935.
———. *Les Carnets de Lucien Lévy-Bruhl.* Paris, 1949.
Tarde, Gabriel. *Le criminalité comparée,* 5th ed. Paris, 1902.
———. *The Laws of Imitation.* New York, 1903.
———. *Penal Philosophy.* Boston, 1912.
———. *Les transformation du droit.* 8th ed. Paris, 1922.
———. *La logique sociale,* 2d ed. Paris, 1898.
———. *L'opposition universelle.* Paris, 1897.

——. *Études de psychologie sociale.* Paris, 1898.

——. *Social Laws,* trans. Howard C. Warren, with a preface by James Mark Baldwin. New York, 1899.

——. *Les transformations du pouvoir.* Paris, 1899.

——. *L'opinion et la foule.* Paris, 1901.

——. *Psychologie économique,* 2 vols. Paris, 1902.

——. *Underground Men.* With a preface by H. G. Wells. London, 1905.

——. *Gabriel Tarde: Introduction et pages choisies par ses fils.* Paris, 1909. Contains a bibliographical introduction and selections from his writings.

PSYCHOLOGY AND PHILOSOPHY

During the preceding period psychology was generally considered to be an independent science, separate from philosophy. Théodule Ribot (1830–1916), founder of the *Revue philosophique* (1876), asserted this independence particularly in *Contemporary English Psychology* (1870). But recently it has undergone significant transformations which have brought it closer in certain respects to philosophy. Even a summary account of these transformations cannot be attempted here, but a few of the principal movements will be mentioned.

Psychology tends for the most part to stress general aspects of psychological life, such as thought, patterns of conduct, behavior, and regulative phenomena. The object is not to divide consciousness into atoms, sensations, or images and then to reassemble them, but to study undivided wholes.

A universal characteristic of mental life—systematic association and immanent finality, which unite the elements of the mind—was emphasized by Frédéric Paulhan in numerous works, the last of them concerned as much with ethics as with psychology: *Mental Activity and the Elements* (1889); *Illusions of Character* (1905); *The Illusion of the World* (1921). Pierre Janet (1859–1947) used the notion of mental synthesis to explain higher mental phenomena in *Psychological Automatism* (*Automatisme psychologique,* 1889). That "psychology should become more objective" is one of the conclusions drawn from all his writings and summarized in Georges

234

Dumas' *Treatise on Psychology* (I, 1923, p. 919). Psychology studies the conduct of men, the partial movements and general attitudes by which the individual reacts to the actions of the objects surrounding him. It observes the general characteristics of his conduct, those which are always present and vary only in degree: psychic tension with all its oscillations, from the lower degree at which an action is conceived and imagined to the higher degree at which it is executed. Here we discover a movement parallel to *behaviorism,* mentioned earlier in connection with American realism. The same observation applies to Henri Piéron who, in *The Brain and Thought* (1923), treats psychology as a part of biology because it is the study of individual modes of reaction or patterns of conduct which are always psychologically conditioned; consequently the psychologist should disregard consciousness. He had supported this view as early as 1912, before the development of the behavioristic method in America.

Present methods in psychology generally prohibit isolating a psychological fact from its psychophysiological context; an emotion, for example, is nothing outside the whole to which it belongs. Dumas, in his book on *Joy and Sadness* (1900), makes it a rule in investigating affective facts to study different affective states or emotional variations in the same individual instead of studying the same affective state in different individuals. The resulting set of characteristics, which is called individuality, determines each phenomenon to such a degree that phenomena designated by the same name—joy or sadness, for example—are never wholly compatible from one individual to another. This would seem to dispel any hope of identifying the "elements" of consciousness.

Problems of genesis, which received much attention earlier, have generally been abandoned in favor of what might be called structural problems. The trend is the same in psychology as in sociology and philosophy as a whole: the idea of evolution, born of romanticism, is gradually disappearing. Here are several proofs.

James Mark Baldwin (1861–1934) considers psychology to be a genetic science. Like Bergson, the American psychologist refuses to concede that the categories of mechanistic sciences can be used to interpret spiritual evolution. Yet his object is not to revive Spencerian evolutionism; on the contrary, he believes that psychic phenomena as well as all other phenomena (for his "pancalism" is a general philosophy) are comprehensible only if the mind refers to a total, immediate experience of itself and by itself. He identifies this total knowledge with aesthetic contemplation, and interprets aesthetic categories as rules of organization to be used in classifying every aspect of experience (cf. especially *Thought and Things, or Genetic Logic*, 3 vols., 1906-11; and *Genetic Theory of Reality*, 1915).[1]

In his book on *The Morbid Conscience* (1913) Charles Blondel assigns the main role in pathological mental states to "pure psychology"—that is, to the homogeneous mass of organic impressions responsible for our individuality, which is irreducible and impervious to the social influence under which judgment and a normal conscience are shaped. Mental diseases originate when this mass is not repressed in the subconscious, as it is in the normal conscience. Here mental attitudes as such are under investigation.

Henri Delacroix tries in his works—*Religion and Faith* (1922); *Language and Thought* (1924); *Psychology of Art* (1929)—to show the impossibility of interpreting any part of the life of the mind without relating it to the whole. "Language is impossible in the absence of a mind; a system of concepts organized according to their relations must be established." By the same token, religion is not pure sentiment. "Religion exists only in so far as the inclination to seek self-satisfaction in an immediate, natural manner is renounced . . . in favor of an indirect approach—magical and religious practices which imply the existence of a system of beings, and notions governing their accomplishment. . . . There is a silent train of thought which precedes its verbal, imaginal expression, or overflows it." "Art seeks to fit into a clear system the harmonious

---

[1] Cf. A. Lalande, "Le pancalisme," *Revue philosophique*, 1915. [*Petit Larousse* defines *pancalisme* as a philosophical system in which beauty is the key to every facet of reality.—Trans.]

swarm of sensorial data. . . . It would be wrong to suppose reason, wisdom, and intelligence on one hand, and on the other to surrender to a kind of supraintellectual intuition. Intelligence labors, cuts, and measures in art as in science." This total involvement of the mind in each of his works is attested by Paul Valéry, who, referring to artistic invention, speaks of the "complex theoretical meditation, a blend of metaphysics and technics," which accompanies the birth of a work.[2]

Psychologists of the earlier period considered the image to be a mental element of some kind, but their analysis was disproved by the psychology of intelligence developed in France by Alfred Binet —for example, in his *Experimental Study of Intelligence* (1903)— and investigated in Germany at the Wurzburg Institute.[3] The theory of forms (*Gestalttheorie*) calls attention to phenomena such as perception of the order or arrangement of three bright dots without referring in any way to the sensation of brightness associated with each of them.[4] Furthermore, introspection reveals the existence of pure thought, devoid of images or words; we do not think without being aware of a task, without assuming a certain attitude, without a certain intention, but we think without images. We can understand the meaning of a sentence even if no image presents itself to our consciousness. The indecomposable whole of the dynamism of thought itself is now coming under investigation, and this tendency is directly opposed to that of associationistic theories.

Child psychology is one study in which problems of genesis played an important role. In a series of works that Jean Piaget has devoted to the subject—*Language and Thought in the Child* (1924), *Judgment and Reason in the Child* (1924), *Representation of the World in the Child* (1926)—infant mentality appears as an irreducible block, which does not facilitate but excludes adult mentality, and which can be described rather than analyzed. It is to

[2] *Bulletin de las société française de philosophie, January* 1928, p. 5.
[3] Cf. A. Burlod, *La Pensée d'après les recherches expérimentales de Watt, Messer et Buhler*, 1927.
[4] P. Guillaume, *La psychologie de la forme*, 1937.

adult intelligence as primitive mentality, according to Lévy-Bruhl, is to the mentality of civilized man.

Generally speaking, even though the diverse currents discussed here are multifarious, they all express the necessity of what might be called a new plan of cleavage in psychological analysis. Here the important thing is to avoid inconsiderate dissociation of elements that are meaningful only when integrated into a functional unit. One last proof of this fact is provided by Freud's pathological psychology or psychoanalysis. The significance that psychoanalysis attaches to imperfect mental functioning—slips of the tongue and pen, forgetting, misplacing objects, dreams—in other words, everything which at first glance seems to be an accident in psychological life but is treated as a symbol at once expressing and hiding deep-seated sexual desire (*libido*), repressed thanks to the censor—evidences the same tendency to make knowledge of the life of the mind depend on an integral, unitary view.[5]

[5] Cf. *Introductory Lectures on Psychoanalysis* (1909), and *The Interpretation of Dreams* (1900).

Bibliography

Baldwin, James Mark. *Handbook of Psychology,* 2 vols. 1: *Senses and Intellect.* New York, 1889. 2: *Feeling and Will.* New York, 1891.
———. *Elements of Psychology. A condensation of Handbook of Psychology.* New York, 1893.
———. *Mental Development in the Child and the Race: Methods and Processes,* 3d ed., rev. New York and London, 1906.
———. *Development and Evolution.* New York, 1902.
———. *Social and Ethical Interpretations in Mental Development: A Study in Social Psychology,* 4th ed., rev. and enl. New York, 1906.
———. *Genetic Logic.* 3 vols. New York, 1906–11.
———. *History of Psychology: A Sketch and an Interpretation.* 2 vols. London, 1913.
———. *Genetic Theory of Reality.* New York and London, 1915.
———. *The Story of the Mind.* New York, 1915. An elementary text.
———. *American Neutrality: Its Cause and Cure.* New York and London, 1916.
———. *The Super-state and the "Eternal Values."* London and New York, 1916.
———. ed. *Dictionary of Philosophy and Psychology.* 3 vols. New ed. with corrections. (Vol. 3, bibliog., comp. Benjamin Rand.) 1901, 1902, 1905.
Binet, Alfred. *The Psychology of Reasoning.* London, 1901.
———, and Féré, Charles. *Animal Magnetism.* New York, 1892.
———. *On Double Consciousness.* Published in English, 1889.
———. *Alterations of Personality.* New York, 1896.
———. *Introduction à la psychologie experimentale.* Paris, 1894.
———. *La psychologie des grands calculateurs et joueurs échecs.* Paris, 1894.
———, and Vaschide, N. "Corrélation des épreuves physiques. *Année psychologique* 4 (1897): 142–72.
———, and Henri, V. *La fatigue intellectuelle.* Paris, 1898.
———. *La suggestibilité.* Paris, 1900.
———. *L'étude expérimentale de l'intelligence.* Paris, 1903.
———, and Simon, Th. "Méthodes nouvelles pour le diagnostic du niveau intellectuel des anormaux," *Année psychologique* 11 (1905): 191–244.
———. *Mind and the Brain.* London, 1907.
———, and Simon, Th. "Le développement de l'intelligence chez les enfants." *Année psychologique* 14 (1908): 1–94.
———, and Simon, Th. "L'intelligence des imbéciles." *Année psychologique* 15 (1909): 1–147.
———, and Simon, Th. "Hystérie." *Année psychologique* 16 (1910): 67–122.
———. *Les idées modernes sur les enfants.* Paris 1911.

———. "Nouvelles recherches sur la mesure du niveau intellectuel chez les enfants d'école." *Année psychologique* 17 (1911): 145–201.

———. "Qu'est-ce qu'un acte intellectuel?" *Année psychologique* 17 (1911): 1–47.

———. *Année psychologique*. Founded by Binet in 1894. Most of his work was published in this journal.

Freud, Sigmund. *The Standard Edition of the Complete Psychological Works of Sigmund Freud,* ed. James Strachey, in collaboration with Anna Freud, assisted by Alix Strachey and Alan Tyson. 24 vols. London, 1954–64. In English translation.

Piaget, Jean. *Le jugement et la raison chez l'enfant.* Paris, 1924. Translated by M. Warden as *Judgment and Reasoning in the Child.* London, 1928.

———. *Le langage et la pensée chez l'enfant.* Paris, 1924. Translated by M. Warden as *The Language and Thought of the Child.* London, 1926. 2d ed. trans. by M. Gabain. London, 1932.

———. *La représentation du monde chez l'enfant.* Paris, 1926. Translated by J. Tomlinson and A. Tomlinson as *The Child's Conception of the World.* London, 1929.

———. *La causalité physique chez l'enfant.* Paris, 1927. Translated by M. Gabain as *The Child's Conception of Physical Causality.* London, 1930.

———. *Le jugement moral chez l'enfant.* Paris, 1932. Translated by M. Gabain as *The Moral Judgment of the Child.* London, 1932.

———, and Szeminska, A. *La genèse du nombre chez l'enfant.* Paris, 1941. Translated by C. Gattegno and F. M. Hodgson as *The Child's Conception of Number.* London, 1952.

———, and Inhelder, B. *Le développement des quantités chez l'enfant.* Paris, 1941.

———. *Le développement de la notion du temps chez l'enfant.* Paris, 1946.

———. *Les notions de mouvement et de vitesse chez l'enfant.* Paris, 1946.

———, and Inhelder, B. *La représentation de l'espace chez l'enfant.* Paris, 1948. Translated by F. J. Langdon and J. L. Lunzer as *The Child's Conception of Space.* London, 1956.

———, et al. *La géometrie spontanée chez l'enfant.* Paris, 1948. Translated by E. A. Lunzer as *The Child's Conception of Geometry.* London, 1960.

———. *La genèse de l'idée de hazard chez l'enfant.* Paris, 1951.

———. *De la logique de l'enfant à la logique de l'adolescent.* Paris, 1955. Translated by Anne Parsons and Stanley Milgram as *The Growth of Logical Thinking.* London, 1958.

———. *La genèse des structures logiques élémentaires.* Paris, 1959.

PHILOSOPHY AFTER 1930

1 Preliminary Considerations

Does a historian have any right to separate the essential from the accidental—complementary, enhancive ideas from divisive ideas —in judging contemporary philosophy as a whole? Myopic by necessity, since he can see things only at close range, does he not cease to be a historian and become a mere critic? At the beginning of this final chapter, we should recall the statements made at the beginning of our study of the history of philosophy since 1850.

One salient but wholly external trait of the decade that began in 1930 is the concerted attempt that was made to develop international relations among philosophers (congresses in Prague, 1934; on scientific philosophy, in Paris, 1935; on Descartes, in Paris, 1937; special congresses on psychology and aesthetics). In their somewhat disconcerting variety, the works presented at the congress on Descartes and published in twelve thick fascicles will stand as a faithful reflection of the state of philosophy in the world during this period. Since 1937 the institute for international collaboration established by the congress on Descartes has published a *Bibliographie de Philosophie,* in principle an annual bibliography on which philosophers from many countries collaborate. At the same time important new journals were founded: in France, *Recherches philosophiques* (1931), particularly receptive to philosophers from other countries; in Yugoslavia, *Philosophia* "Philosophorum nostri temporis vox universa" (1936); in Belgium, *Revue internationale de philosophie* (1938); and in Sweden, *Theoria,* which also publishes many contributions by philosophers from other countries.[1] These are all manifestations of the universalistic mission of philosophy, brilliantly elucidated by Husserl in an important article. "Thanks to philosophy," he wrote, "one can determine whether European humanity is the bearer of an absolute idea and not simply an anthropological specimen such as 'Chinese' or 'Indian,' and on the other hand the Europeanization of all alien forms of humanity is evidence favoring the power of its absolute sense, linked to the sense of the world, and not an accidental absurdity of its history."[2]

II *The Two Tendencies of Contemporary Philosophy*

To understand the general direction of contemporary philosophy, we must return to two theses which, toward the end of the nineteenth century, seemed to be universally accepted. First, wherever there is a structure or form in things, it is due to a unity introduced into diversity. Unification of diversity requires the intervention of intelligence, for things in themselves have no structure or have a structure which is unknown to us. Second, wherever there is a value judgment, there is satisfaction (or dissatisfaction) of human sensibility, individual or collective, and such a judgment simply expresses a relationship between us and things. Philosophical doctrines were intended to reconcile the origin and "subjective" nature of structures and values with permanence and the kind of necessity that these structures and values preserve for man. That is why philosophers turn to auxiliary hypotheses designed to explain, as in criticism, the a priori conditions of experience or the immanent development of the mind and, in sociology, the collective origin of structures and values. But not only are such hypotheses insuf-

---

[1] Also worth noting are *Scientia,* published in Italy; the Viennese journal *Erkenntnis,* continued under the name of *The Journal of Unified Science;* and *Études philosophiques* (Ghent, 1939), a collaborative work by nine writers from France and Belgium.

[2] Husserl, "Die Krisis der europäischen Wissenschaften und die transcendentale Phänomenologie," *Philosophia,* 1936, p. 82.

ficient (the social explanation introduces a factor of inertia and conservation, rather than of development; critical idealism simply records progress in the positive sciences; they are also relative to theses which, if negated, would prove to be useless. These theses are now the subject of much controversy. On one hand, structures and forms appear as a datum which cannot be constructed by the mind but is simply reported or described; on the other hand, its function and meaning in a concrete situation, rather than its origin, provide the basis for attempts to determine the validity of a value. The principal role of philosophy seemed to be correct or to compensate for "subjectivism," linked to these theses; but the very negation of these theses reveals that our contemporaries are unaffected by this accusation of subjectivism, which once seemed identical to the accusation of arbitrariness. Here we shall not consider the kind of militant philosophy which is aimed at justifying certain forms or factors of civilization and belongs rather to politics. Philosophy itself will provide evidence of just such a reversal.

Negation of the two theses and indifference to subjectivism reveal two fundamental tendencies, closely related and yet distinct, which we must examine before taking up their role in publications of the last decade. The first is a general tendency to concreteness; the second, an attempt to discover true reality either in the depths of subjectivity or in the transcendent, leaving aside the relation of subject-object, which had been traditional since Kant.

To be specific with respect to the first tendency, in the frequently repeated statement that philosophical problems are meaningful only in a "concrete situation," the word "concrete" does not designate the individual—for example, a particular historical situation considered *hic et nunc,* in every detail. The individual is opposed to the general, and the concrete to the abstract; these oppositions are strikingly different. The individual, far from being identified with the concrete, is instead analogous to the abstract, for it results from a cut which isolates one aspect of the gradual development of things. The concrete, on the other hand, is not opposed to the general. The concrete vision of things results from an attempt to avoid separating in the mind that which is not separated in reality. It is the sense of a totality of which the elements, if isolated, would be like the sections of a living organism incapable of reconstituting the whole by their reunion (for example, the separation of soul and body, man and the world, thought and behavior, life and death). But here the word totality must be used in a very relative sense, for in the absolute sense a whole is that which is self-sufficient—in other words, the concrete universal in the Hegelian sense. It is an idea rather than a datum, whereas the concrete envisioned by our philosophy is rather a whole which is finite and limited even though it constitutes a unity—for example, an individual human existence understood in terms of its temporal and spatial limits. Moreover, we can comprehend this concrete only by ridding ouselves of the Spinozist or Hegelian prejudice that insists that a limit in the limited concrete is conceivable only in relation to a vaster beyond, whch make the limited concrete an abstract entity; pure imagination originating in the fact that we wrongly follow the example of mathematics, which works with abstract space and, after positing infinite space, delineates limited figures within this space. In truth, we are inside the concrete and do not go beyond it; it is given to us in its finitude. As Jaspers said, there are "circumscribed situations"—death, for example— which we cannot overstep. The concrete could be said to imprison us if prison did not suggest an exterior or a possible liberation which for us is only nothingness. But the concrete, which is neither the individual nor the universal, can be the general. There is nothing to prevent a concrete situation from being a general situation; the concrete is constituted not by the singular aspects of this situation but by the bonds, impossible to construct and experienced directly, which link these three aspects together. The concrete is a structure. Thus recognition of a melody depends not on the perception of individual notes, separately at first and then in their relations to each other, but on a certain quality or style of composition. This quality has a generality which can be detected immediately in melodies which consist of wholly different notes (the common quality in Mozart's melodies for instance, or Schumann's lieder, or Duparc's songs). The same applies to the human concrete, which is susceptible of analysis but in which, contrary to Kant's rule, analysis is not preceded by a synthesis.

The second tendency, which seems to be a characteristic of contemporary thought, should be approached in light of the following considerations. According to a thesis frequently advanced at the end of the nineteenth century, a philosopher of necessity has an intuition of the world which corresponds to his temperament, environment, and education; he believes that he attains to being, and his philosophy is simply a mode of action expressing a determinism; he set out to discover being, but found only himself, and his vision is Narcissus' vision of his own face. Thus determinism leads to skepticism but to skepticism which has its own dialectic, exemplified by our era. Such skepticism implied, in fact, that these philosophical attitudes *should* be judged within the frame of a self-contained reality of which they were simply manifestations. But these attitudes could not be judged within the frame of a self-contained reality inaccessible to us in their absence and therefore meaningless. The contrast between this necessity and this impossibility was the foundation of skepticism. But the contrast, together with the insoluble problems suggested by it, is canceled by the realization that this presumed reality results from an urgent need for unity, which in turn is also an attitude. Then, once we understand that each attitude is inseparable from a vision of the world and that the world envisioned is inseparable from this vision, we see, without trying to discover a transcendent, that each attitude constitutes a domain that cannot be compared with other domains and is for this very reason beyond criticism. A certain freedom of choice is manifested in philosophy, and this freedom is not checked by "principles of reason" or by any reality that might be objective and universal like these principles.

It would seem that this second tendency might lead to a kind of unbridled subjectivism, which would make a doctrine like a confession or confidential disclosure on the part of its author. Still, in spite of certain appearances, nothing of the sort happens. Subjectivity as a sign of arbitrariness exists only in relation to a supposed objectivity. The abandonment of abstract universalism leading to what Nietzsche calls world-truth results instead in the deliverance of men from the objectivistic fiction which imposed external restraints on philosophy and consequently in the unveiling of reality —provided, of course, that attention is no longer concentrated on a subject assumed to contain the conditions governing knowledge of an object but on subjectivity itself, which is given to us as the only type of existence. Under the influence of Kierkegaard, as Jean Wahl convincingly demonstrated, the concrete, complex structure of subjectivity has become the object of philosophical meditation. The significance of this shift of emphasis in contemporary philosophy is seen clearly in these lines written by Husserl (who, incidentally, did not share the opinion expressed here): "The exclusive manner in which modern man's intuition of the world was determined by the positive sciences and allowed itself to be blinded by the success due to them meant the abandonment of questions which, for an authentic humanity, are the decisive questions." [3]

III *Tendencies to Concreteness*

Such shifts of emphasis, traceable in many instances to Bergson, cannot be said to have produced a comprehensive doctrine. They show a revived interest in thinkers like St. Augustine and Pascal, in philosophers like Berkeley and Maine de Biran. Only a few aspects of these widely divergent tendencies are indicated here.

In his critique of abstraction—even more radical than Berkeley's —Jean Laporte, famous for his works on Antoine Arnaud, undertakes to show that an abstract idea is in every sense a fiction: it is not only an impossibility *in re* (since it is universally acknowledged that abstraction consists in separating things which are inseparable in reality) but also an impossibility *in mente*—that is, mind does not have the power to separate what is in reality inseparable in

[3] *Ibid.*

its representation of the real world. At most, he argues in the *Problem of Abstraction* (1940), there is an "abstractive illusion" which is explained by the relation between our representation of an object and our tendencies. "If, in practice, knowledge of an object always means, on one hand, a *datum,* which is what it is and which can be indivisible, and on the other, *tendencies* aroused in us by this *datum,* . . . then it is apparent that such a duality opens the way to splitting, and that since these multiple tendencies constitute the frame or immediate environment of the datum, the divisions to which they lend themselves can seem to apply to the datum itself." Jean Laporte rejects, even in the attenuated form that Berkeley found acceptable, the powers that philosophers attributed to mind, as if by a simple mental manipulation of the given it could penetrate to essences and forms and, as he says concerning the Thomist theory of abstraction, "change a pumpkin into a coach." In another work of similar inspiration—*The Idea of Necessity* (1941)—he showed that logicomathematical necessity and physical necessity can no longer exist as categories of the mind: "neither of them, upon examination, proves to be anything more than a raw datum or convention—in either instance, something empirical which is the direct opposite to something rational. So-called rational necessity, in all of its forms, is a false idea." This is indeed a denial not only of reality but of the possibility of the spiritual structure whose reality Kant proved by making it the necessary precondition of every possible experience. To be sure, he does not contest the reality of our aspiration toward necessity, "but by its very emptiness, this idea symbolizes the emptiness of our hearts, our profound and unsatisfied desire for a transcendent, in the order of knowledge as in other orders." Thus a certain intellectual pride, unbecoming to the human condition, causes us to base our knowledge initially on assertions (abstract ideas, categories) which we cannot possibly verify. Moreover, the practice of referring the mind to a datum which is ours alone has as a counterpart the establishment of a relation to a "beyond"—a transcendent —which does not belong to the same order as the datum.

The fundamental concepts of physical science—the simple notions on which mathematical physics is based (for instance, the concept of mass)—might be set against the results obtained by subjecting abstraction to psychological analysis: thus Newton was opposed to Berkeley. But the insufficiency of these abstract notions was revealed by nothing less than new developments in this science and its appeal to the subtleties of experience as well as to concrete situations. For mass to have played the role it was asked to play, it would have had to be independent of velocity, but this was not the case. Consequently such concepts "can be viewed as simple," wrote Gaston Bachelard, "only in so far as we are satisfied with simplifications. Formerly, it was thought that concepts became complicated in their practical applications, that they were to some degree incorrectly applied. Now philosophers no longer strive for precision at the moment of application but at the outset, at the level of principles and concepts." [4] This means that we can no longer speak of isolating a concept from the conditions under which it is experienced. This assertion seems clearly to indicate the general direction of Bachelard's works on scientific philosophy. Still, in his works we do not find a rank opposition between an oversimplified a priori and a reality apprehended directly by experience, for the experiences which show the insufficiency of this a priori have been prepared by an inner change in the a priori itself, a change that gives them a meaning. This spiritual work of transformation implies the negation of realism, which is not susceptible of true progress; it is "a philosophy that is always right, . . . a philosophy that assimilates everything, or at least absorbs everything. It does not *constitute* itself because it believes that it is always constituted." [5] Thus the concrete is less the given than the result of a "constructive activity" which Bachelard calls a dialectic. This dialectic should lead us toward the concrete, "create complete phenomena scientifically, regenerate all the degenerate or sup-

[4] *Le nouvel esprit scientifique,* 1934, p. 48. Cf. p. 149: "Simple ideas are not the definitive basis of knowledge."
[5] *La Philosophie du Non,* 1940, p. 32.

pressed variables which science, like thought itself had neglected in an initial study." [6] The examples he offers of his dialectic—notions which, like "nonsubstantial atoms" and Dirac's "negative mass," seems to contain their own negations—show that it is pre-eminently polemical, prevents the mind from becoming immobilized in its concepts, and urges it to formulate negations.

The idea of a dialectic of physical notions also predominates in Stéphane Lupasco's last work, *Microphysics and Human Thought* (*L'expérience microphysique et la pensée humaine,* 1941), and suggests to him the creation of a new logic. The idea of "dynamic contradiction" revives (perhaps without the knowledge of the author) an old theory found in Aristotelian physics: every change goes from a contrary to its contrary, with the result that when one contrary becomes actual the other becomes potential. In its own way quantum physics again focuses attention on the forgotten principle of classical physics. In fact, Heysenberg's principle of indetermination does not replace determinism by indeterminism, but it does show their mutual coexistence and antagonism. Classical science places reality at one of the poles—determinism; and although probability is acknowledged along with the exact prevision of a phenomenon, this is only in instances where certain conditions are assumed to be unknown. But "the very constitution of things" causes the quantum phenomenon to rule our deterministic previsibility (p. 148). What can be foreseen is this: of two terms under consideration (position and motion of an electron), each step toward precision in the determination of one is matched by progressive indetermination of the other. Lupasco is careful to separate this dialectic from Hegel's. His desire to avoid giving "dynamic contradictions" a mere instrumental value in the service of a higher synthesis" to "dynamic contradictions" (p. 131) as Hegel had done, sets his philosophy apart from Bachelard's.

[6] *Ibid.,* p. 17. It is indeed the function of the dialectic in Hegel, and Bialobrzeski (*Les nouvelles théories de la physique,* 1939, as quoted by Bachelard, p. 136) wrongly opposes Hegel's dialectic, in which notions are contradictory, to the physical dialectic (which he compares with Hamelin's), in which notions are complementary. Hegel never denied the principle of contradiction.

Lupasco's and Bachelard's interpretation of modern physics is essentially the expression of the first tendency mentioned here. They attempt to achieve, not an absolute, self-sufficient synthesis, but a concrete form comparable to a harmony (a mixture of low tones and high tones) rather than to a melody. Their position on this problem is the reverse of that of J. Laporte, according to whom the abstract is beyond human capacities, and the concrete a datum which is immediately at their level. In keeping with the Spinozist tradition, they hold that the abstract is the result of a deficiency and a stoppage; it is a simplification, and the concrete is reached only at the end of an active dialectic.

The same tendency is manifested in the philosophy of values. "A philosopher," writes Eugène Dupréel with deep insight, "is a thinker who never disregards complementaries."[7] Like Laporte, and even more forcefully, Dupréel links necessity to abstraction. The scientist manages to reach necessary conclusions in his research by isolating and defining facts, but when he tries to apply to reality a notion defined in this way, he is forced to add an obscure motion which reintroduces almost everything eliminated from his data to make it intelligible. For example, to order, which is pure intelligibility or statics, he must add his "complementary"—the confused notion of dynamic activity. "A concept owes its existence to our ability to relegate to the field of indetermination everything not introduced into our comprehension; it summons up the corrective of its *anticoncept*. This word does not mean its contrary but its complement.[8] The scientist can make necessary assumptions concerning this complementary indetermination and still remain faithful to his initial hypothesis. Democritus, for example, posited the void as the complement of atoms because the void alone enabled him to conceive a change compatible with the notion of atoms. A philosopher has the desire, however, not to fabricate complementary concepts to fit the occasion. He is not enslaved to the impersonal mold of principles, but he can gain access to data

[7] *Esquisse d'une philosophie des valeurs,* 1939, p. 239.
[8] *Ibid.,* p. 73.

only through a synthesis of order and activity, "combined elements, which are neither subordinate to each other nor derived from each other."

Knowledge of this duality clarifies the notion of value, which assumes a synthesis of order and force. First, order, manifested in consistency or value; for example, moral conduct, subject to rules, is more consistent than premoral conduct, which depends on the fluctuation of passions. Next, force, since only the adhesion of a will makes this moral conduct possible. These are two wholly independent sources of value. Consistency in itself in no way implies the adhesion of an active subject; in fact, from the first point of view a value is one order (a moral order, for example, or an economic value determined by the existence of a market), superimposed on another (the order of the passions or barter between individuals) but not necessarily derived from it, and that is why the adhesion of a free will is necessary. But as consistency increases, adhesion becomes less certain, that is, values become more precarious. Thus precariousness increases with consistency; the meeting of order and activity has only a probability, which decreases as the requirements dictated by order become more complex and difficult to fulfill.

It is obvious that in this doctrine the corrective of the anticoncept, precariousness, and probability is not the result of an absolute dialectic like Hegel's but proceeds from a sense of the concrete, which rejects the notion of leaving values in the splendid isolation of a heaven in which they are sovereigns without subjects. But there is one difficulty: the degree of consistency of a value, together with order, constitutes the validity of the value. That is a factual assertion which Dupréel accepts as such and which is like a final datum; the necessity of order is an inexplicable absolute, unless it is linked to biological or social conditions. But this proposed explanation, common during the preceding period, is rather a reduction to something that does not belong to the order of values, and it fails to show how a value judgment could be deduced from anything else than a value judgment. This problem remains the Cross of the

philosophy of values. In general, scientists or philosophers concerned with the specialized study of values (economists, moralists,
theoreticians of knowledge, aestheticians) neglect it in favor of the
study of values as they are expressed concretely, in the context of
the activities that they govern, and they seem to think that the
values would be meaningless if isolated from these activities. In
ethics, isolation is nothing less than "the mistake of Narcissus,"
who thought that he could "shut himself up in his own solitude
and associate only with himself." [9] That is the result of what R.
Le Senne so aptly calls "dialectics of separation," based on the
assumption that the obstacles which separate us from God, others,
and the world are absolute.[10] This attitude corresponds in ethics to
the assumption in the theory of knowledge that everything can be
deduced from a few a priori assertions which can be apprehended
in isolation. This unsatisfactory method in the study of values is
giving way everywhere to a more positive investigation, which
brings out the originality of each value. This is exemplified in
Maurice Pradines' last work, *The Spirit of Religion* (1941), which
stresses the specific and irreducible character of religion, notably
its heterogeneity with respect to ethics. In his aesthetics Charles
Lalo has always accepted in principle the impossibility of separating
the beautiful from artistic activities. In a recent work, *Art apart
from Life* (1939), he goes directly to the concrete and determines
the "structural laws" of a certain psycho-aesthetic type, that of the
artist who separates life from art. In *The Aesthetics of Grace* (1933)
R. Bayer maintains that the metaphysical explanation of aesthetic
concepts can be put aside, and qualitative analysis used to identify
the formula on which works of art depend.

This method of investigating concrete structures has been applied
recently in an original manner to an ancient question, that of the
nature of philosophy. Considering the abundance and variety of the
works commonly thought to be philosophical, defining philosophy
has always been a difficult task: an a priori definition is in danger

[9] L. Lavelle, *L'erreur de Narcisse,* 1939.
[10] Le Senne, *Obstacle et valeur,* 1934, chap. vi.

of being arbitrary and failing to fit everything included; an inductive definition obtained by trying to identify the elements common to all works is in danger of finishing up with a scanty residue. Still to be determined is whether a philosophical work as such, in its accomplishment and completion, does not have a certain structure or form in the sense that a drama or symphony is said to have a structure. Étienne Souriau, already known as the author of important works—*Living Thought and Formal Perfection* (1925) and *The Future of Aesthetics* (1929)—attempted to answer that question in *Philosophical Instauration* (1939). By philosophical work he understands, not the verbal execution of a thought, but the inner accomplishment, edification, or "instauration" of this thought, and what he tries to discover are the "universal laws of philosophy." This instauration is like a series of successive retouchings, each representing an attempt to atone for the abandonment of reality imposed, by the necessity of expression, on the philosopher who tries to express it entirely. The fourth chapter, "Architectonic Studies," merits detailed consideration. The philosopher first must choose a point of view which excludes all others; from this point of view, however—this is his second step—he tries to exhaust reality by making each of his assumptions the correlative of an opposite (for example, finite and infinite, phenomena and things in themselves); then these two opposites are harmonized by a middle term (for example, in Kant, practical reason which unifies reality); but this dialectic is too formal and allows "that which is inexpressible in terms of balanced harmony" to escape, giving rise to the need to bring out another "order," in the Pascalian sense, which is like dissonance in music or strong touches of light in painting. An original doctrine is rarely as systematic and coherent, however, as one that has passed into the hands of its critics. In spite of these successive retouchings, the "law of the point of view" necessarily entails the "law of destruction." Any theory of reality imposes certain sacrifices; Bergson, for example, was able to secure the reality of the vital force only by banishing immobility and division. Perhaps the unfinished, "crepuscular" elements of a doctrine (for example, the myth of Hades in Plato) express both the necessity of these sacrifices and the regret which they entail. Such is the design suggested for philosophical speculation, independently of any doctrine.

To these philosophers a structure is not a law of combination or a form wedded to inert matter; it is an indivisible which can be described, not recombined. Nicolai Hartmann, discussed earlier, makes full use of this notion of structure in his recent investigations in ontology.[11] In his theory of categories Hartmann returns, significantly, from Kant to Plato's *Sophistes*; to him categories are determinations of things in themselves, existing independently of the manner in which they are apprehended, and the most important question posed with respect to them is the question of their union and separation. The structure of being is defined, according to him, by the modalities which he assumes. From the application of this principle he deduces new, important views concerning the basis for the distinction between real being (*reales Sein*) and ideal being (*ideales Sein*). He seems to have arrived at these views by trying to preserve the ancient Platonic distinction while avoiding the difficulties of participation. Real being exhibits the three traditional modalities of being—it is possible, actually realized (*wirklich*), or necessary—but these three modes are mutually equivalent. A being of which every condition except the last is realized, is ordinarily called possible, but it should be said to be impossible in so far as this condition is not given; as soon as the last condition is given, being becomes possible but at the same time is actually realized and, consequently, necessarily realized. Like the Megarians of antiquity, Hartmann denies that the Aristotelian notion of potential being has any metaphysical significance. By contrast, the structure of ideal being exhibits new modalities. By ideal being Hartmann understands entities such as Euclidean space and the two non-Euclidean spaces discovered in the nineteenth century. It is only with reference to a being of this kind that one

---

[11] *Zur Grundlegung der Ontologie*, 1935; *Möglichkeit und Wirklichkeit*, 1938; *Der Aufbau der realen Welt*, 1939.

can speak of three new modalities: compossibility, incompossibility, and accident. For example, one can say that identically named figures are compossible in each of three spaces when these spaces are considered separately, that they are incompossible from one space to the next, and that the division into three spaces is accidental. The two kinds of beings—real or given being, and ideal being in which thought can move—exhibit such heterogeneity that the relation which might be established between them is not easily apprehended. That is perhaps one of the difficulties of Hartmann's doctrine.

R. Ruyer's *Outline of a Philosophy of Structure* (1930) is distinguished by its interpretation of mechanism as form or structure. In its traditional sense dating back to the seventeenth century, mechanism implied precisely the negation of structure as an irreducible characteristic of many things and the reduction of any apparent structure to an aggregation of elementary phenomena associated with collision or attraction—in other words, any mechanism was assumed to be materialistic. But the mode of combination and the operation resulting from it are at the very heart of any mechanism, and this accounts for the irreducible distinction between one mechanism and another. "Unlike positivism, true mechanism does not assume stages of heterogeneous realities, but it enables us to understand perfectly that each other form has its own reality, patterns of behavior, and laws." A living being is a mechanism, yet life is not reduced to physicochemical phenomena. Psychological activity is assumed to involve mental images and their distinctive properties or relations (for example, in dreaming or imagining), or their correspondence with the external forms and properties which transform them into signs (in reasoning).

IV *Subjectivistic Tendencies and Their Critics*

To reject the objectivistic point of view is not necessarily to deny rationalism. In the article already cited, Husserl called attention to the distinction between two forms of rationalism—objectivism and transcendentalism. Objectivism is the "naïve" and consequently unacceptable rationalism of the eighteenth century; it converts all reality into an object, mutilates it in the belief that it is dispelling any subjectivistic illusion, and replaces the real by a construction which is not identifiable as such. Transcendentalism, on the other hand, sees the objective world of science as a "formation of a higher degree" preceded by a subjective formation pertaining to prescientific life: "a radical return to the subjectivity which finally produces our whole evaluation of the world, with all its content, before science as in science; a return to questions concerning the nature and mode of the productions of reason alone can enable us to understand objective reality and arrive at its ultimate meaning." [12] Furthermore, this transcendentalism owes its inspiration not so much to Kant as to Descartes. Kant went from object to subject, which he defines only as the condition governing experiential knowledge of an object, previously determined by the sciences; but the object must be disregarded if an analysis of the subject is to be carried out, and this should be phenomenological rather than psychological. Finally, the method is indicated in terms reminiscent of Descartes: "I try to guide, not teach; I only show or describe what I see." [13]

Still, subjectivism has survived as rationalism only in Husserl. When it ceases to study the transcendental subject, which retains an abstract character, and turns to a concrete subject—"being in the world," with all its affective reactions—philosophical inquiry has only the limited scope clearly ascribed to it by Martin Heidegger at the end of *Being and Time* (sec. 83). Here Heidegger was discussing an ontology and did not go beyond an interpretation of human existence. But "the difference between human existence and an existence which is not human existence is only the starting point of the ontological problem, not the stopping point of philosophy"; moreover, "we cannot (like the ancients) investigate the origin and possibility of being by means of a formal logical ab-

---

[12] Husserl, "Die Krisis der europäischen Wissenschaften," p. 144.
[13] *Ibid.*, p. 95.

straction and without a horizon determined by questions and answers. We must try to discover a *way* to clarify the fundamental ontological questions. Is the way presented the only good way? We cannot know until it is too late." The second volume of *Being and Time,* which was to provide the answers to these questions, has not yet appeared, and one wonders whether this "way" is not an impasse and whether finite subjectivity can lead to a term which will provide an escape for us and with which it can be compared. My own subjectivity, which is the center of existentialist reflection, is certainly a reality; but if there is no way of separating my subjectivity as an absolutely real datum from my subjectivity as a standard of judgment concerning things in general, then obviously, as Jaspers discovered time and again, a philosophical doctrine can no longer depend on anything except a personal, arbitrary option. With respect to one of the problems existentialists find most disquieting—the problem of death—how can one justify the Pascalian attitude rather than the Stoic attitude? Of course Kierkegaard, who has had a profound influence on existentialism, escaped from subjectivity by "transcendence"—that is, by a mysterious contact, originating in faith, with another reality.[14]

Among Heidegger's contemporaries, J. Grenier, known for his studies of Lequier, holds the same opinion. "Our center of gravity," he writes, "is so remote from us and so far above our consciousness that we can neither imagine it nor conceive it but at most consent to it with all our being." [15] Hence a change occurs in the temporal character of existence, which, with Heidegger, was linked to anguish in the face of our progressive flight from reality and death. As Jean Guitton indicates, considering the relation between time and eternity, "the supreme office of time is to prepare for each conscious being organs of vision and life which cannot flower in

[14] Concerning these difficulties, see A. de Waelhens, *La philosophie de Martin Heidegger,* 1941, chap. xviii; *Bulletin de la Société française de philosophie,* October 1937; J. Wahl, *Études Kirkegaardiennes.* Martin Buber's work *I and Thou (Ich und Du,* 1923; English translation by R. B. Smith, 1937) expresses a particular form of this existentialism; here subjectivity is replaced by a concrete, personal I-Thou relation (particularly the relation between man and the eternal Thou, who is God).

[15] *Le Choix,* 1941, p. 147.

the present life," and "for the spirit death consists in allowing the complete emergence of the living body." [16] But here we have reached, and perhaps exceeded the limits of philosophy.

"Because I am alive," writes Gabriel Marcel, "I am a being . . . exposed, if you will, open to another reality with which I establish some kind of communication." [17] But for him the discovery, instead of being the solution of a problem and the sign of a profound unity, is the source of many questions concerning this mode of communication. Being influenced by someone else involves many subtleties, depending on whether the recipient is passive or, as the host, makes a gift of himself to "the other." Between the two terms is unfolded the whole spiritual life, ranging from servile imprisonment to complete liberty. In Marcel's doctrine the individual, unless he is socialized and given his proper public function, is "the bearer of certain mysterious energies, cosmic or spiritual, of which he himself vaguely senses the transcendence." [18]

In Louis Lavelle's *The Act* (1937), the difficulties associated with the problem of subjectivty and transcendence seem not to arise, since he begins by placing himself beyond the two terms, in the act, which is "the inner origin of myself and the world." To be sure, the act seems to be a primitive fact, subjective in nature, like the Cartesian Cogito or the Biranian will; but it is in reality "a double fact or, if you will, a relation by which my particular being is inserted into total being, my particular consciousness into a universal consciousness, my finite will into an infinite will" (p. 50). Lavelle does not take into consideration the differences which necessitate an appeal to faith. The relation between the particular being and the infinite, or participation, is given in an "immediate experience," and "the whole metaphysical problem is to define this relation (between the infinite act and our own liberty) or rather to describe the spiritual experience by which we take possession

---

[16] *La justification du temps,* 1941, pp. 128.

[17] "Aperçus phénoménologiques sur l'être en situation," in *Recherches philosophiques,* VI (1936), p. 7; *Etre et Avoir,* 1935.

[18] *Ibid.,* p. 13.

of it" (p. 221). This optimistic solution contrasts with the anguish of separation, which dominates existential philosophies.

But the limits of subjectivity cannot be defined exactly unless an objective reality is defined at the outset. "According to current opinion," writes E. Minkowski, "primary data can relate only to the self. In fact, this self to which primary data are linked cannot be given to me or conceived except in strict relation to the non-self, or better, the universe. Before setting the bounds of my own self, I see myself as I am, or rather as I live in the world." [19] Taking the opposite course, Nickolai Berdyaev shows that "the extinction of the world of things and objects" corresponds to "access to the enigma of existence." [20]

In a general way the cleavage between the psychic and the physical is being modified. "The mental does not lie alongside the physical like a second reality, which might be studied by a second science," writes R. Blanché. "All reality within the province of science is physical. The mental reality is what philosophical reflection identifies as conditions relating to the constitution of science and the objectivity of the real." [21] Also noteworthy are the studies of sensation inspired by the exemplary works of Lavelle—*The Dialectic of the Sensible World* (1921)—and Pradines. Sensation is no longer thought to provide simple data which combine to create the tissue of the psychic life. "The insurmountable difficulties raised by [theories of] the existence of things prior to perception and, on the other hand, by the exteriority of sensible qualities are traceable to an attempt to interpret the sensible world independently and as a primary datum." Furthermore, "we do not have to determine why impressions separate from bodies and appear to us at a distance, for this separation is already implied in the need, so that the natural problem of sensation is the search for a mediation rather than the problem of a mysterious projection of our own states." [22]

[19] *Vers une cosmologie*, 1936, p. 98.
[20] *Cinq Méditations sur l'Existence*, 1936, p. 84.
[21] *La Notion de fait psychique*, 1934, p. 322.
[22] Jean Nogué, *La signification du sensible*, 1936, pp. 71, 73.

And P. Salzi, adopting a different point of view, tries to demonstrate the "paradoxical" hypothesis that sensation and rational conception of the physical world are the same—that sensations spring from the same mental activity that make up our conceptions, that is, from reason.[23]

An unquestionable aspect of this preference for a rich, concrete subjectivity is the rejection in pure logic of mathematics opposed to reality, by virtue of the simple formal connection which deprives the mathematical sciences of any objects, real or ideal.

"Any rigorous mathematical theory," writes René Poirier, "is necessarily algebraic, using this word in the broadest sense." He adds that "any mathematical science is a combination of signs, an algebra of images, which blends in with the algebra of logic. . . . That is also why geometry does not impose laws on experience but offers it formulas or symbolic expressions." Contrary to the belief of the Pythagoreans and Plato, neither the language of mathematics nor language in general reveals the essence of things. "A child thinks he is clever because he knows that the moon is a globe, almost spherical and of a certain size, or because he is able to use literary phrases to describe it. He no longer is able to perceive it as being close to him and almost tangible, while its light falls silently, as by pulsation, and bathes us in its affection. Language envelops us and turns us away from the real world, to which it is philosophy's task to bring us back."[24]

This view of mathematics is linked to the last stage in the development of the doctrine of the "Vienna circle." Under the influence of logical positivism and, later, a tendency labeled "physicalism," the doctrine has assumed a form similar to that of behavioristic psychology in America. Between such distant domains as mathematics, physics, and psychology we discover unexpected relationships which help us to achieve a clearer understanding of subjectivism.

[23] *La sensation: Étude de sa génèse et de son rôle dans la connaissance,* 1934, p. 169.
[24] *Essai sur quelques caractères des notions d'espace et de temps,* 1931, pp. 147, 375, 380. Cf. also his *Le nombre,* 1938.

David Hilbert's axiomatization and the logicalization of the Vienna school are the two closely related forms of this interpretation of mathematics. In the first, a certain number of mathematical assertions (axioms) are given and one must choose the proposition from which all others can be deduced; in the second, primary notions are assumed to be of purely logical origin. The two doctrines are not without difficulties: an internal difficulty if Hilbert's system cannot demonstrate that contradictory propositions will not be reached and if, on the other hand, logicians recognize that it is impossible not to use arithmetical and even physical propositions in stating primary notions.[25] Resistance to the tendency to reduce mathematics to a purely logical scheme is manifested particularly in Brouwer's intuitionism, which makes mathematics depend on arithmetic and the latter on the intuition of time; moreover, creative mathematicians reject ready-made mathematics, reduced to a utilizable mechanism, in favor of an evolving science.[26]

But mathematical formalism, which in one way removes mathematics from the concrete reality, is well suited in another way to bring them closer together. First, in Hilbert's system an axiom is defined by its function (a proposition from which other propositions are deduced by logical transformation and which is not deduced from any other proposition) and not by any criterion of self-evidence; consequently the method of axiomatization "can be applied in fields remote from mathematics—in mechanics, the theory of radiation, or the economic theory of money."[27] The logician, in turn, concedes that "axioms are simple descriptions of operations that can be carried out on expressions constructed according to rules given beforehand." The notion of *operation*, per-

---

[25] On this point cf. Carnap, *The Logical Syntax of Language* (*Logische Syntax der Sprache*, 1934; English translation, 1937), quoted by J. Cavaillès, *Méthode axiomatique et formalisme*, 1938. Cavaillès' work contains a good historical criticism of these questions. See also A. Lautman, *Essai sur les notions de structure et d'existence en mathématiques*, 1937.

[26] See H. Lebesgue, *Sur la mesure des grandeurs*, 1935, pp. 179 ff.

[27] Cf. Chwistek, in *Actes du Congrès international de philosophie scientifique*, 1935, I, 80: two systems of axioms are equivalent when the propositions of the second system can be deduced, by logical transformation, from those of the first system, and vice versa.

fectly concrete, is of capital importance. As it has developed in America during the last ten years, it seems to explain the unexpected relationships mentioned earlier, which give rise to a new hope of realizing the unity of science—a hope that apparently was abandoned for more than a century. According to Percy Williams Bridgman, a concept means nothing more than a system of operations; for example, the concept of length is fixed when the operations through which length is measured are fixed. Length is the system itself.[28] Besides concepts, such as length, that relate to a given situation, we find others that apply to a physical situation which is not given but inferred—for instance, the notion of electrical tension or electrical field. These fabricated concepts (constructs) are uniquely defined by mathematical operations which are supposed to lead to physical operations. Psychology fits in turn into the same frame. In the form that behaviorism assumed with Tolman, the psychological problem is posed in a manner such that it always involves an operational solution.[29] In fact, the behaviorist's aim is to discover the function which relates a certain behavior to stimuli and to the conditions (heredity, prior experience, age, etc.) under which these stimuli operate. His investigation is essentially the same as that of a physicist attempting, for example, to determine the behavior of an inorganic body, endowed with certain properties, in an electrical field. According to Edward Chace Tolman, physics is a system of logical constructions, a system of rules and equations which help us find our way across successive moments of immediate experience. Psychology is merely another, similar system of rules and equations, which, added to those of physics, give us additional help in passing from one moment of experience (stimulus) to the next (behavior).

There is of course one difficulty in this operationalism, and it is identical to the difficulty encountered in "logical positivism." For logical concepts to have a practical meaning, they must be brought

[28] *The Logic of Modern Physics*, 1927. Discussed by Tilquin, *Le Behaviorisme*, 1942, p. 430.
[29] Tilquin, *ibid.*, discussing Tolman, "An Operational Analysis of Demands," in *Erkenntnis*, VI (1937).

face to face with immediate experience. As Moritz Schlick observes, if this condition were met, logical propositions (*Sätze*) could be transformed into statements about things (*Aussage*); but that is impossible since, according to the same doctrine, immediate experience is by nature incommunicable and consequently unverifiable and meaningless.[30] Thus physicalism could become coherent only by affirming that there was no immediate experience; there is nothing resembling the opposition recognized at first by the Vienna circle between knowledge (*Erkenntnis*) and impression (*Erlebnis*). But how, then, can the problem be solved? By affirming that the hypothetical immediate datum is a perceptive judgment which discerns one thing in the midst of others (for example: I see red) and, as such, is communicable. All knowledge is then homogeneous; there is no distinction between language and the real world. Everywhere there are only expressible things.[31]

Notwithstanding the difficulties of this solution, the intention is clear. Far from working in the void, all three tendencies—formalism, physicalism, and behaviorism—indicate a desire to see concrete situations as wholes. To reject apriorism and self-evidence or to deny the existence of phenomena is, in short, to refuse to acknowledge the kinds of abstractions—islands in reality—represented by primitive notions or hypothetical mental facts. Everything is closely interrelated; no assertion can be isolated and given the main place in the formal construction which constitutes mathematical science; and physical phenomena as a whole on one hand, together with human or animal behavior as it relates to the human environment on the other, find expression in the language of this science. Thus subjectivism, which boasts of being so close to reality, succeeds in reaching only fragments of reality, or even empty appearances.

The subjectivists should be persuaded, it seems, to ask themselves the critical question of objectivity in the human science and particularly in history. In *Philosophical Fragments*[32] Kierkegaard,

---

[30] *Actes du Congrès internationale de philosophie scientifique*, IV (1935), p. 13.

[31] Here I am following the excellent exposition of Tilquin, *Le behaviorisme*.

[32] *Filosofiske smuler*, 1844; English translation by David F. Swenson, 1936.

one of their models, takes as the main theme of his critiques the Hegelian assertion according to which man can know himself only by meditating on history; because the requirements of historical knowledge are so complex, this assertion postpones indefinitely the solution of man's most pressing problems. Yet the Hegelian attempt somehow to cause history to be absorbed in the subject by giving it a current meaning is frequently revived, though it assumes quite different forms. Characteristic in this respect is Raymond Aron's *Introduction to the Study of History* (1938). "Man is not only in history, but he carries within himself the history that he explores" (p. 11). That is the fundamental thesis of a work that relates history solely to the present of the one who is writing it and attributes to it only the value it may have for the present. "The past of our intelligence interests us in itself only in so far as it is or would be worthy of being present" (p. 56). "The present illuminates the past" (p. 83) because we understand the present consequences of a past period even though they could not be foreseen by men of that period. "The interpretation of an event depends on the aim adopted by the historian" (p. 103). All these assertions are intended not simply to limit historical objectivity but to deny it outright by making history a justification (necessarily illusory) of our present action. Here subjectivity is not taken in itself as the matter and content of speculation but as something which contributes value and meaning to the study of history. Each group, each individual is assumed to have a unique philosophy of history.

Bibliography

Texts

Berdyaev, Nicholas. *Dream and Reality,* trans. Katherine Lampert. London, 1950.
———. *The Meaning of History,* trans. George Reavey. London, 1923.
———. *The Destiny of Man,* trans. Natalie Duddington. London, 1937.
———. *Solitude and Society,* trans. George Reavey. New York, 1939.
———. *The Beginning and the End,* trans. R. M. French. London, 1952.
Buber, Martin. Publications of the collected works of Buber in German, *Werke,* was begun in 1962 by Kosel Verlag in Munich. The first three volumes appeared by 1964.
———. *I and Thou,* trans. R. G. Smith. New York, 1958.
———. *Between Man and Man,* trans. R. G. Smith. Boston, 1955.
———. *The Prophetic Faith,* trans. C. Witton Davies. New York, 1960.
———. *Paths in Utopia,* trans. R. F. C. Hull. London, 1949.
———. *Two Types of Faith,* trans. N. P. Goldhawk. New York, 1961.
———. *Eclipse of God; Studies in the Relation between Religion and Philosophy,* trans. Maurice Friedman *et al.* New York, 1952.
———. *Good and Evil: Two Interpretations,* trans. R. G. Smith and M. Bullock. New York, 1953.
———. *Pointing the Way: Collected Essays,* trans. and ed. Maurice Friedman. New York, 1957
———. *Martin Buber Writings,* a selection edited and introduced by Will Herberg. New York, 1956.
Carnap, Rudolf. *The Philosophy of Rudolf Carnap,* ed. P. A. Schilpp. Vol. 11 in the Library of Living Philosophers. La Salle, Ill., 1963.
Lavelle, Louis. *La Dialectique de l'Éternel Présent: De l'être.* Paris, 1928, 1932; revised edition augmented by an Introduction to the *Dialectique de l'Éternal Présent,* 1947. *De l'acte.* Paris, 1934 and 1946. *Du temps et de l'éternité.* Paris, 1945. *De l'âme humaine.* Paris, 1955.
———. *Manuel de méthodologie dialectique.* Paris, 1962.
———.*The Meaning of Holiness,* trans. and with introduction by Dom Illtyd Trethowan of Downside. London, 1954.
———. *Traité des valeurs.* Vol. 1. *Théorie générale de la valeur.* Paris, 1951.
———. *Traité des valeurs.* Vol. 2. *Le système des différentes valeurs.* Paris, 1955.
Le Senne, René. *Introduction à la philosophie.* Paris, 1925.
———. *Le Devoir.* Paris, 1930.
———. *Le Mensonge et le charactère.* Paris, 1930.
———. *Obstacle et valeur.* Paris, 1934.

265

———. *Traité de morale générale.* Paris, 1942.
———. *Traité de caractérologie.* Paris, 1949.
———. *La Destinée personnelle.* Paris, 1951.
———. *La Découverte de Dieu.* Paris, 1955.

Texts

Marcel, Gabriel. *Metaphysical Journal,* trans. Bernard Wall. Chicago, 1952.
———. *Being and Having,* trans. Katherine Farrar. London, 1949.
———. *Creative Fidelity,* trans. Robert Rosthall. New York, 1964.
———. *Homo Viator,* trans. Emma Craufurd. Paris, 1945. New York, 1962.
———. *Philosophy of Existentialism,* trans. Manya Harari. New York, 1961.
———. *The Mystery of Being,* trans. G. S. Fraser and René Hauge. 2 vols. Chicago, 1950.
———. *Men against Humanity,* trans. G. S. Fraser. London, 1952. Republished as *Man against Mass Society.* Chicago, 1962.
———. *L'homme problématique.* Paris, 1955.
———. *Présence et immortalité.* Paris, 1959.
———. *The Existential Background of Human Dignity.* Cambridge, Mass., 1963.

Studies

Cain, Seymour. *Gabriel Marcel.* London, 1963.
Clarke, Oliver Fielding. *Introduction to Berdyaev.* London, 1950.
Friedman, Maurice. *Martin Buber: The Life of Dialogue.* New York, 1960.
Piersol, Wesley. "Louis Lavelle—an Approach." *Philosophy Today,* 1965.
Prini, Pietro. *Gabriel Marcel et la méthodologie de l'invérifiable.* Paris, 1953.
Ricœur, Paul. *Gabriel Marcel et Karl Jaspers.* Paris, 1947.
Seaver, George. *Nicolas Berdyaev.* London, 1950.
Spinka, Matthew. *Nicolas Berdyaev, Captive of Freedom.* Philadelphia, 1950.
Troisfontaines, Roger, *De l'existence à l'être.* 2 vols. Paris, 1953.

INDEX